A Haunted Tour Guide to the Pacific Northwest

By Jefferson Davis

Published by Norsemen Ventures

Vancouver, Washington

Printed by Central Plains Book Manufacturing, Winfield Kansas

First Printing 2001

Although the author has researched all sources to ensure the accuracy and completeness of the information contained within this book, he assumes no responsibility for errors, inaccuracies, omissions or inconsistencies herein. Nor does the author presume to pass judgment as to the truth of any paranormal events or stories contained within. Any slights of people or organizations are unintentional.

ISBN: 1-893186-04-0

Library of Congress Number: 2001117265

Davis, Jefferson Dale

A Haunted Tour Guide to the Pacific Northwest

1. Tourist guide
2. Ghosts Oregon
3. Ghosts Washington
4. Ghosts Canada

Acknowledgements

Thanks to the many people who were helpful and hopefully forgave my offences while I was too focused on this book, when I should have been paying attention to my other obligations: Jamie Daniels, Jon Goodman, Katherine London, Roy Susuico, John Warsinske, Annie, Christina, Cindy, Karan, Karen and Kerry, my father, my mother, my wife, my cats, and the many fans who wrote me letters that I did not answer.

On the technical end, thanks to: my cousin Mike, computer expert, Tina for editing, and Janine for final proofing of this copy. Thanks to Howard at Geographic Data Technologies for assisting me in getting rights to produce maps. Thanks to Su at Stone Crow Graphics for my first color cover. Thanks Bruce at Robb Photography for publicity photographs and Karan for being my "ghost gal."

For research help, thanks to: John Adams at Discover the Past, who helped me by telling me stories of some of Victoria's haunts. Rowena Gilbert, who maintains the Castle of Spirits website, which is the largest collection of true ghost stories on the internet. Thanks to Portland's Phantom Seekers for sharing their own collection of experiences. Thanks to my psychic friends Janet and Martina. Thanks to all of the owners, managers and employees of the places I visited, wrote and called; for listening to me ask the same questions over and over again.

Table of Contents

About This Tour Guide

I have been writing books on ghosts and legends of the Pacific Northwest for several years. In three years I wrote three books of collected stories. Every year, from about mid October to Christmas, I spend my weekends in my trusty Ford Festiva, driving to and from book signings across the Northwest. I make a point to get comments from fans about what they want to see in the next book. Whether people have one book or all three, many have had similar comments. They like to visit haunted places, and it would be great if they could get more visitor information in a single volume, rather than having to carry several books with them. So here it is.

This book lists many of the haunted public places that I have heard of in the last ten years. The haunted locales range from hotels, to bed & breakfasts, to restaurants, to museums and even beauty parlors. In my other books, I only discussed Washington and Oregon. Here, I include haunted locales in British Columbia and east into Idaho for one special haunt.

It was hard deciding how exactly to organize this book to be of the best use for vacation planners. Rather than dividing it alphabetically by towns, the book is divided by geographic sections: The first section begins with the southern end of the Northwest Coast. The listing continues northward through Washington. The next section is southern British Columbia. The guide then moves south, into the Puget Sound. It continues south through the Portland Basin and Willamette Valley, then east through the Columbia River Gorge and eastern Washington and Oregon. Within these sections, I have separated the haunts by city, and by type of haunt: lodging, restaurants and clubs, and sights.

I tried to ensure that all of these places are open to the public as businesses, restaurants, hotels or museums. Some places may be familiar, since I describe them in my other books. Some are not. There are nearly 200 locales listed in this book. More than half of them have not been described by me before. In some cases there may be only one or two haunted places in a single town. They are generally listed in alphabetical order. In the case of cities with several hauntings, such as Seattle, the haunts are divided into sections: **Places to Stay; Restaurants, Clubs and Theaters;** and **Shops, Sights and Sounds.**

Each listing includes business information such as addresses, phone numbers, websites, hours, etc. The information in this guide at publishing was correct, given the records available at the time. I also included a brief entry describing the haunts history and the haunting itself. I kept entries brief to fit all of these places into one compact book. If you want longer stories, you can find them in my other books (blatant plug). I have provided maps or directions to many locations mentioned in this book, but not all. Please contact the places you want to visit in advance for updates or alternate directions.

This book is an aid to help you plan a ghost hunting vacation. I cannot guarantee that you will have a paranormal experience in each place. Ghosts do not manifest themselves on command. But if you continue to visit haunted locales, the law of averages will eventually catch up with you and you will eventually have something strange happen.

Ghost Vacation Etiquette & Cautions

Even though the locations I list are reputably haunted, their business is not usually selling ghosts or ghost tours. A haunted restaurant is still a restaurant. If you go in without at least acting like a paying customer, the management will be a little upset. The same thing goes for hotels and other businesses. If you want to chat with the manager or employees, please do it sensibly. Most small businesses like bed & breakfasts are more than happy to talk about their ghosts. They usually treat the ghost as an extra guest. Contacting the management in advance and making an appointment might help. I guarantee that not everyone you talk to will have a story to tell.

Some people won't talk because they do not know anything. Others won't talk because they do not believe in ghosts. Some people will not talk because they do believe in ghosts; and are afraid. I try and list which places are ghost hunter friendly and which are not. For whatever reason, if people do not want to talk about ghosts, please respect them.

I have tried to make sure that I listed places where the ghosts are not dangerous. I have not met anyone credible who has said that a ghost has physically hurt them. What usually happens is when people see a ghost, they are frightened or focused on the event and have an accident. If something strange happens, remember to keep your head, do not panic and you will be all right. I have a similar warning about visiting places like graveyards or other potentially dangerous places.

I want to mention some earthly dangers. Please respect private property rights. Some northwest farmers and property owners carry guns. I also warn against going to some famous haunts for safety reasons. Some haunted places are located in rough neighborhoods. If an area does not look or feel safe, do not stay there. You should check with local law enforcement and perhaps come back when it is safe. This is especially true in graveyards. Some strange people hang out there. I do not mean people like you or me. I am talking about vandals, vagrants and criminals. For that reason I would not go into one at night unless you were with a large group and had permission from whatever people manage the place.

I mention several graveyards in this book. I ask everyone to be respectful when visiting them. Some graveyards have many daylight visitors. Some offer tours.

Other graveyards are small and have suffered from vandals. If you are in a graveyard, please do not add graffiti to thc tombstones or remove pieces as a souvenir, like some people have done at the Maltby Cemetery. That is a felony. The same thing is true when visiting Native American spiritual places like Horsethief Lake and Silver Star Mountain.

Pricing Guidelines

The only symbols that I have used are dollar signs ($), which are a guide to prices: $ = Inexpensive, $$ = Average and $$$ = Expensive.

Lodging:

$	= $0 - $70	double occupancy
$$	= $71 - $130	double occupancy
$$$	= $131 - +	double occupancy

Meals:

$	= $0 - $8	one person w/o drink, tax or tip
$$	= $9 - $21	one person w/o drink, tax or tip
$$$	= $22 - +	one person w/o drink, tax or tip

Museums, Tours, Entertainment, etc:

$	= $0 - $7	per person
$$	= $8 - $15	per person
$$$	= $16 - +	per person

This is only a general guideline. The average price of a meal in downtown Seattle or Portland will be more than in Centralia. Over the next few years' prices will go up, but average should stay average. Facilities, hours and services will also change. Please verify dates, times, prices and any other details by telephone or email before visiting a hotel, restaurant or museum.

Jeff Davis: www.ghostsandcritters.com

What is a Ghost?

What is a ghost? A Gallup Poll found that 30% of the people in America believe in ghosts. This does not include the percentage of people who are willing to discuss the possibility of their existence. The simplest definition of a ghost is that a ghost is the spiritual remains of a deceased person. This soul remains on earth, instead of passing on to a different plain of existence. Or a ghost is a soul without a body. A ghost can manifest itself in many ways, such as being seen, heard, felt, touched or even smelled. A haunting is a series of several paranormal events in a common setting.

Most hauntings are associated with buildings or places. In some cases, when the buildings are torn down, the haunting ceases. In other cases, the hauntings continue in the vacant lot or new structure. There are examples of haunted houses that are moved and the ghost goes with them. Some ghosts seem to be attached to certain objects. Why do we see ghosts mostly at night? Aren't they there during the day? Maybe they are and we just don't perceive them? If ghosts are solid looking, we may think that they are living beings.

The most common type of ghost seems to be a kind of snapshot in time. Frequently, violent or traumatic events seem to release an energy that imprints the action on a place or object. In this kind of haunting, the violent action repeats itself, like a videotape rewound and played over and over again. Sometimes hauntings are not the result of a violent action. It can be the result of someone performing the same actions over and over again. This somehow imprints itself on a place after the person is dead or gone. Some people have seen apparitions of living people.

These hauntings can be seen, heard, felt or even smelled. Ghosts frequently act at the same time every night, or seasons of the year. They do not do anything remarkable, they are just going about their business. Like a night watchman continuing his rounds, after death. These ghosts are not aware that their surroundings change over time. This is why some ghosts appear to be walking though solid walls where there used to be a doorway. They may also walk above or below a modern floor.

The self-aware spirit is another kind of haunting. This spirit stays on because they have business that they want to finish. Sometimes they want to pass on information about their life, death or something more important than life itself (to them). There are guardian spirits, who protect a secret or perhaps treasure. They may have suffered a tragedy in the past and want to warn others in similar circumstances. Some spirits stay on for no apparent reason.

Poltergeist means "noisy ghost". They are quite evident because they cause things to move from place to place, make noise and generally upset the routine of their surroundings. Poltergeists are usually associated with children before or during puberty. Poltergeists usually fade as puberty ends. This is the kind of ghost that seems to be faked most often by people.

Most ghosts seem to fade away over time. At first some ghosts are seen, heard and felt. The visible apparition is both the most frightening and rarest kind of spirit phenomenon. They may be the rarest because it may take a lot of energy to project a visible image. As time goes by, ghosts generally fade away and may only be heard. They may act only on the anniversary of their creation. Even the noises fade over time, until nothing is left of the ghost.

Some ghosts seem able to recharge themselves. Cold spots, light bulbs dimming, drained batteries and electronic machinery going haywire may be caused by spirits gathering energy from around them. These cold spots are sometimes accompanied by erratic magnetic fields. Some people have suggested that these cold spots are actually doorways between a spiritual dimension and our own.

Jefferson Davis

The Northwest Coast

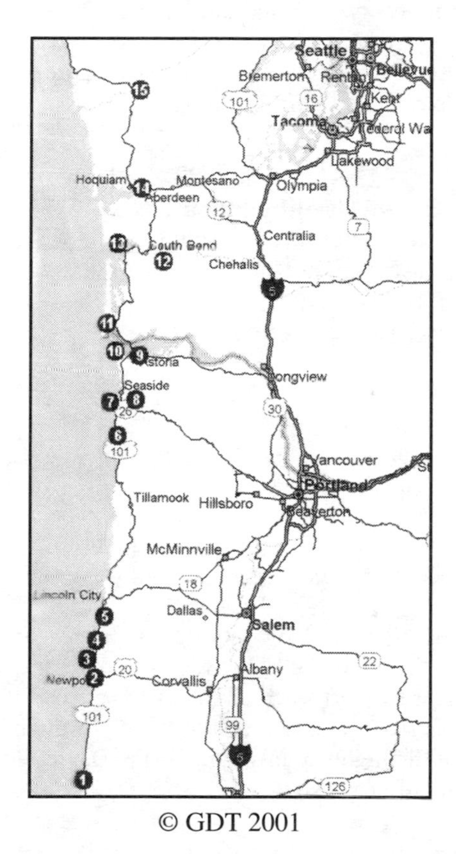

© GDT 2001

1) Yachats, OR, 2) Newport, OR, 3) Yaquina Bay, OR, 4) Depoe Bay, OR., 5) Lincoln City, OR, 6) Neakahnie Mt., OR 7) Ecola State Park, 8) Canon Beach, OR, 9) Astoria, OR, 10) Ft. Stevens, OR, 11) Seaview, WA, 12) Menlo, WA, 13) Tokeland, WA., 14) Aberdeen, WA., 15) Quinalt, WA

The Northwest Coast

The only major highway along the coasts of Washington and Oregon is U.S. Highway 101. With the exception of attractions in larger towns like Newport and Lincoln City, most places in this section are located along the highway. For the other places, I have tried to provide adequate road directions or maps to locate them. This section begins on the southern coast of Oregon and heads in a more or less northerly direction, to the tip of the coast in Washington.

Yachats, Oregon

Name: **Heceta Head Lighthouse**
Address: 92072 Highway 101 south
Yachats, OR 97428
Phone Number: **541 547-3696**
Web site: www.hecetalighthouse.com
Rooms: 3
Prices: $$ - $$$
Theme: Historic lighthouse
Cuisine: Gourmet
Open: Year round
Special Facilities: Full course breakfast, no pets, no smoking, Christmas celebration, and gift shop. The lighthouse is usually booked up a year in advance, so make reservations early.

Directions: Heceta head lighthouse can be reached on Hwy 101 either from the north or the south, between Florence and Yachats. From Hwy 101, there is a turn off to the lighthouse between the 177 and 178 mile markers. This road is on the west of the highway, mid-way through a hair pin curve in the highway in what was the Devils Elbow State park. Look for the lighthouse road signs.

The Heceta Head lighthouse was the most expensive lighthouse constructed. Its 2.5 million candlepower beacon is the most powerful on the coast. It is the most photographed lighthouse in Oregon. The lighthouse and light keeper's quarters at Haceta Head were constructed in 1893, and the lighthouse is still in operation today. In the 1970s, the surviving keeper's quarters were leased to Lane Community College as an extension campus. The keeper's quarters building is in reality divided into two self-contained living quarters. At the same time as classes began, the U.S. Forest Service, who owned the buildings implemented plans to restore the buildings to their original condition.

The lightkeepers residence is currently operated as a Bed and

Breakfast. The current innkeepers are the Korgans, who offer a multi-course gourmet breakfast to their guests.

The Ghosts

This ghost was called Rue and may be the spirit of Mrs. Frank DeRoy, the wife of one of the first lightkeepers. There is a small grave behind the lightkeeper's quarters. Legend says that it is the grave of a child who died shortly after being born. The ghost may be that of the mother, still searching for her lost child. In the mid 1970s contractors were hired to repair the lighthouse. As they worked, tools disappeared, to reappear later. While repairing a window, one man saw the reflection of a woman behind him. He turned round and was confronted by an elderly lady in a long dress, floating toward him.

The ghost also seems to be concerned with keeping the house clean. Broken glass in the attic was found swept into a tidy pile. A psychic visitor stayed overnight, and for some reason water dripped from a chandelier in the dining room. It stopped when she left.

I spoke with Michelle Korgan, who operated the house from 1999 to late 2000. Most couples who visit follow a typical pattern where the wife usually drags her skeptical husband to the coast. By breakfast time, it is usually the husband who admits to being converted. Some have smelled the scent of flowers or rose perfume.

Newport, Oregon

Places to Stay
Name: **Oar House Bed & Breakfast**
Address: 520 SW 2nd St
Newport OR 97365
Phone Number: **800-252-2358**
541 265-9571
Web site: www.oarhouse-bed-breakfast.com
Rooms: 5
Prices: $$
seasonal rates apply
Theme: Nautical
Cuisine: Gourmet
Open: Year round
Special Facilities:
guest living room, sitting room with fireplace, music system

The Oar House was built around 1900 from timbers salvaged from shipwrecks washed up on the beach near Newport. The Oar House began its existence as a boarding house for sailors and transients and later became a bordello. The house grew a little bit over time, so there are interesting turns and jogs in it's architecture. The Oar House is located several streets from the waterfront. The road is steep, and the house overlooks the ocean. The Widows Walk tower on the third floor gives great views of the ocean.

The Ghosts

In the 1930s a young woman from the mid-west came to Newport to meet her fiancé. He was arriving in Newport either as a ship's passenger or a member of the crew. The sympathetic landlady gave her a room on the third floor. In exchange for her room and board, she worked as a maid. From her little room it was a short climb to the Widow's walk, where she could see the harbor. The days turned to weeks and the weeks turned to months. She eventually realized that her fiancé was not going to meet her. She threw herself out the window of her small apartment and died when she hit the ground below.

Jan, the present owner purchased the house in 1993, despite the stories. One evening a guest was in the sitting room reading a newspaper. He began to feel watched and for some reason looked up at the ceiling. There is a small glass hatch leading from the sitting room to the room directly above. He thought that he saw someone looking down at him. He quickly walked upstairs and checked but found the room was empty.

On another occasion the old landlord and his wife planned on taking an afternoon nap in the third floor, ghost room. He walked up to the bedroom and laid down in the bed, waiting for his wife, facing away from the bedroom door. He heard the sound of footsteps on the stairs. The footsteps entered the room, crossed the floor and he felt the bed move as someone laid down beside him. He turned around to talk to his wife, only to find himself lying alone on the bed.

<u>Shops, Sights and Sounds</u>

Name:	**Yaquina Bay Lighthouse**
Address:	Yaquine Bay State Park Newport, OR
Phone Number:	**541 265-5679**
Prices:	$
Theme:	Historic lighthouse museum
Open:	Memorial Day – 30 September 11 a.m. – 5 p.m. 1 October – Memorial Day, noon – 4 p.m.

Special Facilities: Gift shop, period furnishings

The US Lighthouse Service constructed the Yaquina Bay lighthouse in the summer of 1871. The lighthouse is a two-story caretaker's house with an attached, square three-story lighthouse tower. It is the second oldest lighthouse still standing in Oregon. The lighthouse was only used for three years, from 1871 to 1874.

It was de-commissioned in 1874, in favor of the Yaquina Head lighthouse, three miles north of Newport. Over the next 60 years various state and federal agencies used the lighthouse and caretaker's house. The park caretaker lived in the house until 1948 when they decided to demolish the deteriorating structure. A concerned citizen's group lobbied to save the buildings. They were successful, and the Lincoln County Historical Society now runs the lighthouse as a museum and park.

The Ghosts

It is hard to separate history from myths that surround the two ghosts in the old lighthouse. The first ghost is a large redheaded sailor. This spirit may be that of Evan MacClure, captain of a Yankee Whaling ship. In January of 1874, locals stood watching the storm waters break over the Devil's Punch Bowl near Newport. They saw a small boat wash up on the rocks and a man with red hair climbed out. A wave washed over the rocks, taking the boat and man with it. According to legend, when the lighthouse was shut down in 1874, MacClure moved in.

That same year, a ship landed at Newport and a man calling himself Trevenard came ashore. He left his daughter Zina (or Muriel) at a small hotel until he returned. In 1874 she joined a group of teenagers investigating the lighthouse. They discovered a metal door in the lighthouse third floor closet. They were preparing to leave when Zina said she had left her handkerchief in the lighthouse. She reentered, and in a few minutes they heard screams for help coming from inside. A trail of blood drops led upstairs, where they found her bloody handkerchief in the room where they had found the hidden door.

Many visitors have reported eerie sensations when walking through the building. Some have reported a light emanating from a second floor room late at night. I spoke with people at the gift shop. They have not seen or heard anything strange, but are ready to answer questions about the popular stories and history of the area. Other people have spoken with volunteers who confirmed a ghostly presence haunts the lighthouse.

Name: **Yaquina Head Lighthouse**
Address: 4 miles north of Newport, OR
Along Hwy 101
Phone Number: **541 265-5679**
Web site: www.or.blm.cov/salem/html/yaquina/about.htm
Prices: $
Theme: Historic lighthouse
Open: Guided tours noon – 4 p.m., year round
Special Facilities: Located in Yaquina Head Outstanding Natural Area, interpretive center

The beacon of the Yaquina Head Lighthouse shines from the top of the eighty-three foot-high tower, built on an 84 foot high rock face. The Yaquina Head Lighthouse was constructed in 1873. The beacon of the new lighthouse was so powerful that the older, less powerful lighthouse beacon on the bay was shut down.

The Ghosts

The lighthouse was built with an inner and outer wall. When the inner and outer walls were finished, the workers began filling the narrow space between with a mix of dirt and broken rocks. Suddenly, one of the workmen accidentally fell in with the rubble. There was no way to get the man out, so his co-workers were forced to finish filling in the space, entombing their friend within the lighthouse. Some people believe that the lost worker still hammers on the rock inner walls of the lighthouse in an effort to free himself.

In the 1930s, the head lighthouse keeper went into Newport for a drink. He left the second lighthouse keeper and Henry Higgins, the third assistant lighthouse keeper at the lighthouse. The second assistant took the opportunity to get drunk and passed out. Sometime after dark, the head lighthouse keeper went outside and saw that the beacon was out. He rushed to the lighthouse, and up the spiral staircase to find Henry's body on one of the stair landings, dead of a heart attack.

Several years later, lighthouse keepers swore that they have heard the sounds of someone walking up the spiral stairs when they have stood watch over the beacon. When they looked down, there was no one there. When I went to the lighthouse myself, I asked the interpreter if he had seen or heard anything strange. He just smiled a denial. Other people have told me that their guides were willing to discuss the ghosts and their experiences.

Depoe Bay, Oregon

Name: **Spouting Horn Restaurant**
Address:1 10 NE Hwy 101
Depoe Bay, OR 97341
Phone Number: **541 765-2261**
Prices: $$
Theme: Oregon Coast
Cuisine: Northwest & Seafood
Open: Monday 11:30 a.m. – 9 p.m.
Wednesday – Sunday 8 a.m. – 9 p.m.
Chuck Wagon Buffet Thursday & Friday at 5 p.m.
Special Facilities: Views of the ocean and bay

The Spouting Horn restaurant is located on the shores of Depoe Bay. The restaurant was originally a hotel and has two stories, with dining rooms on each floor. Across Hwy 101 is the Devil's Churn and spouting horn. The Devil's Churn is a hundred foot deep hole in the coastal rock. At high tide, the water rushes through the chasm and is forced out into the air. The spouting horn of sea water rises up to 40 feet in the air.

Betty Tauton and her husband Vaughn moved to Depoe Bay and bought the Spouting Horn in 1951. The building was built sometime in the 1930s and used as a boarding house and was the U.S. Coast Guard Headquarters in World War II. Though Vaughn has passed on, Betty and her family still run the restaurant. She is an accomplished chef, having studied cooking in Portland as well as France. She attended cooking schools in Provence (near Nice) and the other school was in Perigord. Her baking skills have earned her pies local fame.

The Ghosts

The Tauton family call their ghost Ralph and have become comfortable with his practical jokes. When Betty and her family were converting the old hotel into the Spouting Horn they had to remodel the upper floor. While they were doing this, one person was pelted with an old nail. People have heard disembodied footsteps and dishes and pans in the kitchen fall with a clatter. On the second floor there is a quiet back lounge. The bartender and others have reported seeing a ghostly man walking across the hallways. In 2001, psychics and paranormal investigators detected a strong male presence in the hallway leading from the second floor dining room to the back bar. On a tape recorder they captured a voice saying, "I'm not goin' in there!". This was mocking the psychic, who refused to walk through the hallway.

Name:	**Francis Drake's Landing**
Address:	Drake in Oregon Society PO Box 412, Depoe Bay, OR 97341
Phone Number:	**541-574-6309**
Fax Number:	541-765-3040
Web site:	www.whalecove.com/drake.html
Prices:	$
Theme:	Historic Mystery
Open:	Year Round

From 1577 to 1580, Drake sailed around the world on a journey of exploration and pillage. In 1579 Drake decided to sail from South America to England, by heading westward across the Pacific to England. Although a longer route, it was safer. He had spent over a year on the east coast of South America and the Spanish Fleet was looking for his ship the *Golden Hind*. Following Magellan's route, he sailed around the tip of South America. As he continued north, the *Golden Hind* across the Pacific, the ship had to be beached to make repairs. When Drake landed his ship, he and his crew stayed ashore for some time and made friends with the local Native Americans. He christened the land, New Albion. This is all part of the accepted historic record.

The location of New Albion is the current controversy. Based on Drake's logs, most historians believe he landed somewhere near San Francisco. Bob Ward, of the Drake in Oregon Society believes that Francis Drake landed in Whale Cove, south of Depoe Bay. He has many interesting historic artifacts and documents to support his theory.

Not Quite Ghosts

Although there are no ghosts associated with Drake's voyages, there are some supernatural connections. There are stories that claim Drake was a warlock. While he was at sea, the father of his fiancée tried to marry her off to a rival. As they were standing in church, a meteor crashed through the window. The startled wedding party assumed that Drake shot a cannon ball from his far away ship to stop the wedding. In another legend, Drake and other ship captains beat a magical drum, which brought the storm that wrecked the Spanish Armada. This drum is still in possession of the Drake family. The drum beat on it's own during the Battle of Britain, to aid the British RAF pilots.

Lincoln City, Oregon

Name: **Devil's Lake State Park**
Address: U.S. Hwy 101, east of Lincoln City, OR
Phone Number: **800 452-5687**
Prices: $
Theme: Native American legend, State park
Open: Year Round
Special Facilities: 32 RV sites, 68 tent campsites, 2 disabled persons campsites, restroom, showers, hiker/biker camp, boot moorage, fishing dock.

Directions: Devil's Lake State Park is 1/4 mile east of Lincoln City and Hwy 101. Look for signs. The campground is located off of NE 6th Drive, and the boat ramp is located on East Devil's Lake Road..

The Ghosts

According to legend, many years ago Chief Fleetfoot sent a canoe of warriors across the lake one moonlit night. When they reached the center of the lake, the still waters churned and a giant creature rose out of the lake and sunk their canoe. It is said that crossing the lake during the full moon will bring the creature to the surface. There have been many night boating accidents there, so I would recommend against testing the power of the legend, or the elements!

Name: **Wildflower Grill**
Address: 4150 N Hwy 101
Lincoln City, OR 97367
Phone Number: **541-994-9663**
Prices: $$
Theme: Historic home restaurant
Cuisine: Home cooking
Open: Daily 7 a.m. — 4 p.m.
Special Facilities: Open for dinner late 2001, home baked desserts

The Wildflower Grill restaurant opened in mid 2001 in a converted home. The owners have tailored their menu and décor to make people feel comfortable when they eat a leisurely meal at the beach.

The Ghosts

When the owners were converting the 1930s home into a restaurant they began feeling like they had a ghost or two. A female ghost haunts the ground floor. She looks after the restaurant. A male ghost haunts the upper floor, which is not open to the public. Shortly after the restaurant opened the chef was in the kitchen late at night. He glanced into the seating area and saw a shape walk through the restaurant. When he investigated he found himself alone.

Name: **Ghost Ship**
Address: near SW 51st Street and Hwy 101,
Siletz Bay, Lincoln City, OR

When visitors visit the bay today they often have a hard time believing that a ship could ever fit in the bay. In the 1940s or 1950s a spit was constructed, blocking half the bay. Seal sun themselves on the sandy bar, to the delight of tourists. The spit caused the bay behind it to silt up. The channel used to be deep enough for sailing ships over 100 feet long to enter the bay. There have been several boating accidents and at least one, perhaps three shipwrecks there.

The Ghosts

Several people have seen a ghostly sailing ship in the Siletz Bay since at least the 1940s. On the 26th of July, 2001, a woman watched a three masted ship enter the bay and head toward the shore, at full sail. She went to get her husband. When they returned, the ship had vanished. Two psychics were asked to point out the location of where they felt the ship might have wrecked. Later, a long-time resident confirmed that when he was a child, the ribs of an old ship had been visible in the same spot at low tide.

Nehalem, Oregon

Name: **Neahkahnie Mountain**
Address: Oswald West State Park
Near Manzanita, OR
Phone Number: **800 452-5687**
503 842-5501
Web site: www.ohwy.com/or/o/orpd.htm
Prices: $
Theme: Native American Spiritual
Center, buried treasure

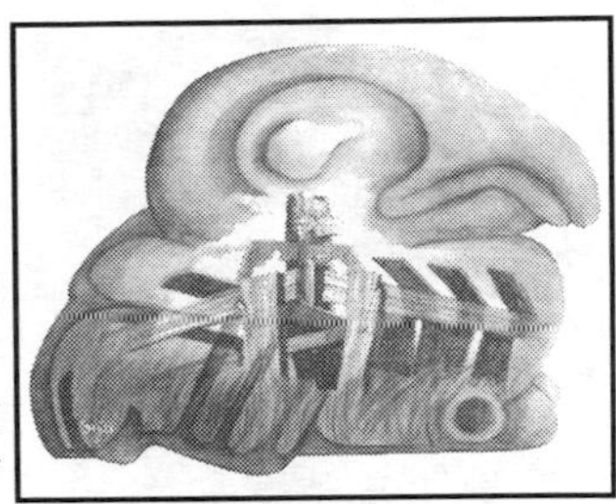

Open: Year Round
Special Facilities: 36 unimproved campsites, nature trails

Oswald West State Park is named for former Governor Oswald West. He was responsible for the State of Oregon turning much of the State's beach front property into parks rather than opening it up for development. Neahkahnie Mountain is located inside the park and is a Native American spiritual center. In the local Chinook dialect, Neah-Kah-nie can be translated as "Home of the fire God." It is the highest point for miles round and strange things have been reported there.

More recently, it has been a haunt of treasure hunters. According to Native American stories, sometime in the past a European ship wrecked upon the coast, and the sailors came ashore. They eventually attacked the local peoples, who killed them in self defense. Before that, the Europeans, probably Spaniards, buried a giant treasure chest on the mountain, leaving strangely carved stones as markers.

This oral tradition has been mixed with historical reports by people such as Lewis and Clark, and later settlers. Lewis and Clark met coastal people with light skin and red hair, supposed descendents of the Spaniards. Pieces of beeswax with mould marks from the Spanish Pacific trade routes were found along the beach.

What is not myth is the fact that for many years treasure hunters have dug massive holes and trenches across the mountain slopes in search of gold. Some have died, when their excavations collapsed on them. There is a trail to the top. The trailhead is located between mile markers 41 and 42 on Hwy 101. There is a gravel turn off, with a brown trail sign. Take the road and drive up the road for about ½ mile until you come to the Trailhead parking sign. The trail leading to the top of the mountain is about 1 ½ mile long. If the air is clear, the view from the mountain top is worth more than gold, in my opinion.

Canon Beach, Oregon

Name: **Bandage Man**
Address: The intersection of hwy 26 and hwy 101
Canon Beach, OR
Open: Year Round

People driving pick ups at the intersection of Highway 26 with

U.S. Highway 101 should be on the look out. A man like figure, wrapped in bloody bandages, may jump in the back of their vehicle. He sometimes pounds on the cab of the truck, or breaks windows. He then jumps out of the vehicle or simply disappears. He usually leaves behind a bloody bandage or the smell of rotting flesh. I contacted the Oregon State Police and no one has reported any Bandage Man incidents in over a decade.

The details of Bandage Man have gone beyond a folklore origin or ghost story into a super urban legend. He has been described as the ghost of an injured logger, a maniac, a Sasquatch wrapped in bandages and soon a space alien!

Name: **Ecola State Park**
Address: U.S. Hwy 101, north of Canon Beach, OR
Phone Number: **800 452-5687**
Prices: $
Theme: State park
Open: Year Round
Special Facilities: Hiking trails, pay parking, restroom, picnic areas, viewpoints

Directions: Ecola State Park is one mile south of the junction of Hwys 26 and 101. Look for signs. There are two parking areas.

The word Ecola is from the Chinookan, meaning whale. In 1806, Captain William Clark and members of his expedition went in search of food to supplement their diet of dried salmon. They found a group of Chinook Indians in the vicinity of the present Ecola state park, butchering a large whale. Clark purchased 300 pounds of blubber for his party to eat over the winter.

The Ghosts

At least one group of hikers has had a strange encounter along the trail that passes Indian Beach. In the mid-1990s a teenager and his aunt were hiking up a trail. At one point the trail was very narrow and enclosed by dense brush and trees. They were surprised to see a couple walk up the trail a few feet ahead of them. They called out to the couple, who were walking hand in hand, and asked for the time. The people stopped, turned and told them the time, 3:15 p.m.. The couple vanished.

The curious hikers tried to catch up with the elusive couple. They walked up the trail and nearly fell over a drop-off, when the trail ended at a cliff.

The boy and his aunt were convinced that the couple had not doubled back around them, nor had they jumped off the cliff face. They turned around and stumbled down the trail in terror. A few minutes later, when they returned to the trailhead, worried relatives informed them that it was after 5:30 p.m. In the late 1980s, a landslide had closed off the trail for over a year. This happened before the teenager and his aunt took their near fatal trip on the Indian Beach Trail.

Was this a strange episode of lost time, where two separate groups of hikers had somehow intruded into the same space and time for a short while?

From Ecola State Park and Canon Beach you can see **Tillamook Rock lighthouse**. The lighthouse was built on a rock outcrop some distance offshore, between Canon Beach and Seaside. The rock was considered sacred to Native Americans. At least one person was killed during its construction. It was one of the most isolated lighthouses, receiving re-supply at six month intervals. The lighthouse was reputedly haunted, and is now a storage facility for cremated remains. It is not open to the public, but is still an inspiring sight on clear days.

Astoria, Oregon

Name: **Uppertown Fire House Museum**
Address: 2986 Marine Drive
Astoria, OR 97103
Phone Number: **503 325-2205**
Prices: $
Theme: Historic Fire House museum
Open: May – September 10 a.m – 5 p.m.
October – April 11 a.m. – 4 p.m.
Closed Thanksgiving, Christmas & New Years
Special Facilities: Gift shop

The Uppertown Fire Station was built in 1896 as the North Pacific Brewery, which closed during Prohibition. It was purchased by the City of Astoria and converted into a fire station in 1920. The building was used as a fire station until 1960. The third floor was used a combination storage facility and youth club until it was re-opened as a museum in 1990.

One fixture of all fire stations is the brass pole that fire fighters

slide down to get to the engines. When I visited the museum a staff member pointed out the sealed opening around the brass pole. Tradition has it that a firefighter who used to sleepwalk fell through the hole and died. His ghost is supposed to haunt this building. This may be mixed up with the story of Paul Marion, a firefighter who worked out of the old fire station at 4th and Astor Street. Marion fell down the hole there and died one night in 1928.

The Ghosts

Most of the firefighters knew there was something wrong with the building. They heard the sounds of things being dragged across the floor. Sometimes the ghost would come down to their quarters on the second floor. In the middle of the night the doors on the fire crew's equipment lockers would rattle and shake. The noise was loud enough to awaken the fire fighters. When the firehouse was closed gear was stored there. A work crew checked the old furnace every afternoon. Several times they reported strange noises on the third floor. They never found anyone in the building. The museum staff are willing to discuss the haunting in historical terms but they believe every story.

Name: **Fort Stevens State Park**
Address: Ridge Road, Hammond, OR
(outside of Astoria, OR)
Phone Number: **503 861-1470**
Web site: www.visitfortstevens.com
Rooms: 9 yurts, 213 RV hookups, 128 electric campsites
6 campsites for disabled persons, 7 group campsites
Prices: $
Theme: Historic military facility
Open: Year round
Special Facilities: Museum, boat ramp, restroom, shower, yearly re-creation military encampment

During the War of 1812 British warships blockaded the mouth of the Columbia River and cut off supplies to Fort Astoria. The Civil War motivated the War Department to look to the security of the Union in the Pacific. In the summer of 1863, Captain George Elliot began work on several gun emplacements at the mouth of the Columbia. He constructed roads, earthworks and emplacements for over 40 guns at Fort

Stevens.

On the 21st of June 1942, a Japanese submarine surfaced and fired several rounds at Fort Stevens from their deck gun. The closest hit the beach in front of Battery Russell. This was the only instance of United States soil being attacked by a foreign enemy in the 20th Century. In 1947 the gun emplacements were decommissioned and the guns were removed. A few years later Ft Stevens State park was opened, There are re-creations of the Civil War era gun emplacements being constructed as well as reproductions of the original canons.

The Ghosts

Visitors walking along the old road near Battery Russell have heard the sound of a metallic ringing or clanging, like a swinging chain or metal banging on metal. The light of a flashlight moving along the road usually accompanies this sound. The light and sound will approach people on the road and get so close that people have seen the outline of a man, holding the flashlight. At that point, the light and noise always cease and disappear. Some people think that this may be the ghost of a park night watchman or guard patrolling the road.

Seaview, Washington

Name: **Lamplighter Restaurant**
Address: 39th and L Street
Seaview, WA 98644
Phone Number: **360 642-2375**
Prices: $$
Theme: Historic restaurant
Cuisine: Northwest
Open: Year Round
Special Facilities: Lounge

Directions: To get to the Lamplighter, Take Highway 101 west to Seaview/Holman, turn right on the 103 loop, then left on 40th Place, and left onto L Street. The Lamplighter is in the middle of the first block.

The Ghosts

The Lamplighter Inn has been a part of the Long Beach community for over 125 years. The primary candidate for the ghost is Louie Sloan. Louie owned the restaurant for decades, before selling it in 1963. He stuck around as a regular until he died in 1977. One night shortly after Louie's death, the manager had to turn off the bar lights to chase out some late customers. She walked away from the light switch and was surprised when the lights came back on. She walked back to the switch and found it was still in the off position.

In 1990, an employee heard a clicking noise and looked at the pool table. She watched as the pool balls began moving across the table, bumping into each other without anyone nearby. This continued for several minutes. When he died, Louie was cremated and his ashes went unclaimed until 1992. The owners of the Lamplighter accepted the urn containing Louie's ashes and placed it in the lounge. Since that time most of the physical manifestations have ceased. The manager is too busy to talk about any recent happenings, if any.

Menlo, Washington

Name:	**Willia Keil's Grave**
Address:	Menlo, WA
Prices:	$
Theme:	Historic grave marker
Open:	Year Round

Directions: A Washington landmark sign on SR 6, between Raymond and Menlo, marks the grave. If you are on Hwy 101, turn south on SR 6 and head south, you will see the marker just north of Menlo.

Willie Keil's grave is not a monument to his life, but to how his death saved the lives of his family. Willie was the son of William Keil, SR, who emigrated to New York from Prussia in the 1830s. The elder Keil first settled in New York, then moved to Pittsburgh and eventually moved to Missouri in 1844, where he became a prominent member of the Bethelite religious community. In 1855, Keil decided to spread his form of gospel to the Pacific Northwest. His son Willie asked permission to ride in the lead wagon. He died a few days before the trip began.

The elder Keil had Willie's coffin lined with lead and he filled it with whiskey from the Belthelite distillery. He put the coffin in the front seat of his wagon, draped in black and bells and set out along the Oregon trail. Along the way they were approached several times by Indians from many tribes, including Sioux, Cayuse and Yakima warriors. Each time Keil took the lid off the coffin to show them his son, and the gathered pioneers sang dirges in German for them. Each time they were allowed to pass safely to northwest Washington.

They settled along the Willapa River and buried Willie on the day after Christmas. Unfortunately, the weather was too much for them, and the colony relocated to what is now Aurora, Oregon.. The only thing left of their colony is Willie's grave.

Tokeland, Washington

Name: **Tokeland Hotel**
Address: 100 Tokeland Road
Tokeland, WA 98590
Phone Number: **360 267-7006**
Rooms: 18
Prices: $$
Theme: Historic Seaside Hotel
Cuisine: Country
Open: Hotel usually closes during the week from the 1st of December through early spring. The restaurant is open while the hotel has guests.
Special Facilities: No room #13, meeting room, TV, non-smoking rooms

Directions: The Tokeland hotel can be approached along Hwy 105 from either the north or the south. From the highway, turn south on Tokeland Road, into Tokeland. The hotel is located on this main road.

The town of Tokeland was built on a little peninsula on the north entrance of Willapa Bay. The hotel was originally a farmhouse, built by William and Lizzie Kindred. Visitors arrived in Willapa Bay by carriage or steamer, in great numbers at the turn of the 19th century. In 1899, the Kindred's added on to their house, turning it into a summer beach resort. It is the oldest operating inn in Washington. The hotel restaurant is the only restaurant in Tokeland.

The Ghosts

According to local legends, in the early 20th century Tokeland's position along Willapa Bay was a great drop off point for ships smuggling illegal Oriental immigrants into the United States. Charlie was one of the many who traveled through Tokeland. He hid in the fireplace room, where he died while hidden in the back of the fireplace. Guests in Room 3 have felt someone sit on the bed. Others have told the staff it was nice to have a cat sitting at the foot of their beds… A psychic had bad vibrations from Room 7.

Aberdeen, Washington

Kurt Cobain was born in Aberdeen and is one of the City's most recent celebrities. People often come into Billy's Bar & Grill, asking for directions to the house where he was born. Most do not know about an earlier celebrity; Billy Gohl.

Name: **Billy's Bar & Grill**
Address: 322 E Heron St.
Aberdeen, WA 98520
Phone Number: **360 533-7144**
Prices: $$
Theme: Bar & Grill
Cuisine: Famous burgers and seafood
Open: Monday — Sunday, 7:00 a.m. — midnight
Special Facilities: Microbrews, 11 beers on tap

Billy's is not haunted, but it was named for one of Aberdeen's earlier celebrities, Billy Gohl. Gohl was a common sailor and laborer who came to Aberdeen in 1903. He became the representative for the Sailors' Union of the Pacific. He had an office on a wharf, near the present day restaurant. This location allowed him to practice his secret avocation as a serial killer.

Billy liked to target sailors and laborers. Many men came to his office for interviews or to leave valuables in Billy's care. If the man met his profile, Billy would shoot, poison, strangle or bludgeon the man and take his valuables. He dumped the body through a trap door in the floor where it fell into the Wishkay River. The river carried the corpse to Gray's Harbor. Between 1909 and 1912, 41 'floaters' were found in the bay. Among the annals of serial killers, this is a kind of record. There are estimates that in a ten year period Gohl killed at least 124 people. When Gohl was caught he was sentenced to life in prison.

The entire affair left a bad memory for the city of Aberdeen. He was not talked about or mentioned in local history journals. In recent years, Aberdeen has been more open about this part of its history.

Name: **The Lady Washington**
Address: Grays Harbor Historical Seaport
712 Hagara St (offices)
Aberdeen, WA 98520
Phone Number: **800 200-5239**
Fax Number: 360 533-9384

Web site: www.ladywashington.org
Capacity: 48 passengers
Prices: $$$
Theme: Historic Sailing Ship
Open: See website for schedule
Special Facilities: Cabins and bunks below decks, running water

The *Lady Washington* is a reproduction of the original *Lady Washington*, the ship of Captain Robert Gray. In 1788, it was the first United States ship to visit the Pacific Northwest. The *Lady Washington* is a two masted Brigantine ship, built in 1989. She is 112 foot in length and 22 feet wide. Her actual deck length is 68 feet, the tallest mast is 90 feet high and she weighs 195 tons. The *Lady Washington* is capable of traveling at 9 knots when under full sail. She is armed with two 3-pound deck guns and four swivel guns. She has a crew of 12 and a maximum passenger capacity of 60 people.

The *Lady Washington* has a long itinerary of good will missions, sailing up and down the Pacific Coast. The ship usually makes day trips with passengers, though there are week long family packages, two week crew training cruises as well as being available for chartered cruises.

The Ghosts

I spoke with one of the volunteer crew members who had an interesting series of experiences. He does not believe that the ship is haunted. But when she comes into old ports, the historic ghosts that remain on the docks seem to gravitate to the tall ship. He told me that he saw, or thought he saw ghosts dressed in 19th century costume come from a dock, onto the deck of the *Lady Washington* in one Oregon port.

Lake Quinault

Name: **Lake Quinault Lodge**
Address: PO Box 7
Quinault, WA 98575
Phone Number: **800 562-6672**
360 288-2900
Web site: www.visitlakequinault.com
Rooms: 92 with bath
Prices: $$ - $$$ Seasonal rates
Theme: Historic Lodge
Cuisine: Northwest Gourmet $$
Open: Daily for Breakfast, Lunch and Dinner

Lounge opens Monday – Friday 4 p.m., Saturday & Sunday, Noon
Special Facilities: Lounge, gift shop, game room, no phones, no TV, some rooms have fireplaces, lake recreation facilities

Directions: Lake Quinault Lodge is located in the Olympic National Forest, between Neilton and Queets. The lodge is easy to find when driving north or south on Highway 101. At the southwest corner of Lake Quinault, take South Shore Road east. It is two miles to the lodge.

In 1926, Lumber baron Ralph Emerson decided he wanted Lake Quinault Lodge built in a hurry. In two weeks, Joseph Skoog, a Seattle Architect drew up plans for this Georgian-Tudor style hotel. In six weeks, crews working evenings and weekends completed this 92 room hotel overlooking Lake Quinault. Despite the rush job, the craftsmen added many finishing touches to the log beams in the lobby. They carved ornate dogs, ducks, deer and dancers on the woodwork.

In 1937, President Franklin Roosevelt toured the Olympic Peninsula. He was lobbied by local preservationists, who wanted him to turn the area into a National Park. A rainstorm drove them into the hotel, where he was served lunch and entertained by local school children. Their lobbying paid off, the Park contains nearly one million acres and includes the north shore of the Lake. The Lodge is a little rustic, but many guests like the way it forces them to get out and enjoy the scenery.

The Ghosts

According to stories perpetuated by the staff, the resident ghost of the hotel is named Beverly. Unlike many ghosts, Beverly was not murdered she died in her sleep. She must have liked her room, because she has never left. In 1991, one of the guests saw Beverly standing at the foot of her bed. The night watchman had a run in with her when she kept on turning the radio on in his office one night.

British Columbia

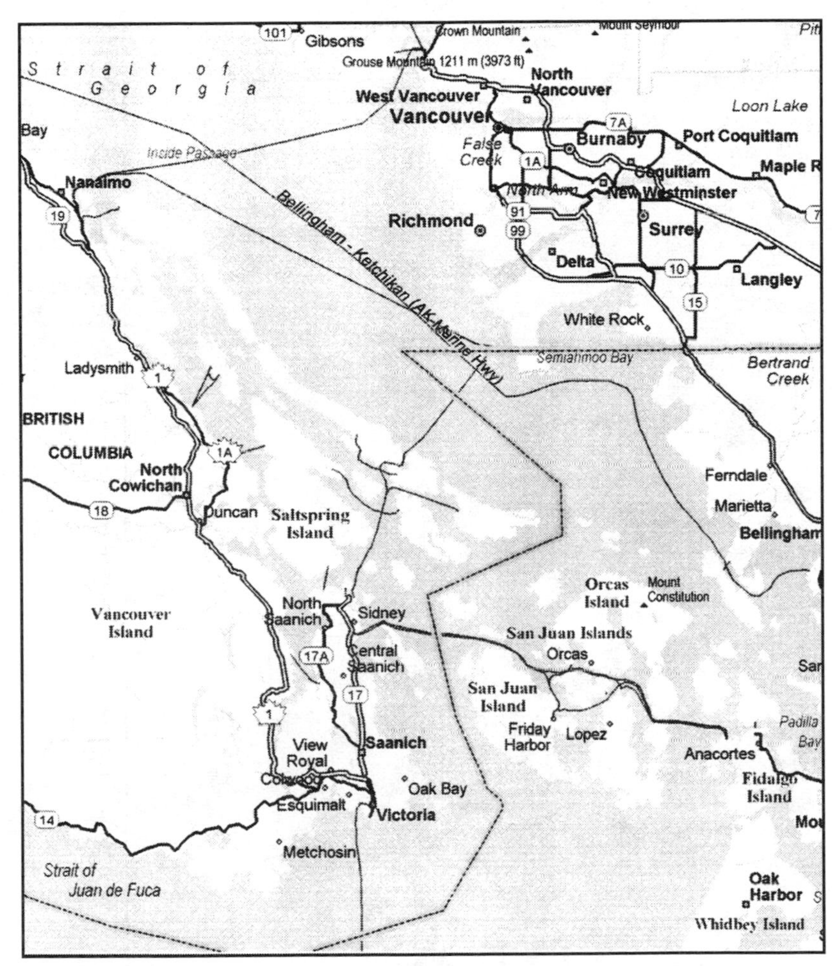

New Westminster, B.C.

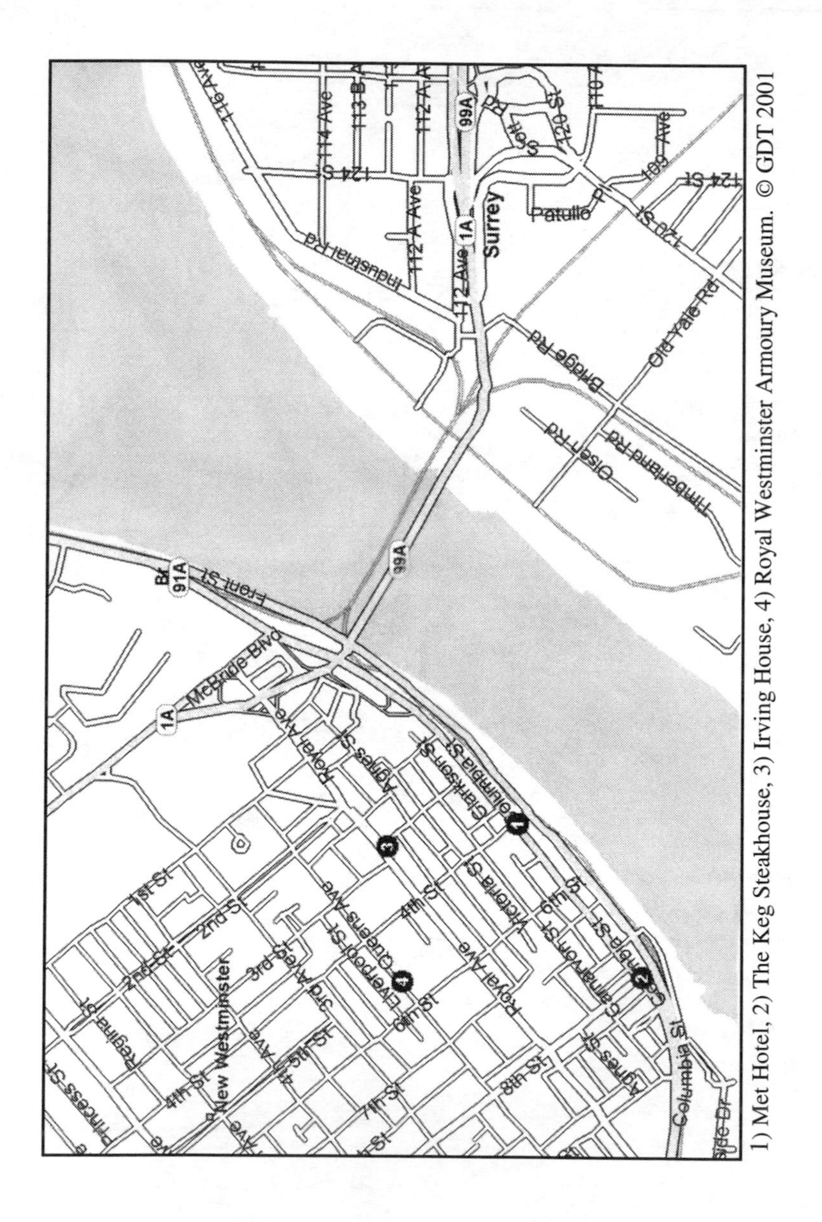

1) Met Hotel, 2) The Keg Steakhouse, 3) Irving House, 4) Royal Westminster Armoury Museum. © GDT 2001

Downtown Vancouver B.C.

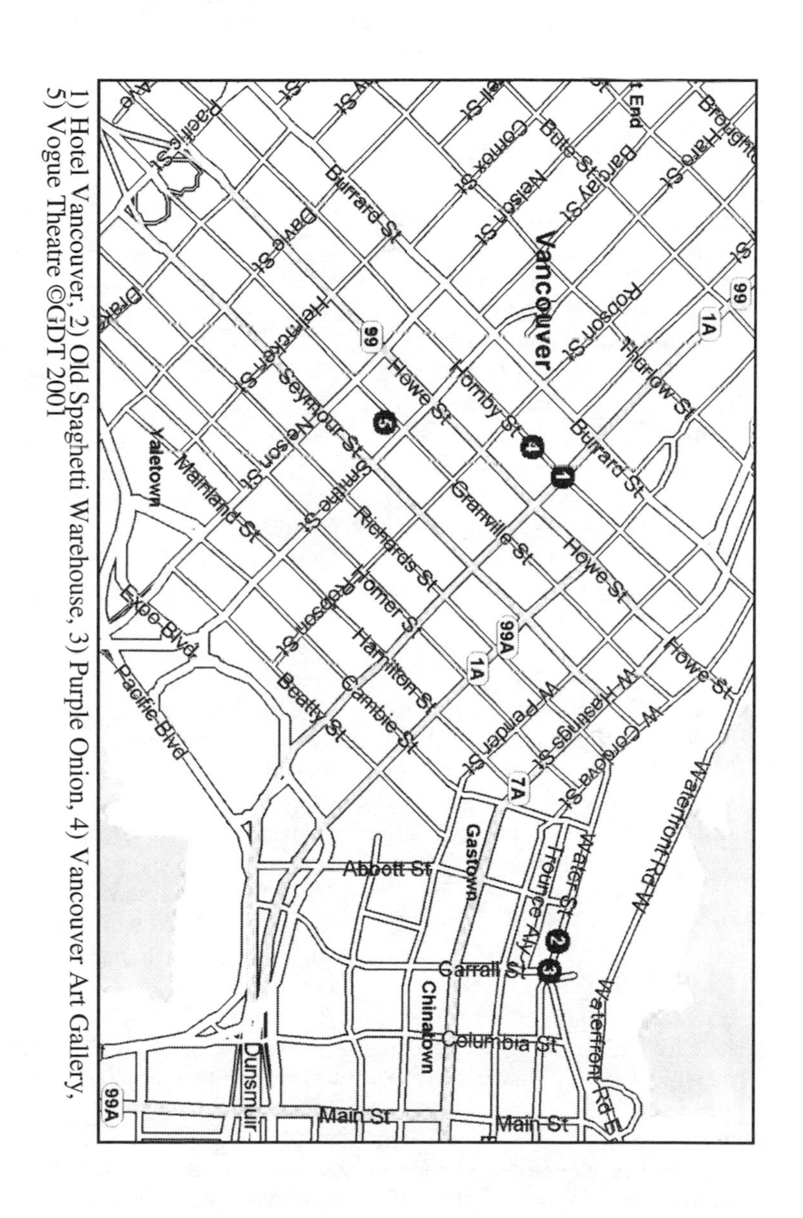

1) Hotel Vancouver, 2) Old Spaghetti Warehouse, 3) Purple Onion, 4) Vancouver Art Gallery, 5) Vogue Theatre ©GDT 2001

British Columbia

I came across a common problem for United States tourists, what is the U.S. / Canadian Dollar exchange rate? I have tried to take the international money market into account when determining the price guide here.

Vancouver B.C. and Surrounding Cities

Places to Stay

Name:	**Hotel Vancouver**
Address:	900 West Georgie Street Vancouver, B.C. V6C 2W6
Phone Number:	**800-441-1414** **604-684-3131**
Fax Number:	604-662-1929
Prices:	$$$
Theme:	Elegant European Hotel
Cuisine:	Gourmet Griffins Restaurant $$$ West Restaurant & Wine Bar $$
Open:	Daily

Special Facilities: Gift shop, indoor pool, hot tub, concierge, fitness center, lounge, two restaurants, High Tea, conference facilities

The seventeen story Hotel Vancouver was built in 1939. It was a luxurious throwback to the hotels built by the Canadian National and Pacific Railways in the late 19th century. It was modeled after a French Chateau, with a copper roof and ornate windows. The hotel looks a little Gothic because of the Gargoyles and simplistic carvings decorating the outside. The European style lobby is lavish, with crystal chandeliers, wood paneling, marble inlay floors and columns.

The hotel was remodeled in 1999 and the rooms were modernized, but the hotel management was careful to maintain the old-world elegance. My wife and I took High Tea in the lounge. We sat in high backed chairs that were more comfortable than they looked as our server brought us an assortment of teas, and a multi-tiered tray with clotted cream, petit fours, and crust less sandwiches. To be honest, she had High Tea and I had a very good pastrami sandwich.

The Ghosts

The ghost of a woman dressed in a red dress haunts the hotel. She was seen on the 14th floor of the hotel when it was being constructed in 1939. This is actually the 13th floor, but the hotel does not officially have an unlucky 13th floor. She has been seen in the main lobby, where she's told people to get out of her seat. Other times she's been seen boarding the elevator and disappearing before it reaches her floor.

Name: **Met Hotel**
Address: 411 Columbia Street
New Westminster, B.C. V3L 1A9
Phone Number: **888-512-5511**
604-520-3815/
Fax Number: 604-520-0657
Web site: www.themethotel.com
Rooms: 20
Prices: $$ (includes continental breakfast)
Theme: European style hotel
Cuisine: Northwest
Met Bar & Grill $$
Open: Lunch and Dinner
Special Facilities: Business meeting rooms, catering, exercise room, room service, television.

The Met Hotel survived the Great Fire of 1886, which destroyed most of New Westminister. It is one of the oldest buildings in the Vancouver B.C. area. The Met is a classic example of Victorian Romanesque architecture and 19th century, small luxury hotels. Each level of the four- story building has its own lobby, and all of the rooms have 11-foot high ceilings. The hotel has been redecorated and its furnishings include hands free telephones and internet connections as well as a color television in each room.

The Ghosts

There are two unrelated hauntings in this old fashioned hotel. One ghost is George. He was a long time resident who died in his room. A few years ago, a workman saw flashes of light coming from George's old room one night. When he checked out the room, he could not find a reason for the light effects. George has been seen floating down the hotel hallways, passing through solid walls.

The second haunting is the ghosts of an elderly couple. They have been seen on the fourth floor as well as by the hotel elevator. They are usually seen talking with each other. They disappear when approached. Some people experience a feeling of peace when the ghostly couple is seen.

Restaurants, Clubs and Theaters

Name: **Bridge House Restaurant**
Address: 3650 Capilano Road
North Vancouver B.C. V7R 4J1
Phone Number: 604-987-3388
Prices: $$
Theme: Historic Home restaurant
Cuisine: West Coast gourmet
Open: 11 a.m., last seating at 7 p.m.
Special Facilities: Intimate dining, banquet room, hours can change so call ahead for reservations.

The Capilano Suspension Bridge built by George Grant Mackay in 1889 was a swinging rope bridge that many were afraid to cross. It is still there, 450 feet long, swaying 230 feet above the Capilano River. The Bridge House was built in 1934 as the home of Mac and Elizabeth MacEachran. They owned the bridge and Elizabeth was property caretaker. Today the bridge and surrounding area is a public park.

The house, including the original stone fireplace has been preserved and turned into a restaurant. The living rooms have been turned into small, secluded dining areas. The restaurant promotes casual, gourmet-dining specializing in local foods.

The Ghosts

There are many stories of Elizabeth, who haunts the restaurant building. Elizabeth seems to want the house looked after. She watched an employee iron linen in the basement once. Footsteps are heard by employees and customers and bottles have been pushed off shelves by invisible shelves.

Name: **Hart House Restaurant**
Address: 6664 Deer Lake Avenue
Burnaby, B.C. V5E 4H3
Phone Number: 604-298-4278
Fax Number: 604 298-0124
Prices: $$$
Theme: Mansion turned into restaurant
Cuisine: Northwest, local delicacies
Open: Lunch, Tuesday – Friday, 11:30 a.m. – 2:30 p.m.
Dinner Tuesday – Thursday & Sunday, 5:30 p.m. – 9:00 p.m.
Friday & Saturday, 5:30 p.m. – 10:00 p.m.
Special Facilities: Wheel Chair Access

Hart House was built on a 12-acre estate by Frederick Hart in 1910. Hart wanted something of old England to retire to. He had architect Frank Macey design this Tudor style mansion with exposed beams and leaded glass windows. He called the house 'Avalon,' after the Avalon Peninsula in New Foundland. Montague Moore purchased the house in 1916 and his family lived there until 1950. His wife designed the famous Rosedale Gardens on the estate grounds.

After the Moore family sold the house, it changed hands many times. Later owners modernized the interior and in the process some of the older features were removed. The Corporation of the District of Burnaby bought the house in 1979. In 1989 Paul & Carol Smolen and their partners leased the house and turned it into a restaurant.

The Ghosts

The ghost at Hart House is very discrete. Long time employees talk about small incidents. The most notable is the grandfather clock in the lobby. Periodically it begins tolling, even though it does not work.

A few years ago, actor Richard Gere filmed a movie at the Hart House and gave Paul Smolen an autographed picture. This was hung in the ladies lounge. In early 2001 it disappeared. It reappeared a few weeks later, in a new, ornate frame. If the ghost did this, I can guess at it's gender.

Nearby is the Burnaby Village Museum, a 10 acre open air museum that depicts a Canadian village of 1925. There is supposed to be a ghost haunting one of the historic buildings that was moved to the village site.

Name: **Jake's Crossing**
Address: 2414 St. Johns
Port Moody, B.C.
Phone Number: **604-939-7811**
Theme: Railroad saloon f
Cuisine: Pub grub
Open: Lunch and dinner
<u>Special Facilities:</u> Bar

The Ghosts

When Jake's Crossing was known as the Port Moody Arms, the unofficial caretaker was a man named David "Slim" Kirkpatrick. Slim lived in the basement, near the beer keg storage area. In the late 1970s Slim became ill and died in the hospital. After that, some of the employees felt strange in the basement area, but that may have been memories of the departed Slim rather than a true ghost.

In the mid-1980s, the owners sold the Port Moody Arms and management changed. The new owners and clientele began seeing a tall man dressed in a plaid shirt in the restaurant lounge. He always disappeared when confronted. One night a broken record player began to work on its own. Liquor bottles fall off the bar of their own accord, appliances turn on or off without being touched. Doors are also opened when they were locked. Slim seems content to play tricks on the staff and customers. I visited Jake's Crossing in 2000 and was told that he's still active.

Name: **Old Spaghetti Factory**
Address: 53 Water St
Vancouver, BC V6B 1A1
Phone Number: **604 684-1288**
Web site: www.oldspaghettifactory.co/gastown.html
Prices: $$
Theme: antique and stained glass
Cuisine: Pasta
Open: Monday – Thursday 11:30 a.m. – 10 p.m.
Friday & Saturday: 11:30 a.m. – 11 p.m.
Sunday: 11:30 a.m. – 9 p.m.
Special Facilities: Patio seating, parking is free on weekday evenings, all day on weekends. Meal costs include salad, bread and ice cream, tea or coffee.

The Old Spaghetti Factory is located in a warehouse built around 1900, by the W.H. Malkin Company. At the time, they were famous importers of teas and coffee. This area is known as Gastown, and is the center of the oldest part of Vancouver B.C. Visitors can see a steam powered clock nearby. The warehouse was converted into an office building in the 1930s. In the 1960s, the Gastown neighborhood suffered from urban decay, and so did this building.

In the 1970s the first Canadian Old Spaghetti Factory restaurant opened in the old warehouse building. The Spaghetti Factory finds old buildings in historic districts, and renovates them. They do their best to keep the historic character intact. The Gastown Old Spaghetti Factory's chief attraction is a restored trolley car, dating to the late 1800s.

The Ghosts

The historic trolley may be the center of the haunting at this restaurant. A shadowy figure was captured on film, sitting in the trolley in a picture taken in the 1950s. The problem is that the trolley was empty when the picture was snapped. A copy of the picture used to hang in the restaurant. Some employees have reported seeing a figure sitting in the trolley. Other people have heard their name called.

A red haired man dressed in red clothing sometimes hides in an empty stall in the ladies restroom. He will surprise women by bursting out of the stall, laughing and exiting the restroom and disappearing. When I visited in 2000, I spoke with a maintenance worker and a manager. Both denied any knowledge of the red haired ghost. One of them told me he would quit if he found a ghost there.

Name: **Purple Onion**
Address: 15 Water Street (2nd floor)
Vancouver B.C. V6A 1A1
Phone Number: **604-602-9442**
Fax Number: 604-602-1270
Web site: www.purpleonion.com
Prices: $$
Theme: Cabaret
Open: Monday – Sunday, 9:00 p.m. - Midnight
Special Facilities: Reservations needed, two rooms, DJs, live music.

The Purple Onion is located on the second floor of an old Gastown building. It used to be a comedy club called Punchlines. A few years ago, it was converted into a Jazz club named the Purple Onion. There was a fire recently, which damaged the club interior. The owners took the opportunity to make changes in the clubs décor and venue.

The Purple Onion is now a cabaret, featuring a wide variety of acts. The stage has been extended and booths have become cozier. There are two rooms, a main room and a smaller, more intimate room. The sound and lighting system have also been upgraded. Visiting movie stars and musicians have been known to hang out there.

The Ghosts

When the building was a comedy club named Punchlines, the owner reported some strange incidents. When he arrived at the club in the mornings, the candles at the tables would already be lit. He once heard someone call his name from the empty back room. A worker once asked him who the old man in the back room was. The room was empty.

Name: **The Station Keg Restaurant**
Address: 800 Columbia Street
New Westminster, B.C. V3L 1A9
Phone Number: 604-524-1381
Prices: $$$
Theme: Historic building converted into restaurant
Cuisine: Steak and seafood
Open: Monday — Thursday, 4:00 p.m. — 11:00 p.m.
Friday and Saturday, 4:00 p.m. — Midnight
Sunday, 4 p.m.— 10 p.m.
Special Facilities: Hours can vary, call for reservations

The Keg is located in the original Canadian Pacific Railway station building. The train station is built of stone and brick, and resembles many of the English train stations constructed at the same time.

The Ghosts

This haunt seems to have wound down, with few recent incidents. The basement seems to be the focus of the hauntings. In the slightly spooky setting, several staff members heard their name called by disembodied voices there. I do not know if the haunting extends to the main floor and guests are not allowed in the basement.

Shops, Sights and Sounds

Name: **Irving House Museum**
Address: 302 Royal Avenue
New Westminster, B.C. V3C 1H7
Phone Number: 604-527-4640
Fax Number: 604-527-4641
Web site: www.city.new-westminster.cb.ca/cityhall/museum
Prices: $ (donation)
Theme: Historic house museum
Open: May 1st –Mid-September, Tuesday – Sunday,
11:00 a.m.– 5:00 p.m.

April 30th – Mid-September, 1:00 p.m. – 5:00 p.m.
Special Facilities: Knowledgeable tour guides in period clothing.

Captain William Irving had the Royal Engineers build this wonderful house in 1862. Irving spent years living at the sea and had them incorporate nautical designs in the house. This included caulking the floorboards, so that the old house is nearly "creak" free. Irving lived there for ten years before he died of pneumonia. Irving was a large man and his specially built bed is on display. In 1887 there was one period of major renovation done on the house when new utilities were added.

This is the period reflected in the museum displays. The Irving family were active in local society and lived in the house until 1950. The local government acquired the house and turned it into a museum. A knowledgeable staff conducts tours and do not mind discussing ghosts.

The Ghosts

Captain Irving and his family may still be attached to their fine home. During one tour, a child asked her mother why a man was allowed to lie down in one of the beds. It was Captain Irving's room. No one saw a man in his bedroom before. When museum staff investigated they saw that the covers on his bed had been rumpled.

When the staff stays late at night, they sometimes hear the sound of someone pacing in the upper floors. This is probably not the floor settling, since the caulking prevents random creaks and cracks. This may be Mrs. Irving, who has also been seen.

Name: **Ghost Hitchhiker**
Address: Near the Corner of Blanca &University Avenue
Vancouver B.C.
Theme: Murder scene
Open: Year Round

The Ghosts

Every region has a story of a ghostly hitchhiker who haunts the vicinity of his or her death. Vancouver has one as well. This wraith is a woman , who wants nothing more than to go home. She flags down motorists asking for help. When someone stops to help, the ghost disappears.

Name: **Royal Westminster Regiment Armoury Museum**
Address: 530 Queen's Avenue
New Westminster, B.C. V3L 1K3
Phone Number: 604-526-5116

Prices: $ (donations accepted)
Theme: Historic military museum
Open: Tuesdays, 11:00 a.m. – 3:00 p.m.
Thursday, 11:00 a.m. – 3:00 p.m., 7:00 p.m.- 9:00 p.m.

This Armoury is the home of the Royal Westminister Regiment. It was first formed in 1863, by volunteers to protect against Native American uprisings and threats from the United States. The Regiment has served in South Africa, and Europe in World War I and World War II. In that time, it has earned 28 battle honors and two of its members were awarded the Victoria Cross.

The Regiment was assigned to the present Armoury in 1893. The building has remained its home ever since. Elements of the Regiment still meet there, as well as the 2316 Royal Westminster Regiment Army Cadets. The museum is located in the old gunroom, which was built around 1895 and is staffed by volunteers. It has displays of artifacts such as weapons, uniforms, medals, awards, trophies and memorabilia dating back to the original founding of the Regiment.

The Ghosts

I do not know much about the ghosts that reputably haunt the museum. They may be attached to the exhibits or some old soldiers who refused to merely fade away, and may still occupy the buildings. The staff is suspiciously quiet about ghosts.

Name: **Vancouver Art Gallery**
Address: 750 Hornby Street
Vancouver B.C. V6H 2V4
Phone Number: **604-662-4719**
Fax Number: 604-682-1086
Web site: www.vanartgallery.cb.ca
Prices: $$
Theme: Historic building turned into art gallery
Open: April 25th – October 12th
Monday – Sunday, 10:00 a.m. – 5:30 p.m.
Thursdays open until 9:00 p.m.

Jefferson Davis

October 13th- April 24th.
Monday – Sunday, 10:00 a.m. – 4:30 p.m.
The gallery is closed Mondays

Special Facilities: Modern and historic art, gallery shop, cafe

The Vancouver Art Gallery is located in the old Vancouver City courthouse, built in 1910 or 1911. Like many judicial buildings, the Courthouse has a Greco-Roman theme. Outside, heavy columns support a pediment front. Behind the pediment is a high dome. Lions guard the main entrance and broad steps. Inside, the walls are decorated with plaster designs and the doors are heavy, dark-wood. The glass topped rotunda dome lightens this dark effect.

In 1983 a new courthouse was built and the old one was turned into a museum. The gallery had a permanent collection that includes both modern Canadian and 18th and 19th century art. This includes Dutch as well as British paintings and sculpture. A portion of the collection is always on display in the four floors of exhibits.

The Ghosts

Sometimes justice is not only blind; it can be taken by surprise. Immigration officer William Charles Hopkinson was at the courthouse, many years ago. He was waiting to give evidence against a prisoner held in the lower cells. The defendant knifed him in the basement before Hopkinson could testify. Charlie now haunts the lower level, and is heard by the security guards as he wanders around in the dark.

Name: **Visual Arts Burnaby/Gallery at Ceperley**
Address: 6344 Deerlake Avenue
Burnaby B.C., V5G 213
Phone Number: **604-205-7332**
Fax Number: 604-205-7339
Web site: www.burnabyparksrec.org
Prices: $
Theme: Historic house art gallery
Open: Tuesday – Friday, 10:00 a.m. – 4:30 p.m.
Saturday & Sunday, noon – 5:00 p.m.

Special Facilities: Special art displays, individual and corporate art rentals possible

Between 1909 and 1911 Henry and Grace Ceperley built their retirement home, Fairacres, on the shore of Deer Lake. From the lake, the large stone porch adds an interesting effect to the Tudor style building. The interior of the building was finished with handcrafted

woodwork and stained glass.

Grace Ceperley died in 1917. She stipulated in her will that when the house was sold; the money would go to children's charities. A group of Benedictine monks bought the house as a monastery in 1939. An American evangelical minister who called himself Archbishop John the Ist was next. He established a church headquarters and school. According to some rumors, his religious order practiced ritual child abuse there. He was eventually arrested by U.S. and Canadian authorities for bigamy and embezzlement. The city of Burnaby soon acquired the house and after a brief stint as a fraternity house, converted it into an art museum in the 1960s.

The Ghosts

The gallery staff has seen the wispy figure of Grace Ceperly walking the hallways at night. A spectral man has also been seen at the top of the stairs. The sound of children crying has been heard on the third floor. This is where John the Ist' people punished their children. An employee heard the sound of furniture scraping the floor from his second floor office. In the 1980s, a ghost hunter spent the night there and was awakened by a heavy weight on his chest.

Nearby is the Burnaby Village Museum, a ten acre open air museum that depicts a Canadian village of 1925. There is supposed to be a ghost haunting one of the historic buildings that was moved to the village site.

Name: **Vogue Theatre**
Address: 918 Granville
Vancouver B.C. V6Z lL2
Phone Number: **604-331-7902**
Fax Number: 604-331-7901
Web site: www.voguetheatre.com
Prices: $$
Theme: Historic theatre
Open: See box office

Special Facilities: There are 1,144 seats in three levels, with four wheelchair accessible seats.

The Art Deco style Vogue Theatre was built in 1941. Its designers wanted to make it an intimate theater, along the same lines as theatres in New York or London's West End. The Vogue has hosted a variety of live acts over the years and is the home of the Vancouver International Jazz Festival and the Vancouver International Film Festival.

The Vogue was renovated in 1998 to refurbish the interior décor as well as upgrade the technical specifications of the theatre. This restored the Vogue to its place as the foremost live performance venue in Vancouver. Many non-profit groups use the theatre for their venues.

The Ghosts

Three or four ghosts haunt the Vogue Theatre. The heavy steel basement doors sometimes open and slam shut on their own. People working there feel as if they are being watched. Staff in the stage area has seen an old man in a trench coat, walking back and forth through a door that turns out to be locked. People sitting in the fifth and sixth rows near the orchestra can hear the sound of a handful of coins dropping on the floor. It always turned out no one has dropped their change.

Lake Okanagan

Ogopogo

Lake Okanagan hosts its own Loch Ness monster known fondly as 'Ogopogo.' Lake Okanagan resembles Loch Ness in some ways. It is long, nearly 80 miles in length and the water is very deep. Stories of Ogopogo go back to Native American times and continue into the homestead period. Ogopogo is supposed to be from 30 -70 feet in length. Its head is either horse or sheep shaped. Some witnesses reported a beard

or whiskers. Most witnesses reported that the body was humped or coiled and these parts showed above the surface of the water when it moved.

Sightings of Ogopogo became publicized in the 1950s and continue to this very day. Lake Okanagan has become popular as a tourist recreation area. In the summer it is covered with boats of all sizes and the sound of powerful outboard motors is a nuisance to local people. This may have caused the sightings to decline over time.

Victoria, British Columbia

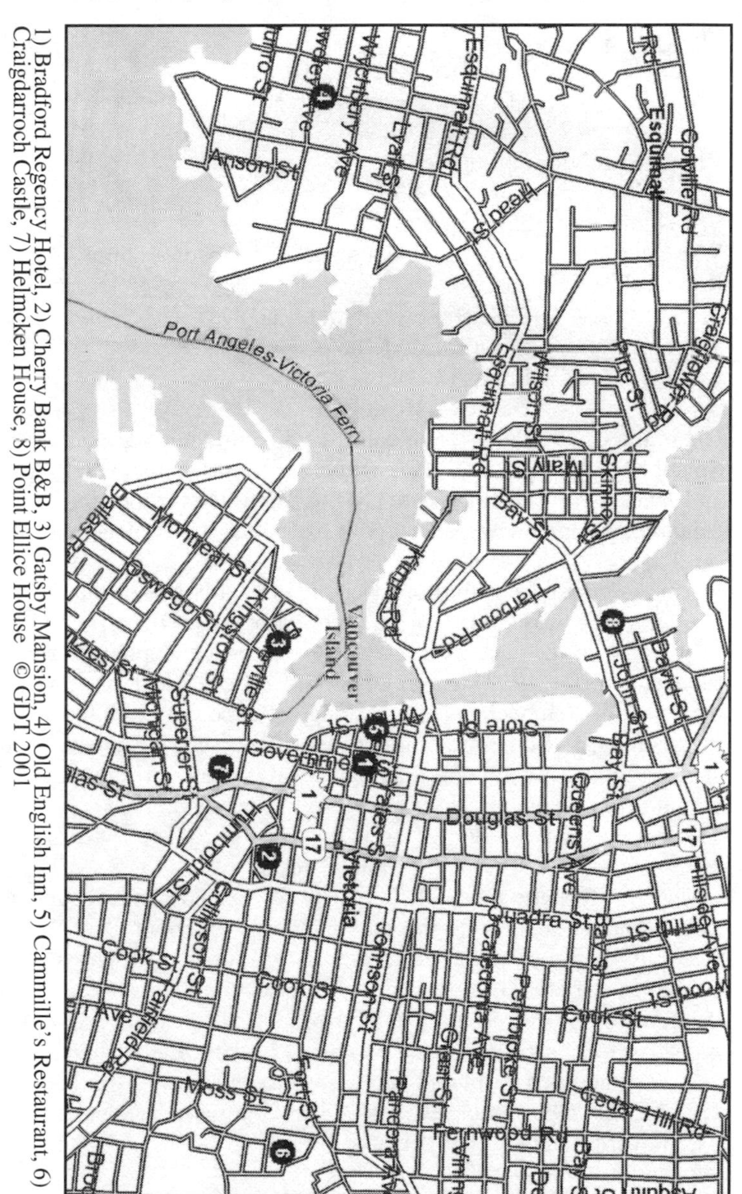

1) Bradford Regency Hotel, 2) Cherry Bank B&B, 3) Gatsby Mansion, 4) Old English Inn, 5) Cammille's Restaurant, 6) Craigdarroch Castle, 7) Helmcken House, 8) Point Ellice House © GDT 2001

Victoria B.C. and Vicinity

Places to Stay

Name:	**Bradford Regency Hotel**
Address:	1140 Government Street Victoria B.C. V8W 1Y2
Phone Number:	**800-665-6500** **250-384-6835**
Fax Number:	250-386-8930
Web site:	http://victoriabc.com/accom/bedford.html
Rooms:	40
Prices:	$$ - $$$ seasonal rates apply
Theme:	European style hotel
Cuisine:	English Cooking Garrick's Head Pub $$
Open:	Pub is open daily, 11:30 a.m. Sundays, noon

Special Facilities: Three styles of rooms, some with fireplaces and Jacuzzis, coffee or tea delivered to rooms in morning, valet dry cleaning, morning newspaper, room packages, conference facility

The six-floor Bedford Regency Hotel is one of the oldest hotels in Victoria. It was built near the inner harbor, near the arriving passenger ships. It is in the center of Victoria's old town shopping district. It was renovated in the 1980s to bring it up to modern standards. As might be expected, the remodel has had a strange effect on the architecture of some of the rooms. Some are compartmentalized, like a train. Sometimes a sitting room is joined with a bedroom by a small corridor. Other rooms are quite large. It's just the right place for old ghosts.

The Ghosts

Before the remodel, the Bedford Regency had a reputation as a sleazy hotel. The pub in the basement was the worst part of the place. The pub is gone, replaced by meeting rooms. When not used for functions, the employees use it as a break room. That is when they see the ghost of a former bar fly named Brady. He was stabbed to death one night, over his girlfriend, who everyone knew as "Lady Churchill."

She lived in a hotel room upstairs, which she still haunts. You can tell her when you see her. She is usually accompanied by the overpowering smell of her perfume.

Name:	**Cherry Bank Bed & Breakfast Hotel**
Address:	825 Burdett Avenue

Victoria B.C. V8W 1B3
Phone Number: 800-998-6688
250-385-5380
Fax Number: 250-383-0949
Web site: www.bctravel.com/cherrybank.html
Rooms: 28 some with shared baths
Prices: $$ breakfast included, seasonal rates
Theme: English style Inn
Cuisine: English breakfast; BBQ
Bowman's Rib House $$
Open: Lunch and dinner
Special Facilities: No phone, no TV, non smoking rooms, refrigerators, no wheel chair access, children welcome

The Cherry Bank Hotel was built as a mansion for local architect James Brown in 1897. In addition to a home, he had a separate guesthouse constructed. They were constructed in a Cherry orchard, which is how the hotel got its name. By 1912, the estate had been converted into a boarding house. In the 1940s, its facilities were upgraded with a coffee shop and it was turned into a hotel. The hotel restaurant is named Bowman's Rib House, and has been in operation for 40 years. It recently won local awards for the quality of its barbecue.

The Ghosts

One former resident of the hotel was Miss Kathleen Hamber. She was the unmarried sister of BC's former Lieutenant Governor, Eric Hamber. She died while staying there. She haunts her old room, which is now a banquet hall. There is a haunted table there. Is it her favorite? She or another ghost haunt locales through the entire building. The kitchen has a ghost that plays in the walk-in refrigerator. The bartender has to deal with a ghost that plays with the telephone. There are ghosts in the upstairs bedrooms. Room 4 has an active girl ghost-guest who has been seen and her disembodied voice has been heard by living guests.

Name: Gatsby Mansion
Address: 309 Belleville Street
Victoria B.C. V8V 1X2
Phone Number: 800-563-9656
250-388-9191
Fax Number: 250-920-5651
Web site: www.travelscout.com/victoria/ved/gatsby/gatsby.htm
Rooms: 20 most with bath
Prices: $$ - $$$ includes breakfast, seasonal rates

Theme: Elegant, period hotel
Cuisine: Gourmet $$$
Special Facilities: Cable TV, some rooms have balconies, children welcome, non smoking rooms

The Gatsby Mansion is a Victorian hotel constructed near the dock of the Port Angeles Ferry. It was built by the Pendray family in 1897, and once served as a convent. It has been a hotel for several decades The lobby resembles a Victorian era museum. The hotel still has original hand frescoed ceiling paintings and stained glass windows. There are several crystal chandeliers and dark wood paneling on the walls. Many rooms have canopy beds. The overall effect has recreated a 1920s era seaside hotel.

The Ghosts

One guest sleeping in the master suite woke up to see a disembodied head revolving around her bed. It appeared, coming from the wall on one side of the bed. It circled around her and disappeared in the wall on the opposite side. She was so frightened, she demanded another room in one of the hotels other buildings. The room had been the bedroom of William Pendray, who died there after a severe head injury.

Name: **Olde England Inn**
Address: 429 Lampson Street
Victoria B.C. V9A 5Y9
Phone Number: **866-388 4353**
250-388-4353
Fax Number: 250-382-8311
Web site: www.oldeenglandinn.com
Rooms: 51 rooms
Prices: $$ - $$$ seasonal rates apply
Theme: Tudor period England
Cuisine: Traditional English $$
Open: Lunch, daily 11:30 a.m.– 3:30 p.m.
Dinner daily 5:00 p.m.– 9:00 p..m.
Special Facilities: Gift shop, historic village, antique furnishings, cable TV, smoke free

The Olde England Inn was originally part of an estate named Rosemead. In 1909, developer Harry Slater had architect Samuel Maclure design this Tudor Revival style house. The large paneled front hallway, was designed by Maclure and has remained intact. A reconstructed English Tudor village and grounds were built around the house when it was converted into a hotel. A replica of Anne Hathaway's cottage and Shakespeare's birthplace were constructed and are open for tours. The gardens are functional as well as beautiful. The chefs get their cooking herbs from the garden.

In 1950, Sam Lane converted the bulding into an Inn. He made several trips to England where he bought the furnishings. The rooms at the Olde English Inn are furnished in a medieval style. Some include 16th and 17th century antiques. The king of Portugal used one four-poster bed. The inn restaurant also has a medieval theme. Dishes are meat oriented, with heavy sauces.

The Ghosts

One of the Inns ghosts may have emigrated to Canada with a 4-poster bed. Guests who sleep there have reported seeing the apparition of a man, floating above the bed. I do not know if this has happened while they were lying down.

Restaurants, Clubs and Theaters

Name:	**Camille's**
Address:	45 Bastion Square Victoria B.C. V8W 1J1
Phone Number:	**250-381-3433**
Fax Number:	250-381-3404
Web site:	www.camillesrestaurant.com
Prices:	$$
Theme:	Romantic fine dining
Cuisine:	Northwest gourmet
Open:	Daily, 5:30 p.m.

Special Facilities: Live music most Fridays, wheelchair access, vegetarian dishes, non-smoking, reservations only

Camille's is located in the basement of the old Law Chambers Building in Victoria's Bastion Square. Its architect, F.M. Rattenbury, tried to model Bastion Square along the lines of a European Piazza. In 1899 he designed the Law Chambers with an Italian flavor. Many of the court buildings were vacated in 1962, when a new courthouse was built. In 1970, Peter Neve Cotton restored and renovated the building using many regional architectural motifs.

Camille's opened in the basement of the old Law Chambers in 1988. Camille's favors low lighting, provided by stained glass lamps, and the brick walls blend in well with the antique décor. The mood is set by jazz or blues music which is sometimes played by live musicians.

The Ghosts

The haunting at Camille's is ongoing, and the staff has learned to live with it. The most common facet of this haunting is the smell of cigar smoke mixed with women's perfume. This happens frequently and centers in one spot. The staff moved the table where it appears, because the smell disturbs patrons. They do not know who the ghost or ghosts might be. There were public executions in the square when it was a fort and people are buried there. The staff takes it in stride. They greet the ghosts when they walk in and the place smells like it is full of cigar smoke. Camille's frequently hosts Dinner Ghost tours.

Name: **Four Mile House**
Address: 199 Island Highway
Victoria B.C. V9B 1G1
Phone Number: **250-479-2514 (restaurant)**
250-479-3346 (pub)
Prices: $$
Theme: Historic Inn
Cuisine: Pub and fine dining
Open: Daily, 11 a.m.— 11 p.m.
Special Facilities: Tea served, daily special

The Four Mile House was built in the 1850s as a stage coach stop on the Metchosin Road. The roadhouse fell on hard times after the coming of the car. The low point in the inns history came after World War II, when it was patronized by drunken servicemen and prostitutes. The upstairs was a combination rooming house and bordello. Several pieces of silk lingerie were found in the attic when it was renovated.

Graham and Wendy Haymes purchased the dilapidated building in 1979. They turned it into a combination antique store and tearoom. They made extensive repairs throughout the building, which soon resembled a rustic Tudor style cottage. They shut down the antique business in the late 1980s and opened a combination pub and tearoom. The restaurant serves gourmet food, and the pub serves typical pub grub.

The Ghosts

There are several ghosts at the Four Mile House and its vicinity. When the building was being renovated, the Haymes frequently heard the sound of ghostly workmen hammering and sawing in the deserted second floor. Several people saw a man wearing a trench coat over a 1940s suit, sitting at a table in the tearoom. Whenever anyone tried to talk to him, he disappeared. Some mornings before opening, the staff hear a clinking sound, as if someone is stirring a cup with a spoon.

The first property owner, Jake Matteson may haunt the house and property. Jake put all of his money in a secret hiding place before he died. His presence may watch over the hiding place. Margaret Gouge was a houseguest in the late 19th century. She loved flowers, and has been seen in the laundry room overlooking the garden. She may be the White Lady who haunts the grounds around the house. The White Lady may also be the wife of a sea captain who never returned from the sea. She died of loneliness waiting for his return.

Shops Sights and Sounds

Name:	**Craigdarroch Castle**
Address:	1050 Joan Crescent (off Fort Street) Victoria B.C. V8S 3L7
Phone Number:	**250-592-5323**
Fax Number:	250-592-1099
Web site:	www.craigdarochcastle.com
Prices:	$$
Theme:	Historic mansion museum
Open:	June 15th – September 9th, 9:00 a.m.– 7:00 p.m. September 5th –June 14th, 10:00 a.m.– 4:30 p.m. Closed Christmas, Boxing Day & New Years

Special Facilities: Special events, gift shop, no wheel chair ramps (87 stairs)

When he died in 1890, Robert Dunsmuir was the richest man in British Columbia. Dunsmuir and his family moved from Scotland to Vancouver Island in 1851. He eked out a living overseeing the Hudson's Bay Company's coalmines. In 1869 he helped develop a rich coal seam in Nanaimo. He soon built a railroad to transport the coal, which netted him a land grant of nearly 25% of the land around Victoria. He eventually owned his own iron foundry, newspaper and merchant fleet.

In 1887 he began work on his 60-room house, Craigdarroch Castle. It has been called Romanesque, but it is so vast and ornate, that it goes beyound Romanesque. Dunsmuir died before the house was completed, though his wife and three unmarried daughters moved in. Joan Dunsmuir lived in the house until her death in 1909. The castle was later used as a soldier's hospital and as Victoria College for many years, before being opened as a museum.

The Ghosts

When it was Victoria College, students detected a ghost in the house. Most people think that the ghost is Joan Dunsmuir. Some people report a strong invisible presence in her bedroom. Piano music is heard in the old ballroom, and a woman in white has been seen looking out of the ballroom windows, even when the house was closed for the night. Sometimes people have reported smelling candles burning.

I toured the house several years ago and it definitely has a spooky air. Despite the high ceilings and open spaces, the dark wood interiors and stained glass windows can seem repressive in a Gothic way. The movie *Spooky House* was filmed there. In 2001 Edgar Allan Poe's play *The Fall of the House of Usher* is on the playbill.

Name: Discover the Past
Address: 34 Battery St
Victoria, B.C. V8V 1E5
Phone Number: 250 384-6698
Web site: www.discoverthepast.com
Prices: $$
Theme: Historic ghosts
Cuisine: variable
Open: Check website for details

From the end of June through Labor Day, Discover the Past conducts ghost walks every night, beginning at 7:30 p.m.. The ghost walk meets at the Visitor Information Centre at the corner of Wharf and Government Streets in downtown Victoria. Tickets can be purchased from the tour guide or at the Visitor's Centre. During the last two weekends in October, start locations and tour times change, so check with Discover the Past for more details.

Historian John Adams has been conducting tours in Victoria since 1970. He operates his own historic tour and education company, Discover the Past. He has gathered stories about Victoria's wacky, strange and macabre citizens and haunts for many years. He offers Ghost Walks during the summer and late October, and will give tours for groups of ten or more people year round. He also conducts serious historical tours and talks throughout the year, specializing in Victoria's diverse neighborhoods.

John Adams also hosts a program called Dinner Ghosts. For this, people meet at one of the many haunted restaurants in Victoria for a full course dinner and a talk on the history and ghosts of the restaurant and vicinity. Other activities might include a talk on making ghost protection oil and a walk around the neighborhood to visit other haunts. The evening program usually ends in a haunted pub or other haunted place for an informal discussion. The dinner programs begin at 6:30 p.m. and take around three hours. Dinner ghost programs are offered on selected Saturday evenings from January through March and by special arrangement at other times. Reservations are required because group size is limited.

Name: **Helmcken House**
Address: 10 Elliot Square
Victoria BC V8V 2P8
Phone Number: **250 361-0021**
Fax Number: 250 356-7796
Web site: www.tbc.gov.bc.ca/culture/schoolnet/helmcken/
Prices: $$
Theme: Historic house museum
Open: May – September, 10 a.m. – 5 p.m.
October – December noon, – 4 p.m.
February – April, noon – 4 p.m.
Closed: January
Special Facilities: Gift shop, English & Japanese self guided tour tapes, ghost tours

Dr John S. Helmcken was hired in London by the Hudson's Bay Company as a physician. They sent him to North America, and he traveled to Victoria, in 1850. He originally intended to stay in the wilderness of Vancouver Island for a few years to fulfill his obligations. He was then going to return to England. Instead he remained in Canada for 70 years, until his death in 1920.

In 1852 Helmcken married the daughter of Governor James Douglas. He built a three room log cabin for his family and medical practice. As his family and fortunes grew, so did his house. Helmcken became involved in politics. He served as the first speaker of the colony of Vancouver Island's House. He became speaker for British Columbia and in 1870, he helped negotiate British Columbia's union with Canada.

The Ghosts

Dr Helmcken and members of his family have remained behind in their house. The spirits are very active, as evidenced by the Halloween ghost tours. In 2001, the staff began a program called "This Old Haunted House." The tours begin on 1 July and ended on 31 October. They are offered Thursday to Saturday, beginning at 8 p.m.. In October there are two tours, 7 p.m. and 8:30 p.m.. More tours are offered in the last two weeks before Halloween. The tours highlight the ghostly experiences of the staff at Helmcken House. After 2001, I suggest contacting the

Helmcken House staff for information about any changes to the schedule.

Name: **Old Cemeteries Society**
Address: Box 50004, #15 – 1594 Fairfield Rd.
Victoria, BC V8S 1G1
Phone Number: **250 598-8870**
Web site: www.oldcem.bc.ca/body.html
Prices: $$
Theme: Historic cemetery tours
Open: Check website for details
Special Facilities: Historic walks, bus tours

Victoria's Old Cemeteries Society has a year round program of guided tours of Victoria's Roy Bay Cemetery, which opened in 1873. The cemetery is about 30 acres in size and contains 28,000 graves. Many of Victoria's oldest and most famous citizens are buried there. During the summer the Cemetery Society conducts Lantern tours of Victoria's "Old Burying Ground," beginning 1 July to 31 August. The tours begin at the Cherry Bank Hotel at 9 p.m. and last one hour.

For ghost hunters, their fall schedule is of the most interest. In late October, there are walking ghost tours beginning at 1 p.m.. The tours start every 15 minutes; the last one starts at 3 p.m.. On selected days, they conduct Ghost Bus-tours. These tours begin at 6:30 and 9:30 p.m. with tickets available at selected locations. These are annual events, but I strongly recommend checking the Cemetery Society's website or contacting them by mail or phone for any changes to times, dates and places for the tours.

Name: **Point Ellice House Museum**
Address: 2616 Pleasant Street
Victoria B.C. V8T 4V3
Phone Number: **250-380-6506**
Fax Number: 250-356-7796
Prices: $$
Theme: Historic house museum
Cuisine: English High Tea
Open: May 12th – September 9th, noon – 5:00 p.m.
Special Facilities: Extensive gardens, gift shop, tea served from noon to 4:00 p.m. Halloween ghost tours

Peter O'Reilly built the Point Ellice House in 1867. He served as a magistrate and as gold commissioner for the Caribou District. Instead of living in the interior, he chose to build in Victoria. The house is now a bit at odds with the current waterfront setting. In the past the neighborhood was more picturesque. The single story house has an Italianesque design, with many long, low windows. The O'Reilly family surrounded the house with an extensive garden and hosted formal teas with local society there.

The O'Reillys lived in the house for several generations. The last family members opened it as a museum in the late 1960s. It became a provincial historic site in 1974. With its furnishings, gardens and intact architecture, it is considered one of British Columbia's premiere Victorian homes.

The Ghosts

Shortly after the house was opened as a museum, a woman dressed in a long blue dress took visitors on a tour of the house. When the woman finished, the tourists spoke with a museum volunteer complementing the tour guide. The volunteer told them that no such tour guide worked there. The dress they described had belonged to Kathleen O'Reilly, who died in 1945. Two other visitors were later shown the house by a woman matching her description.

An American psychic visited the house and claimed to have detected several spirits in the house. Ghostly incidents seem to have slowed down since the government took ownership of the building. In October the staff offer haunted house tours. Check in advance for details.

The Puget Sound

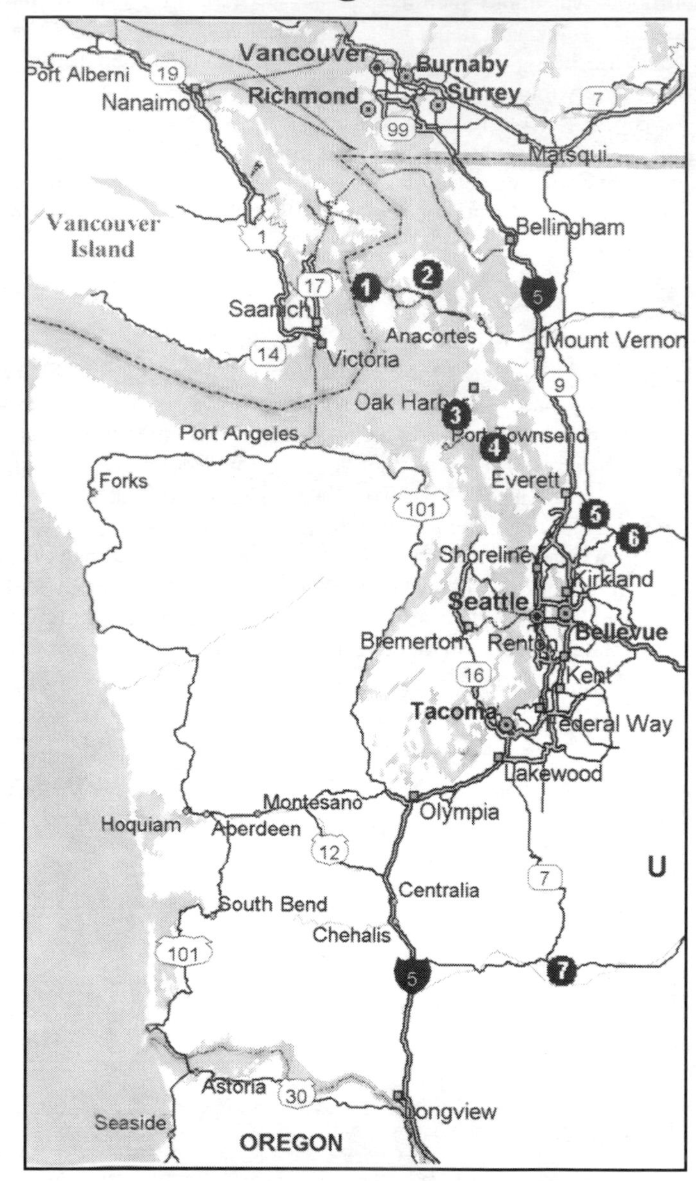

1) Roche Harbor, 2) Orcas Island, 3) Coupeville, 4) South Whidbey Island, 5) Snohomish, 6) Skykomish, 7) Morton Other cities and towns are shown without numbers © GDT 2001

Bellingham

Name: **Mt. Baker Theatre**
Address: 104 North Commercial Street
Bellingham, WA 98225
Phone Number: **360-734-6080 (ticket office)**
Website: www.mtbakertheatre.com
Prices: $$- $$$
Theme: Moorish Spanish
Open: Variable. See website or call the ticket office.
Special facilities: Open to use by outside organizations.

This 1500 seat theater was built in 1927. It was one of the last theme theaters built in the Puget Sound before the Great Depression. It was a multi-purpose theater, including a vaudeville stage, orchestra pit and pipe organ as well as a movie screen. After World War II and television's golden age, the Mount Baker Theatre was obsolete as a movie house. By 1970 it could not compete with multiplex movie theaters located in modern malls.

Fortunately, the citizens of Bellingham banded together to save their beloved theater. In 1978 it was listed on the National Register of Historic Places as a historic landmark. In 1996 it underwent extensive remodeling to restore its use as a live performing arts center under a non-profit group. Entertainment and acts vary.

The Ghosts

One ghost has been named Judy by staff and stagehands at the Mt. Baker. According to legend, Judy lived in a house located on the site of the Mt. Baker. Against her wishes she was either evicted or otherwise forced to move in 1926, to make way for the new theater. Judy is very active in the corridor that connects the balcony and mezzanine. She seems very fond of male employees. Many of them have heard a disembodied female voice, calling out their names. In addition to the voice, employees and customers have reported hearing the rustle of a woman's skirt. They have also felt gusts of cold air, and seen balls of light. Some have claimed that she is a fictional character, invented to give the theater notoriety.

Everett

Name: **The Equator**
Address: 10th Street Boat Launch
14th Street Yacht Basin
Everett, WA 98201
Phone Number: **425-257-8010 (Everett Library's Northwest Room)**
Theme: Historic sailing vessel
Open: unknown
Special Facilities: While not strictly speaking a tourist attraction, *The Equator* is docked at the Port of Everett. Although a historic landmark, it is slowly decaying due to a lack of funds to restore it.

The Equator is a two-masted schooner, constructed in San Francisco in the late 1880s as a "copra" trader. Copra traders went from port to port, picking up cargo at one port in the hopes that it might be sold at the next port. Two important people who were aboard the ship were Robert Louis Stevenson and King Kalakaua of Hawaii. Stevenson spent several months living in Waikiki and was a frequent guest in the palace of Hawaii's king, Kalakaua. Stevenson booked passage on *The Equator* for himself and his family. King Kalakaua escorted the Stevenson party on their way and had a final luncheon on the ship. Stevenson lived aboard the ship for six months, before settling in, and later dying in Samoa.

The Ghosts

In the 1980s and early '90s, observers reported seeing strange people on her deck, and workmen's tools began disappearing. Floating lights were also seen above her decks. This led to her caretakers allowing a séance to be held on *The Equator*. During the séance, two glowing lights appeared and hovered near the psychics. The psychics stated that the two glowing lights were the ghosts of Robert Louis Stevenson and King Kalakaua of Hawaii.

Name: **Everett Theatre**
Address: 2911 Colby Avenue
Everett, WA 98201
Phone Number: **425-258-6766 (ticket office)**
Website: www.everetttheatre.org
Prices: $ - $$
Open: See website or call ticket office for hours
Special Facilities: Open for rental. It has a movie screen, stage, orchestra pit, organ, multiple lobbies, and an elevator to the balcony.

The Everett Theatre was built in 1901. It has been through a complete renovation, including the lobbies, seating, façade and elevator. This took some time, because it was financed from a variety of sources, including the Everett Theatre Society. The efforts took time too but improvements were done with loving care. The theatre hosts a mix of live theater, Community Theater and classic movies.

The Ghosts

I do not know too much about the ghost here. It is supposed to be a male ghost, perhaps an old theater worker who has stayed on to make sure the theatre stays in business.

Whidbey Island

There are many, many haunted locations in Whidbey Island. Unfortunately most of them are not generally open to the public. They included haunts around the Navy bases on Whidbey Island, several haunted houses and even a mystery burial or two. Having teased you, I can only direct you to a few of the public places in this book.

Name: **Captain Whidbey Inn**
Address: 2072 West Captain Whidbey Inn Road
Coupeville, WA 98239
Phone Number: **800-366-4097**
360- 678-4097
Website: www.captainwhidbey.com
Rooms: 25 rooms, seven cabins and cottages
Prices: $$ - $$$ Full breakfast is included
Theme: Rustic Log Cabin
Cuisine: Classic country inn cooking $$
Special Facilities: All rooms have feather beds and down comforters and antique furniture. The lounge is stocked with regional beers and wines. There is a conference facility, and a 52-foot sailing ship with charter packages.

Directions: The Inn's website has excellent directions on how to get there.

In 1906, Lester Still had builders use timbers from a large stand of madrona trees growing nearby to build his Inn. Madrona does not grow straight, so the inn walls were built in sections and then pieced together. Originally called the Whid-Isle Inn, it was renamed the "Captain Whidbey" in the 1960s, by the new owners, the Colbys.

The Colby family have owned and run the Inn since that time. They have added separate cabins or cottages. Inn rooms have shared baths, and two suites are available. Lagoon rooms have private baths. Cabins have bedroom, sitting room, private bath and fireplace. The Cottages have fireplaces or wood stoves and kitchens. The present owner is John Colby Stone. In the years he has been at the Captain Whidbey, he has not seen a ghost and remains skeptical about it. Sort of…

The Ghosts

Over twenty years ago, a man was the only guest at the Inn. One night he left his room to use the bathroom down the hall. He was washing his hands, when he felt a presence behind him. Outside the bathroom he saw a woman walk into room number eight. The next morning, he asked the staff about the woman. They told him that he was alone and no one was staying in room eight.

One of the housekeeping staff walked down a pathway to clean one of the cabins. She saw a woman ahead of her enter a cabin that needed cleaning. When the housekeeper walked in, it was empty. Since then, a woman dressed in white has passed many guests in the hallways of the Captain Whidbey. After walking by guests, the woman simply disappears. People still report the ghostly woman's presence.

Name: **Meerkerk Gardens**
Phone Number: **360-678-1912**
Website: www.meerkerkgardens.org
Prices: $
Theme: Rhododendron gardens
Open: Seven days a week, 9:00 a.m. to 4:00 p.m.
<u>Special Facilities</u>: There are three different rhododendron gardens as well as a 43 acre woodland preserve with five miles of nature trails. Guided tours are only available from March through May. No pets.

Directions: Follow State Route 525 to Resort Road, Turn right on Resort Road ½ mile to Meerkerk Lane. Turn left and follow the signs to the visitor's parking area.

In the 1960s Ann and Max Meerkerk began collecting ornamental trees and rhododendron hybrids. As time went by, their interest became a passion and they sought rare "rhoadies" from across the world. They developed their own hybrids, some of which have grown to tree size. They surrounded their rhododendron plantations with fir, cedar and hemlock trees as a privacy screen. Those trees have grown into the 43-acre woodland preserve. After the Meerkerks died, they passed their gardens to the Seattle Rhododendron Society, who opened the gardens to the public in 1979.

The Ghosts

It seems that the Meerkerks have decided not to leave their beloved gardens just yet. People walking through the gardens have reported the strong smell of cigar smoke. The gardens are non-smoking. Upon a search, no one has been found smoking. People who knew the Meerkerks report that Max was fond of fragrant cigars.

In the 1980s, the garden caretaker found Ann's displays of orchids and cacti rearranged at frequent intervals. In the late 1990s there was a gathering of Ann Meerkerk's old friends, who agreed to tape record old stories about the Meerkerks. The night before the interviews, all of the recording equipment was moved. After some searching, the equipment was found and the interviews were done. When the historian listened to the tapes, all of them were blank.

The three year-old child of the caretaker told his mother that he heard music playing in the gardens. He also saw an older couple wandering among the rhododendrons.

Roche Harbor

Name: **Roche Harbor Resort**
Address: Roche Harbor Resort
248 Reuben Memorial Drive
P.O. Box 4001
Roche Harbor, WA 98250
Phone Number: **800-451-8910**
360-378-2155
Fax Number: 360-378-6809
Website: www.rocheharbor.com
Rooms: Hotel de Haro has 16 rooms, four suites
Prices: $$ - $$$ Seasonal rates apply.

Theme: Turn of the century hotel, two restaurants.
Cuisine: Northwest gourmet
Madrona Grill, Bar & Grill $$
McMillin Restaurant, gourmet $$ - $$$.
Open: Prime season is from May 18th to June 14th and September 7th to September 27th.
Quiet season is September 28th to May 16th.
Restaurant hours: Vary depending on the season
Special Facilities: Swimming pool, gift shop, gardens, tennis court, nature walk to McMillin Mausoleum. The McMillin Suites, condos, and other more luxurious facilities have some extras such as kitchens, fireplaces, multiple televisions and extra-large tubs.

In 1881, lime mining began near Roche Harbor. Shortly afterward John McMillin of Tacoma discovered the northwest's richest lime deposits nearby. By 1886, the Tacoma and Roche Harbor Lime Company became a northwest economic force. McMillin built the 22 room Hotel de Haro in 1886. It was a place where his customers and guests could stay to observe mining operations. After 1956, it was sold to a succession of wealthy owners and investors who restored the hotel to its original state and added many facilities. Special guests included Teddy Roosevelt and John Wayne.

The Ghosts

Most people believe that the mischievous ghost that haunts the Roche Harbor Resort is that of Ada Beane. Ada was the personal secretary to John McMillin. She had her own cottage next to the family house. Some rumors hold that she committed suicide, but local historians maintain that she died of natural causes. After she died, she was cremated. The family kept her ashes for a time, and later interred them in the family crypt. This crypt is located a short walk from the hotel and I shaped like a family dining room table. Many of the McMillin family, and Ada, are buried inside the stone chairs.

Ada is very active in certain portions of the hotel. Her cottage has been incorporated into the hotel and is now the McMillin Dining Room. In the 1990s, a security guard and a chef watched the door to an old storeroom open on it's own. Appliances in the kitchen turn on and off of their own accord. One employee has heard the sound of a woman's clothing rustling when no one was there.

The gift shop is also part of Ada's stomping grounds. Again, though alarming, the ghostly incidents are mischievous rather than frightening. One night an employee watched several glass shelves crack and shatter, one-by-one. The back storeroom was even more active with its contents and stored furniture periodically moving and shifting.

Orcas Island

Name:	**Rosario Resort (Orcas Island)**	
Address:	One Rosario Way East Sound WA 98245-2201	
Phone Number:	**800-562-8820** **360-376-2222**	
Fax Number:	360-376-3680	
Website:	www.roasarioresort.com	
Prices:	$$$	
Theme:	Turn of the century mansion	
Cuisine:	Northwest gourmet	
	Compass Room, formal dining	$$$
	Orcas Room, informal dining	$$$
	Cascade Bay Café, deli &grill	$$$
	Poolside Bar & Grill (seasonal)	$$
Open:	Variable times.	

<u>Special Facilities:</u> Lounge, exercise room, gift shop, one indoor pool, two outdoor pools, spa, marina, retail outlets, banquet facilities. There are seasonal packages as well.

Robert Moran came to the Pacific Northwest as a young carpenter and soon became one of the regions top industrialists. Moran's shipyards were the largest in the Pacific Northwest. In 1904, Moran purchased 7,000 acres of land on Orcas Island and built his retirement home, which he called Rosario. The mansions roof is made of copper, and exotic woods like Honduran mahogany and Indian teak were made into paneling, and parquet floors throughout the mansion. Before he died in 1938, Moran sold Rosario to Donald Rheem.

Rheem was a wealthy industrialist and inventor. Rheem and his wife, Alice, spent over a million dollars adding to and maintaining Rosario. Alice Rheem would sometimes drive her Harley Davidson motorcycle from the mansion into the nearby village of Eastside and play cards with the locals.

The Ghosts

The maids at the Rosario are often the victims of paranormal practical jokes. Faucets in the laundry room turn off and on, on their own. Laundry is messed up by unseen hands. Employees and guests have reported hearing a woman wearing high-heeled shoes walking across the hardwood floors. In the 1980s, an employee stayed in Alice's old room. She saw a shadow cross the wall of the room. It moved across the wall toward her. She felt invisible fingers caress her hand. She left then, around midnight. The next morning, the guests who had the room next door complained that starting around midnight the sound of passionate lovemaking coming from that room kept them up all night long.

I did a radio interview on Halloween in 2000. One on-air caller had been a Rosario employee. Alice's room was vacant one night, and he decided to take a nap in it. He woke up and looked around the darkened room. A woman came out of the shadows toward him. She halted some distance away and asked him calmly, "Did you enjoy your nap?" She disappeared. He turned on the lights but the room was empty.

Port Townsend

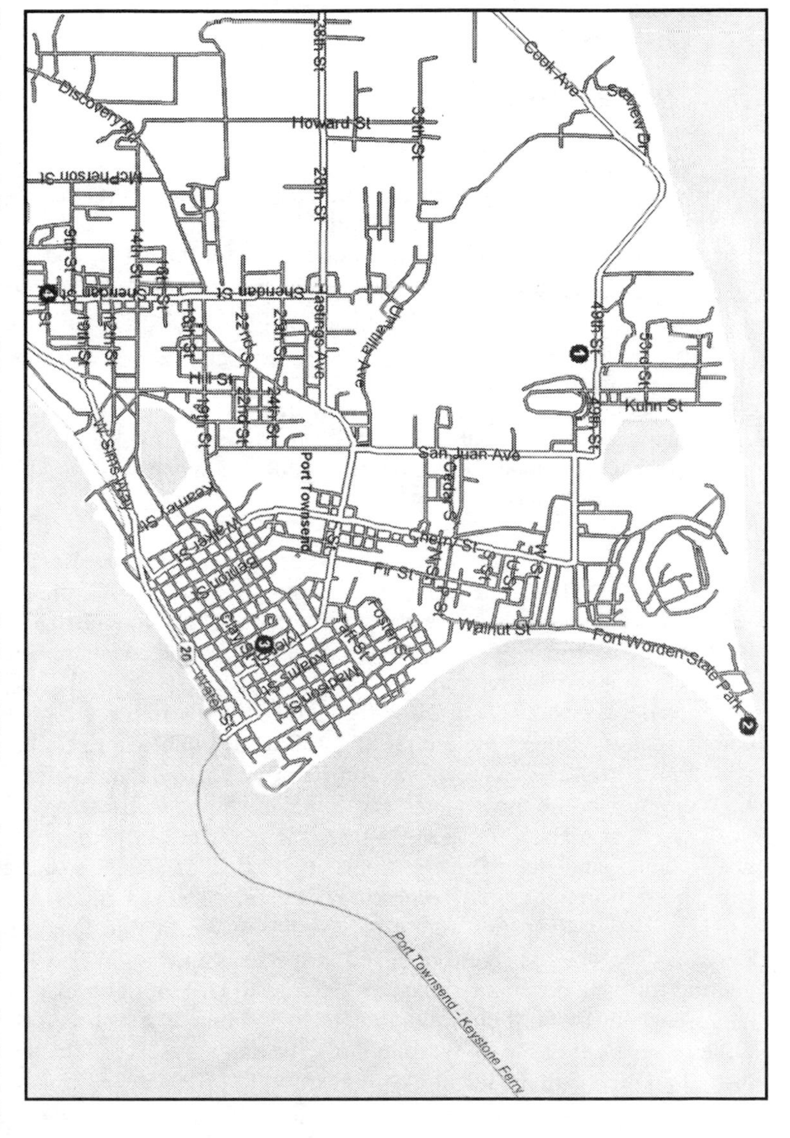

1) Fort Worden State Park Headquarters, 2) Point Wilson Lighthouse, 3) Holly Hill House, 4) Manresa Castle © GDT 2001

Port Townsend

Places to stay

Name:	**Fort Worden State Park**
Address:	200 Battery Way Port Townsend, WA 98368
Phone Number:	**360-385-4730**
Fax Number:	360 385-7248
Website:	www.olympus.net/ftworden
Rooms:	83 campsites, 3 dormitories, 33 officer's quarters a hostel and grand building known as 'The Castle.'
Prices:	$ for camping and hostel, $$$ for dormitory and individual houses.
Theme:	Turn of century military complex
Cuisine:	Catering available.
Open:	Year round

Special Facilities: Museum, beachfront, boat ramp, two buildings are Americans with Disability compliant, no pets, no TV, and most buildings have a phone. Reservations should be made well in advance. All facilities are NON-SMOKING.

The oldest building at Ft. Worden State Park is Alexander's Castle, built in 1892. The Castle was supposed to be a combination retreat and honeymoon house for Alexander and his intended bride in Scotland. Unfortunately, when he returned to Scotland to fetch his bride, he found she had married someone else.

Between 1897 and 1911 the United States military built three defensive forts around the mouth of the Puget Sound to protect against armed invasion. Fort Worden was finished in 1902 and named after John L. Worden, who commandeered the ironclad ship, *The Monitor*, during the Civil War. Each fort was its own small town. In addition to the heavy guns and their fortifications, they had residences, barracks, workshops, warehouses and some kind of entertainment facilities.

The smaller guns were removed during World War I and sent to Europe. The big guns were removed at the beginning of World War II, and the fort was decommissioned in 1953. The U.S. military maintained a presence there until the mid-1970s, after which the entire fort was turned over to the state of Washington. The state preserves it as historic district and recreational facility.

The Ghosts

The principal haunted building at Fort Worden is Alexander's

Castle. The ghost there is often heard by guests but never seen. Guests are restricted to rooms on the first floor and the ghost inhabits the upper floors. Guests and park employees have heard the sound of footsteps in the top floor bedroom. Sometimes they hear the sound of something heavy being dragged across the floor. Unfortunately for would be ghost hunters, Alexander's Castle has been closed for some time, pending much needed repairs. It is not the only haunted building on Fort Worden. House number 10 as well as the Point Wilson Lighthouse seem to have their own ghostly residents.

Name: **Holly Hill House B&B**
Address: 611 Polk Street
Port Townsend, WA 98368
Phone Number: **800-435-1454**
360-385-5619
Website: www.hollyhillhouse.com
Rooms: Five with private baths
Prices: $$ - $$$, full breakfast
Theme: Victorian
Special Facilities: Parlor, non-smoking rooms and a porch dining room.

Holly Hill House is named after Robert Hill. His descendents lived there for over 90 years. Hill moved to Port Townsend from Whidbey Island and invested in Port Townsend. He opened the First National Bank, and served as mayor of Port Townsend in 1885. After Robert Hill died, his son William and his wife Lizette moved in and lived there until their deaths. The house has large fireplaces, ornate moldings, built in hutches and the original light fixtures.

Some modifications were made while William (or Billy) and Lizette lived there. Billy Hill, suffered a stroke. At that time doctors thought that after a heart attack or stroke patients should stay in-active rather than building up their stamina. They thought that it would not be safe for him to climb up the stairs to their normal bedroom. They converted the downstairs ladies parlor into a bedroom with bath for him. Billy slept in the converted parlor for many years. He never fully recovered from the stroke.

The Ghosts

As you might expect, Billy Hill haunts the house where he spent most of his life. What is unexpected is that he does not haunt his sick room. Perhaps because he was an invalid, he dreamed of his carefree days as a boy, living in his childhood room. Guests staying in the Billy

Room have experienced varied paranormal phenomenon. The most common thing is the smell of cigar smoke even though no one in the house smokes now.

Some guests claim to have had late night conversations with him. Other guests have reported hearing ghostly music playing at night. None of them have described what melodies they heard, or how they knew a ghost created it though. The people who have reported these ghostly contacts have always reported that Billy seems to be happy. He's just indulging himself.

Name:	**Manresa Castle**
Address:	Seventh Street and Sheridan Avenue P.O. Box 564 Port Townsend, WA 98368
Phone Number:	**800-732-1281** **360-385-5750**
Fax Number:	360-385-5883
Website:	www.manresacastle.com
Rooms:	Standard room, water view room, small suite, and Jacuzzi suite, tower suite.
Prices:	Winter season is October 15th - April 30th, rate- $$. Summer season is May 1st - October 14th, rate- $$ - $$$
Theme:	Victorian
Cuisine:	Fine dining. $$
Restaurant open	Dinner every night during the summer season. Wednesday - Saturday nights during the winter season. Buffet breakfast served every Sunday.

Special Facilities: Banquet and weddings facilities, 30 person meeting room, lounge, mountain views, gardens.

In 1878, Charles and Kate Eisenbeis began construction on their dream home. They brought in skilled woodworkers and artisans who finished the Rhineland castle style house with imported tile and ornately carved wood trim. After several years, the 30-room house known as the Eisenbeis Castle was completed in 1892.

Charles died in 1902 and Kate soon remarried and moved away. In 1925 the house was purchased as a retreat for nuns. In 1927, it was sold to an order of Jesuit priests who used it as a seminary. In 1928 they added a wing to the house, including a chapel and dormitory rooms. They covered the red brick with white stucco, and changed the name of the building to Manresa Hall. In 1968, they sold it to investors who converted the building into a hotel. It has changed hands several times, but each owner has tried to maintain its 19th Century charm.

The Ghosts

According to legend, a Jesuit priest hung himself in the attic above room 302, the large round tower. He may be the ghost that appeared as a translucent figure in room 306 and vanished, leaving behind a rotting stench. Footsteps have also been heard in the round tower. The footsteps may be those of a second ghost, named Kate.

Kate was a young woman who was staying at Manresa when the Eisenbeis family owned it. She was waiting for her fiancé to arrive by ship. After a long time she was so despondent that she flung herself from one of the tower room windows. She has been seen and heard by a family who conducted séances in the third floor of the tower.

Wineglasses have spontaneously shattered in people's hands in the bar. In 2000, I received a letter from a woman who stayed in room 302. When she woke up in the morning, she felt a weight on her back, pressing her down. The pressure gradually went away and she was able to get up. Later, a reporter from the Seattle Weekly stayed in Manresa Castle and reported a weight on her bed, which held her down by her hair.

According to the Jefferson County records, there are no reports of a priest committing suicide at Manresa. The Eisenbeis family deny any stories about suicide when they owned the building. Some people counter that any suicides could or may have been covered up. A hotel bartender claimed that he invented the ghosts to tell people about when they asked about any ghosts in the hotel. Of course, what prompted people to ask about ghosts?

Shops, Sights and Sounds

Name:	**Guided Historical Sidewalk Tours**
Address:	820 Tyler Street Port Townsend, WA 98368
Owner:	Joyce Cox
Phone Number:	**360-385-1967**
Prices:	$ group rates for seven or more people. Children half-price
Theme:	Old Town Port Townsend
Open:	Call for tour times.

Your tour guide?

There are three separate tours Waterfront Tour, Homes Tour, and the Saloon & Brothel Tour. After the formal tour ends, Joyce might be persuaded to tell some ghost stories. For a modest fee, Joyce sells a Historic Homes Self-Guided Tour Book, so you can walk around yourself.

Name: **Kathy Hill Step-on Tours**
Phone Number: 360-385-4356
Prices: $50 per hour
Open: Tours are by appointment only.

Kathy works with large groups who have their own bus. She boards their bus and guides them on a tour of historic Port Townsend. She highlights people, interesting buildings, the eclectic and strange, but no ghosts.

Name: **Point Wilson Lighthouse**
Address: **Phone Number: 206-385-4730**
Open: The lighthouse grounds are open to tourists at this time.

Directions: The lighthouse is located at the entrance to Admiralty Inlet on the Puget Sound, within the confines of Ft. Worden State Park.

As this book goes to press, Fort Worden and the U.S. Coast Guard are negotiating to transfer ownership of the lighthouse and open it for tours.

In 1879 the United States Government established the lighthouse at the mouth of the Puget Sound. The original wooden lighthouse tower was attached to the light keepers quarters. In 1914, the old wooden tower was demolished and the present tower was built not too far from the old one. The U.S. Coast Guard maintains the lighthouse. It was last used as a residence by crewmen from the Coast Guard Cutter, *Osprey*, whose home port is Port Townsend.

The Ghosts

One of Fort Worden's night watchmen has seen the ghost. He reported seeing the glowing apparition of a woman wearing a long gown wandering the grounds around the lighthouse. The 100+ year old lighthouse keeper's residence is also haunted. The two-story building is subdivided into two separate houses, like a duplex. The ghost seems confined to the second story of one apartment

Downtown Seattle

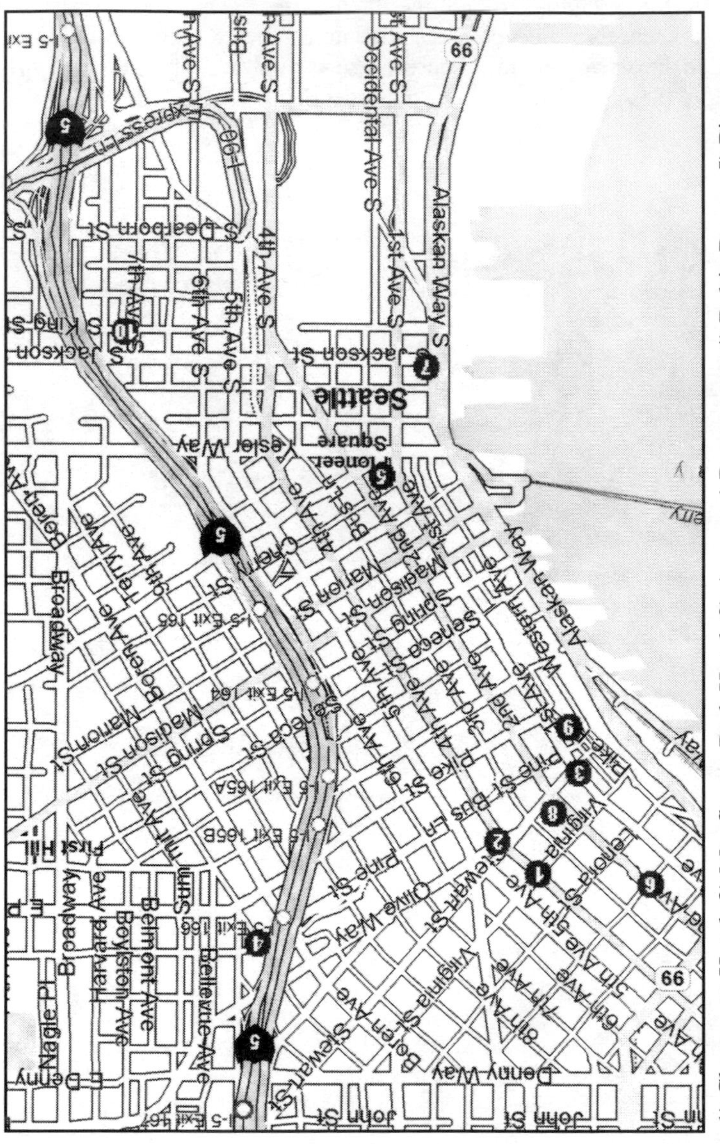

1) Claremont Hotel, 2) Mayflower Park Hotel, 3) Avenue 1 Restaurant, 4) Baltic Room, 5) Pioneer Square, 7) O.K. Café, 8) Moore Theater, 9) Pike Place Market, 10) Wing Luke Museum © GDT 2001

Renton

Name: **Greenwood Memorial Park**
Address: 350 Monroe Avenue NE
Renton, WA 98056
Phone Number: **425-255-1911**
Open: Monday – Friday, 8:00 a.m. - 4:30 p.m.
Saturday & Sunday, Noon – 4:00 p.m.

The chief attraction here is Jimi Hendrix Gravesite. The grave is hard to find, since it is a simple flat grave marker. The Hendrix family may improve the gravesite for Hendrix's fans.

Seattle

Places to Stay
Name: **Claremont Hotel**
Address: 2000 4th Avenue at Virginia Street
Seattle, WA 98121
Phone Number: **877-448-8600**
206-448-8600
Fax Number: 206 441-7140
Website: www.claremonthotel.com
Rooms: Rooms range from deluxe to executive suites.
Prices: $$$
Theme: 1920's Elegance
Cuisine: Italian
Assaggio Restaurant, $$ - $$$.
Open: Lunch: Monday – Friday, 11:30 a.m. - 2:30 p.m.
Dinner: Monday – Saturday, 5:00 p.m. – 10:00 p.m.
Special Facilities: Cable TV, fax and copy machines, same day valet service, in-room massage, and fitness room, Americans with Disabilities compliant rooms.

The ten-story Claremont Hotel is one of the few remaining family owned hotels in downtown Seattle. The present owners recently had the hotel remodeled in keeping with its original European style. Its decor includes high ceilings, marble floors, handmade Italian chandeliers and brass accents. The hotel has a two-story ballroom with mock skylight.

The Ghosts

In August of 2000, I received an email from Sean. He and his girlfriend had spent a night in one of the deluxe rooms at the Claremont Hotel. He was awakened in the middle of the night by the sound of a man's voice mumbling in the bathroom. He got up and went into the bathroom to investigate. The sound was not from an adjoining room. He went back to bed, where he told his girlfriend he thought they had a ghost. She covered her head with the covers, but was not too frightened to go back to sleep.

After listening to the noises for a short while, Sean fell asleep too. He awoke to see the shadow of a man standing at the foot of his bed. Instinctively, Sean thought that this was a thief rather than a ghost. He jumped out of bed to confront the stranger. His girlfriend sat up, slowly waking up. The figure turned and ran away from the bed, through a wall. Sean realized that he had not confronted a thief, but a ghost.

Name: **Mayflower Park Hotel**
Address: 407 Olive Way
Seattle, WA 98101
Phone Number: **800-426-5100**
Website: www.mayflowrerpark.com
Rooms: 71 rooms with 13 luxury suites.
Prices: $$ - $$$
Theme: 1920's Elegance
Cuisine: Northwest
Andaluca Restaurant $$$.
Open: Breakfast: Monday – Saturday, 6:30 a.m. – 11:00 a.m.
Sunday 7:00 a.m. to noon.
Lunch: Monday – Saturday, 11:30 a.m. - 2:30 p.m.
Dinner: Monday – Thursday, 5:00 p.m. – 10:00 p.m., Friday and Saturday, 5:00 p.m. - 11:00 p.m.
Sunday 5:00 p.m. - 9:00 p.m.

Special Facilities: Complimentary coffee and newspaper, air conditioning, large screen television, cable TV, electronic security keys, same day laundry service, non-smoking floors, Americans with Disability compliant rooms.

The Mayflower Park hotel is the oldest restored hotel in downtown Seattle. It was built in 1927, originally called the Bergonian. It was designed and outfitted to remind visitors and guests of a small but luxurious Old World hotel. In keeping with the refined and understated theme of the hotel, the ghosts here seem to be quiet and polite too.

The Ghosts

The ghosts were fairly discrete and quiet at the Mayflower until April of 1997. Three different guests stayed in Room 1120 and told management of a ghost. This ghost did not do anything spectacular, but it made itself felt as a presence in the room. All three guests felt that the spirit was benign.

Restaurants Clubs and Theaters

Name: **Avenue One Restaurant**
Address: 1921 First Avenue
Seattle, WA 98101
Phone Number: 206-441-6139
Website: www.savvydiner.com/seattle/avenueone/menu
Prices: $$ - $$$
Cuisine: French Bistro
Open: Lunch: Monday – Saturday, 11:30 a.m. – 2:00 p.m.
Dinner: Sunday – Thursday, 5:00 p.m. – 10:00 p.m., Friday & Saturday 5:00 p.m. – 11:00 p.m.

Special Facilities: Full bar with copper top, extensive wine list, high-ceiling dinning room, and special seafood dishes.

Funeral home director E.R. Butterworth is supposed to have invented the term's 'mortuary' and 'mortician.' Business was so good that he had a custom funeral home built at 1921 1st Avenue, in 1903. The main entrance is located at street level of the four-story building. There were separate doors at street level, with mosaic tiles, denoting chapel and business office entrances at street level.

The bodies of the deceased moved through the building in stages. When they arrived, they were taken to the top floor where they were embalmed. They were moved to chapel services on the next floor down. After the service, they moved to the basement. Some of them were cremated on-site. Others were put into a hearse and taken to a graveyard. The Butterworth family moved their business to Capitol Hill in 1923. Since that time shops and restaurants occupied the building.

The Ghosts

Before it became the Avenue One, the restaurant was named the Café Sophie. Years ago an electrician was repairing some wiring in a chandelier late one night. Two men sitting in a booth were having an animated conversation. A woman dressed in an unearthly white dress walked into the dining room. The men stopped talking and began yelling insults at her and then at each other. The electrician ran out without finishing the job.

Arnie Millan did extensive remodeling to the main floor of the Café Sophie before he reopened the restaurant as the Avenue One. Sometimes remodeling can cause ghosts to either become more active or disappear. In this case, the ghosts seemed to hold their breath and then became active again. It began with small things, such as place settings out of place, cold spots, and something that seems to "hang out" near the ladies' bathroom. Nothing frightening has ever happened, but it keeps the staff on their toes.

Name: **Baltic Room**
Address: 1207 Pine Street
Seattle, WA 98101
Phone Number: **206-625-4444**
Prices: $$
Theme: Jazz, rock, hip-hop, and electro-techno music
Cuisine American music club
Open: Sunday – Saturday, 5:00 p.m. – 2:00 a.m.

The club recently changed focus from a low-key piano-wine bar to a more contemporary mix of music. It still retains the low lighting and round booths of its former incarnation. It has also changed from selling strictly wine and beer to a full bar.

The Ghosts

There are two ghosts that haunt the Baltic Room, a man and a woman. The woman used to stand in the balcony and watch the piano player when this was strictly a jazz bar. She was dressed either in a negligee or frilly evening dress. The man used to appear after she had disappeared, as if he was following her. I don't now how they took the change in venue here.

Name: **College Inn Pub**
Address: 4006 University Way NE
Seattle, WA 98105
Phone Number: 206-634-2307
Website: http://nwbrewpage.com/wapubs/collegeinn.html
Theme: College Pub
Prices: $
Cuisine: Pub grub
Open: Daily, 11:00 a.m. – 2:00 a.m.
Special Facilities: Basement pub divided into two sections, pool tables and wooden booths, smoking allowed but bad ventilation, 14 beers on tap, a favorite hangout of U of W students.

The College Inn Pub is located in the basement of the University of Washington College Inn building. The upstairs houses a traditional B&B, a café and a small grocery store. Because it is located on the campus, parking can be confusing. There are several nearby university parking lots with parking sticker requirements.

The Ghosts

The ghost of Howard Bok is supposed to haunt the University pub. Bok was a sailor who was staying at the University Inn. He was murdered there, perhaps in the basement, before the pub was opened in the 1970s. Howard usually confines himself to the Snug Room in the back of the bar. There is a piano there, which he sometimes plays. Most of the time he is felt as a presence, especially after hours or on slow nights.

Name: **Crocodile Cafe**
Address: 2200 Second Avenue
Seattle, WA 98121
Phone Number: 206-441-5611
Fax Number: 206-448-2114
Website: www.thecrocodile.com
Theme: Classic cafe
Prices: $$
Cuisine: Bar & Grill
Open: **Café**: Tuesday – Thursday, 8:00 a.m.– 11:00 p.m.;
Friday & Saturday, 8:00 a.m. - Midnight;
Sunday, 9:00 a.m.–3:00 p.m. (Brunch only)

Club times: Tuesday – Saturday, 8:00 a.m. – 2:00 a.m.
Sunday, 9:00 a.m. – 3:00 p.m.
Special Facilities: Live music, up and coming bands, rock stars hangout, located in Belltown, which can be rough at night. There is a cover charge. Special events cost a little more to attend.

The owners of the Crocodile Café are pro-active in promoting all the services at their club. They advertise an ultra-diverse clientele, and highlight not only their live music but their restaurant and its full meal menus.

The Ghosts

The ghosts at the Crocodile seem to be very discreet. They seem limited to creaks and groans and other sound effects noticed mostly by the staff.

Name: **Doc Maynard's and The Underground Tour**
Address: 610 First Avenue
Seattle, WA 98101
Phone Number: 888-608-6337
206-682-4646
Website: www.undergroundtour.com
Prices: $$
Theme: Historic Seattle
Cuisine: Northwest
Open: Tour times vary depending on season. It is best to call ahead and make reservations.
Special Facilities: The Underground Tour, 15 draft beers. Tour prices are moderate. The tours end at the gift shop.

At night Doc Maynard's has live music, mostly rock. You can purchase a $7.00 co-cover charge that will let you into any club in Pioneer Square. The bar portion of Doc Maynard's remains nearly unchanged, but the parts of the building where the Underground Tour tickets are purchased is a combination of neon and white walls. Frankly I miss grungy walls and cobwebs.

The Ghosts

Several years ago, Seattle newspaperman Bill Speidel began the Seattle Underground Tours, which began at Doc Maynard's, one of the oldest buildings in Seattle. One employee told me about the ghost that used to haunt Doc Maynard's. His first job was to come in early and make soup for the morning tourist crowd. At that time, the kitchen was on the first floor in the back of the building. Sometimes he felt a dramatic drop in the temperature, and a presence standing over him. Sometimes the kitchen utensils hanging on the walls would swing from their hangers.

He thought that he was going crazy, until another employee witnessed it once. He found that playing loud music would quiet the ghost. The growing popularity of the Underground Tours made it necessary for a massive remodel of Doc Maynard's in 1996. Since that time, all poltergeist activity seems to have ceased. Even so, the morning cooks still turn the radio up loud, just in case.

The Underground Ghost

Ten or fifteen years ago, the tours opened what the guides refer to as the *new section*, under the Denny and Yesler buildings. After that, people began to see the apparition. The most common apparition is that of a man in formal dress, including a top hat and cape. Was this the spirit of Yesler or Denny, returning from some ghostly formal ball? Other tour guides have reported seeing the ghost of a man in uniform near what used to be a bank vault. One tour guide nearly walked into a solid looking man dressed as a turn of the century miner.

Name: **Kells Irish Restaurant and Pub**
Address: 1916 Post Alley, Pike Place Market
Seattle, WA 98101
Phone Number: **206-728-1916**
Website: www.kellsirish.com/seattle
Prices: $$
Cuisine: Irish pub
Open: Seven days a week, 11:30 a.m.
Special Facilities: Micro-brew, live music, Irish theme.

Kells Irish Pub occupies the bottom floor of the old Butterworth Funeral Home (see the Avenue One Restaurant). The funeral home's stables, hearse garage and crematorium occupied the bottom floor. This seems to have had some lasting effect on operations in the pub that now occupies the same space.

The Ghosts

In the early days of Kells, a plumber was working on some pipes under the floorboards. He found little piles of ashes under the floorboards. Were they left behind from the crematorium? Perhaps in memory of the crematorium, candles sometimes light on their own. The ghost or ghosts liked to pull practical jokes.

Customers used to find bar straws in their hair and locked doors were sometimes found open. The owner's son was working in the bathroom and was frightened by the sound of a disembodied voice mumbling. It became louder and louder, until he finally ran out of the room. The owners had an exorcism performed several years ago and that seemed to put an end to most of the happenings.

Name: **O.K. Hotel and Cafe**
Address: 212 Alaskan Way S
Seattle, WA 98104
Phone Number: **Unknown**
Theme: Turn of century bar
Prices: $ - $$
Cuisine: Pub food
Open: At the time this book was written, the O.K. is shut due to earthquake damage. I hope that it will open later.
Special Facilities: Microbrew, live music.

The O.K. is also known as the Old Klondike Hotel, after the miners who stayed there, waiting to head to the Alaskan gold fields. There were 25 rooms on each floor, with only one common bathroom on each floor. Eventually only the ground floor hotel lunch counter remained in operation. The O.K. opened in the 1980s.

The O.K. is a combination café, bar and art gallery. It can be a rough place because of its locality. It had a varied clientele, from dockworkers to small parties of wine bar patrons who sometimes slip in to listen to the live music. Their stories make the O.K. a candidate for Seattle's most haunted nightspot.

The Ghosts

People have seen transparent apparitions. They have felt strange presences and even been touched by invisible hands once or twice. One afternoon a couple from the Midwest stopped at the O.K. They were following the trail of an ancestor who had stayed at the O.K. in the past. They left in a hurry when the wife saw an older couple walk down the stairs from the second floor, arm in arm. As they neared the foot of the stairs, the couple became transparent and disappeared.

The owner has an apartment on the second floor. Several times he has been awakened in the middle of the night by the sound of someone whistling in the bar below. Each time he has found the bar dark and locked up tight. An employee named Pat seems to attract one of the resident ghosts. One employee has seen a shape they described as a black tornado following him.

Name:	**Sit and Spin Laundromat and Club**
Address:	2219 4th Avenue Seattle, WA 98104
Phone Number:	**206-441-9484**
Fax Number:	206 448-2710
Website:	www.sitandspin.net
Price:	$ - $$
Theme:	Eclectic mix of New Age art and linoleum.
Cuisine:	Café with alcoholic and non-alcoholic drinks.
Open:	Sunday – Wednesday, 10:00 a.m. to 11:00 p.m. Thursday – Saturday, 10:00 a.m. to 1:30 a.m.

Special Facilities: Laundromat in front, live music in back. Internet café.

The Sit & Spin Laundromat is one of those eclectic places that you may see portrayed on a sit-com, but never expect to see in real life. It is a combination club and Laundromat. The club has a definite grunge look that contrasts with its linoleum floor and Formica-topped kitchen tables. In the late 1920s, Seattle band leader, Vic Meyers opened a jazz nightclub in the Sit & Spin building.

As a joke, Meyers ran for mayor and campaigned with a vengeance. Even though he lost, he was sixth out of a total of ten candidates. A few months later Meyers drove down to Olympia where he planned to file to run for governor. He could not afford to file for governor, but lieutenant governor cost much less. Meyers told the clerk that although he could not spell lieutenant, he would take it. Meyers later beat his opponent by 40,000 votes.

The Ghosts

When the jukebox is put on random play, it always seems to play jazz music. One employee I spoke with always felt a chill when she went into the back hallway by the bathroom. Another employee was cleaning the bathroom when he saw an apparition with no head, vanish into a stall. A woman was performing on the small club stage when she saw a man next to her, out of the corner of her eye. When she turned to look directly at him, there was no one there.

The owner saw the ghostly shadow when she was alone in the club's band room around 4:00 a.m. The light was behind her and she saw her own shadow and the shadow of a man wearing a large Fedora-type hat standing behind her. She whirled around to face him, to confront empty air.

Theaters

Name: **Harvard Exit Theater**
Address: 807 East Roy Avenue
Seattle, WA 98102
Phone Number: **206-323-8986**
Theme: Meeting hall turned theater
Price: $$
Open: Check with the box office for show dates and times.
Special Facilities: Comfortable lounge, snack bar, two movie screens.

Built in 1924, the Harvard Exit Theater was the original home of the Women's Century Club. This was founded by Bertha Knight Landes, Seattle's first and only woman mayor. In 1926 she ran for mayor and was elected on an anti-crime platform. Despite her success in cleaning up corruption in Seattle, she was not re-elected in 1928.

Landes remained active in both women's and social issues. She died in 1945, at the age of 75. In the late 1960s, the organization sold their building, which was converted into the Harvard Exit Theater. As part of the sales agreement, the lobby must stay the same as when the Women's Century Club owned it. This is because they still meet there twice a month. The lobby fixtures include a large fireplace, grand piano, and several comfortable couches.

The Ghosts

Janet Wainright was the manager of the Harvard Exit Theater from 1970 to 1979. One morning she opened the theater to find re-arrangements had been made to the lounge. The fireplace, which should have been cold, was filled with a large fire. The chairs and couch were arranged in a circle around the fire, as if a group of people had been sitting for several hours.

One morning she opened the door to the lounge and saw a strange woman. She was dressed in a long, flowered silk dress with her hair pulled up off of her shoulders. The woman was also transparent. Other people claim to have seen the ghost of a middle-aged woman wearing 1920s clothing. She hovers or floats a few feet off the ground before disappearing through walls. People taking photographs of empty rows of seats in the third floor theater were surprised to find images of people sitting in the seats, when their film was developed.

Name: **The Moore Theatre**
Address: 1932 Second Avenue
Seattle, WA 98121
Phone Number: **206-467-5510 (business)**
206-628-0888 (Ticketmaster)
Theme: Traditional Gothic Theatre
Price: $$ - $$$
Open: Check website or Ticketmaster for prices and times.
Special Facilities: Live theatre, comedy acts, plays, concerts.

James A. Moore, the major developer of the Capitol Hill neighborhood, built the Moore Theater in 1907. Moore wanted to woo major business interests away from the Pioneer Square area. The grand lobby had tile floors of marble and onyx. The richly carved wood paneling impressed early customers. Giant statues of the muses of Drama and Music support the lofty ceilings. The theater interior was decorated with more stained glass windows, thick wall hangings and chandeliers.

In the mid-1970s it was converted into the Moore-Egyptian Movie Theater, after the gilt Egyptian artwork on the walls. It showed foreign and classic films and became the first home to the Seattle International Film Festival. In 1980 the facility became the Moore Theatre and returned to live performances and shows.

The Ghosts

The more popular ghost stories about this building date to the 1970s, when it was a movie house. The two owners, Dan Ireland and Darryl MacDonald, lived in the old dressing rooms below the stage. One night Ireland went up to the control room to turn off some equipment. He stopped when he heard the sound of heavy breathing and smelled the heavy odor of human urine. After waiting in the dark for several seconds, he lost his nerve, and ran toward the projection booth. He passed through something that left him feeling cold and tingling. He locked himself in the projection booth and spent over half an hour calling for his partner. He later fired several employees who were having a séance in the lobby.

Name: **Neptune Theater**
Address: 1303 NE 45th Street
Seattle, WA 98105
Phone Number: 206-633-5545
Prices: $$
Theme: Nautical motif
Open: Variable, check the ticket office phone number.
Special Facilities: Seats 1000 people. It has a single screen and was remodeled in 1994, with upgraded seats and sound system.

The Neptune Theater was built in 1921 as a combination silent movie theater and vaudeville house. The original owner was a ship builder. He used aquamarine colors with stained glass panels in the theater. The god Neptune and mermaids cavort on the walls and ceilings.

The Ghosts

Two or three ghosts haunt this theater. One is the ghost of a young woman wearing a white, flowing dress. A manager saw her bathed in light in the organ loft. One night a janitor was treating himself to a free cola at the snack bar when he saw a woman walk through the lobby. He called out to her, saying that the theater was closed. She became transparent and disappeared. He dropped the cola, cracking the countertop. The gray woman has been seen and felt in many locations. Backstage workers or performers sometimes smell tobacco smoke, even when no one is smoking.

Shops, Sights and Sounds

Name: **"Metaphysical Street"**
Address: NE 65th Street from 8th to NE 25th Avenue
Seattle

This is a neighborhood phenomenon. Many of the shops and stores lining the street specialize in New Age and alternative goods and services. One special feature was a labyrinth on the corner of 65th and Roosevelt. I do not know if it is still there.

Name: **Pike Place Market**
Address: The main entrance is, "Under the Clock,"
Near the corner of Pike Street and 1st Avenue
Seattle, WA
Phone Number: 206-682-7453 (market information)
Website: www.pikeplacemarket.org
Theme: Farmer's market
Open: The market is open year round but hours and days of the week vary, depending on the type of merchandise sold. Fish and produce stalls generally open and close early, restaurants generally open late and close later.

Pike Place Market began as a statement of outrage in 1907, when the price of onions went from 10 cents, to one dollar a pound. On August 17th, 1907, eight farmers parked their wagons at the corner of First and Pike Street and sold directly to their customers. Since then, the market has expanded to five stories and out buildings. Some of the traditional shops have occupied the same stalls for the last 90+ years.

If there was ever a place that reminds me of a doorway into an alternate universe, it is Pike Place Market. I always find a new shop, just around the corner or down another narrow stairway. Sometimes I walk down stairs that end at solid walls. Other passages open into galleries. Many tourists assume that the market is contained within the main building. It actually extends through several buildings on and around Pike Place Way. I recommend that visitors pick up a copy of the *Pike Place Market News*, for the list of shops and map of the market usually printed inside.

The Pike Place Market Merchants Association conducts walking tours of the market every day. You must make reservations a day in advance at 206-587-0351. Tours are $7.00 for adults, $5.00 for children under 12. There is also a discount rate for 15 persons. The tours begin at the pig and last about an hour. Where's the pig? Just ask anyone; she's been there since 1987.

The Ghosts

There are many ghosts that inhabit both the hallways and shops of the Pike Place Market. There seem to be three or four ghosts that most people have seen, heard, or felt. They are an elderly Native American woman, a little boy, an overweight woman, and an African American man.

The Native American ghost is the most well known spirit at Pike Place Market. She spends a lot of time in the "Down Under," shops below the mezzanine, or ground floor of the Main Market Building. Some people believe this elderly ghost is Princess Angeline or Kickisomolo, the daughter of Chief Seattle. She died in 1896 at the age of 85. She is described as being elderly, with her gray hair tied up in long braids. One person reported that she was glowing with a white light. Princess Kikisomolo is also buried in Lake View Cemetery, with many pioneers and Bruce and Brandon Lee.

If you talk to merchants, Princess Kikisomolo has been seen everywhere... just yesterday, as a matter of fact. In the past she was associated with the Old Friend Memorabilia Shop, the Goodwill and Shakespeare and Company Bookstore. The Goodwill is now the Market Child Care Facility and Shakespeare and Company is now Lionheart Books. Princess Kickisomolo is not confined to the lower levels of the market. She has been seen at the Sound View Café, in the Leland Building, along Flower Row, and in the Craft Emporium in the Main Market Building.

The Craft Emporium is also known as the Bead Shop. It stocks a complete selection of modern as well as traditional beads. Several years ago, the owner of the shop, Lynn Roberts, saw an elderly Native American woman looking at the collection of seed beads. When Roberts asked the woman is she could help her, the woman disappeared. The Craft Emporium has a second ghost that spends most of its time there.

This is the ghost of a little boy. One day he walked up to Roberts, tugged her sleeve to get her attention and... disappeared. The next day, a radio turned on of its own accord. She unplugged it. Even without power, it played. The little tyke has a tendency to throw beads at employees and customers. I visited the shop in 1998 and I was told that a shaman had performed an exorcism there. This

stopped most of the strange goings on. Maybe they just moved to another shop?

There is a candy store in the Main Market Building. At the end of the day, the employees are told put the candy scoops away in a storage cupboard. In the morning the scoops are sometimes out of their storage area, in the candy. At night people have reported hot and cold spots in the hallways. Cold spots can be explained as drafts, but what about the hot spots?

There is also the ghost of a tall African American man associated with the Vitium Capitale Restaurant. The only problem is that the Vitium Capitale is no longer at the Pike Place Market. No one I spoke with knows which building or space they used to occupy.

Left Bank Books is located in the Corner Market Building. According to an unconfirmed report, when some employees are alone in the store, they hear footsteps walking down the empty aisles. The ghost of the large woman dates to the time when an overweight female customer fell through a weak floor, onto a table or floor on the lower level, before dying. I have not been able to find anyone who actually knows where or if this happened.

Name: **Lake View Cemetery**
Address: 1554 15th Avenue East
Seattle, WA 98112
Phone Number: **206-322-1582**
Theme: Pioneer Cemetery
Open: 9:00 a.m. – 4:30 p.m., Monday - Saturday
Special Facilities: A map showing prominent gravesites is available at the cemetery office. At certain times of year local historical societies run graveyard tours.

Many of Seattle's prominent founders and citizens are buried in Lake View Cemetery. They include pioneers Henry Yesler and the Denny family. Some of the people buried here may haunt other places in the Pacific Northwest. They include Robert Moran, who built and may now haunt the Rosario Resort. Princess Angeline, or Kickisomolo, the daughter of Chief Seattle may haunt Pike Place Market. "Doc" Maynard is buried here, but he probably does not haunt the kitchen of his old building on Pioneer Square. The two most famous residents of Greenwood Cemetery are Bruce and Brandon Lee (Grave lot 276).

Martial arts legend Bruce Lee died of a cerebral hemorrhage in 1973, at the age of 32. His son, Brandon Lee died at the age of 28, while filming the movie, *The Crow*. Fans and devotee's visit the Lee graves year round. Many leave offerings at the graves, such as cigarettes, coins

This is not Lake View or Maltby Cemetery. Can you guess where it is?

and miniatures of both men. On the average, ten people a day visit the gravesites, which were vandalized in the past. Their gravesites have been improved with a bench, and a flagstone path covers the grass, which was worn away by visitors.

Name **Maltby Cemetery**
Address: Withheld
Phone Number: Withheld

The Maltby Cemetery is a small family cemetery located outside of Seattle. It has a reputation for being haunted. People searching the web can read fantastic stories about climbing thirteen steps (to Hell) lead into the cemetery. Or, that there are 13 gravestones, for the Damned Souls there. Stories about Maltby have grown until they have become an urban legend.

One thing that is not an urban legend is that this is a very small, very old cemetery that has been vandalized by curiosity seekers. I have been told that the owners have to hire guards to shoo away tourists at Halloween. I discourage any curiosity seekers from visiting this cemetery, if only as a matter of respect.

Name: **Private Eye Seattle Tours**
Phone Number: 206-622-0590
206-365-3739
Website: www.privateeyetours.com
Prices: $20 to $25 per person
Theme: Investigative tours
Open: By appointment

Tours are conducted by vans, though there are places where tourists can get out and walk to sites. The tours offered by Seattle Private Investigators include a Queen Anne Tour, Capital Hill Tour, and a Church Tour. New in 2001 is a Ghost Tour. Tours take 2 — 2 1/2 hours with the exception of the church tours. The tours focus on the strange, macabre and amazing.

Name: **Armonica Musical Recordings and Concerts**
Address: P.O. Box 33119
Seattle, WA 98133

Phone Number: 206-364-8042
Website: www.glassarmonica.com
Prices: $$
Theme: 18th century music
Open: Check website for live concerts
<u>Special Facilities</u>: Three Music CD's of Armonica music are available from the website.

Benjamin Franklin designed a musical instrument with a horizontal rod, which had a series of glass bowls of varying sizes nested within each other. The rod spun around in a circle, so that the when a musician touches the bowls, it generated sounds. He called it the 'armonica,' which is Italian for 'harmony.' People said it sounded like the music of heaven. Franklin brought his armonica, to France during the American Revolution. It was an instant hit.

At least 300 works of classical music were written for the armonica. The armonica developed a reputation for being able to soothe different kinds of mental illnesses. This brought it to the attention of Franz Mesmer. Mesmer used the armonica as an aid in calming patients before hypnotizing them. Later the armonica was reputed to cause depression and thought to summon the spirits of the dead.

This reputation surrounding the armonica led to its downfall as a popular musical instrument by the middle of the 19th century. William Wilde Zeitler lives in Puget Sound and gives armonica concerts in the northwest. He has not yet had a ghost summoned to his presence by his playing.

Name: **Kinnear Park**
Address: 899 W Olympic Place
Seattle, WA 91833
Phone Number: 206-684-4075
(lost and found information)
Price: $ (free)
Open: 4:00 a.m. - 11:30 p.m.
<u>Special Features</u>: Children's playground, restrooms, and tennis courts.

George Kinnear moved to Seattle in 1874. He was the driving force behind the first wagon road from Seattle, east through Snoqualmie Pass. He eventually owned great chunks of land in and around Seattle. In 1889, some of his friends suggested he sell some of his land to the city for a park. He sold the City of Seattle 14 acres for one dollar.

The Ghosts

I have heard only one unconfirmed report that in the 1920s park visitors were frightened by the sound of a baby crying at night.

Name: **Lake Washington, Seattle and Bellevue**
Special Facilities: Magnuson Park, and other parks and recreation centers.

There are many strange stories associated with Lake Washington. They include a hermit, whose ghost still inhabits an island in the lake where he lived. Visitors have reported hearing moaning sounds coming across the lake. Some have attributed this to UFOs, which have been sighted over the lake in the past. Many do not know about the 'sound garden' at the National Oceanic Atmospheric Administration (NOAA) reservation, north of Magnuson Park. The sound garden is a sculpture of open tubes, which creates these noises when the wind blows across their open ends. There is a trail from Magnuson Park to the 'sound garden".

Sea monster hunters should be impressed with the history of Lake Washington. In the late 1960s there were reports of alligators chasing ducks on the lake. In 1987 an eleven-foot long sturgeon was found dead in the lake.

Name: **Suicide Bridge, Seattle WA**

The Aurora Bridge is officially named the George Washington Bridge and is sometimes called the 'Suicide Bridge.' It was built near the Freemont neighborhood, above Lake Union. There have been over 200 suicides who jumped off the bridge from 1932 to the present day. Some people swear they see the ghosts of some of the dead jumpers and in one case, a ghost dog, to this day.

In contrast to this dark history, tourists can visit the giant concrete troll statue built under the north bridge abutment. At first condemned by the artistic community, many city residents love 'The Statue,' which holds a VW bug in its hand.

Name: **Wing Luke Museum**
Address: 407 Seventh Avenue South
Seattle, WA 98104
Phone Number: **206-623-5124**
Website: www.wingluke.org
Price: $
Open: Tuesday – Friday, 11:00 a.m.- 4:30 p.m.
Saturday & Sunday, 12:00 p.m. – 4:00 p.m.

Special Facilities: Admission on the first Thursday is free. In addition to general admission, there is a guided tour for a modest fee.

This museum is named after Wing Luke, the son of an immigrant oriental laundryman. In 1962 he was the first Asian Pacific American elected to the Seattle City Council. Three years later he died in a plane crash. As part of his vision, the museum was created in 1967 and named in his honor.

The Wing Luke is the only Pan-Asian American museum in the United States. Its focus is on the preservation and display of artifacts relating to Pacific American history, culture and art. It is not focused on one Asian culture, but all of them. There are many displays from different places, cultures, and times.

The Ghosts

Past hauntings of the Wing Luke may be due to its multi-cultural focus. Some times in the past, displays have combined spiritually conflicting items with each other. In 1987, a display from Tibet combined artifacts from shamanistic, pre-Buddhist times with later, Buddhist period objects. A few minutes after the conflicting objects were combined, the display case shattered. There have not been any recent reports about the Wing Luke museum. Even if there were, it is doubtful that the staff would answer questions. Ghosts or no, the museum is worth the visit.

Snohomish

Name: **Cabbage Patch Restaurant**
Address: 111 Avenue A
Snohomish, WA 98290
Phone Number: **360-568-9091**
Prices: $$
Theme: Turn of the Century antique.
Cuisine: Northwest (many seafood dishes)
Open: Monday — Friday, 10:00 a.m. — 10:00 p.m.
Saturday & Sunday, 8:00 a.m. — 10:00 p.m.
Special Facilities: Catering, Lounge

The city of Snohomish probably has the greatest concentration of historic homes that I have ever seen in any northwest setting. The Cabbage Patch Restaurant is one of these fine old homes that has been turned into a restaurant, as opposed to an antique store. Instead, the antiques are part of the décor of the restaurant.

The Ghosts

Although the restaurant employees are not afraid of their resident spirit, Sybill Sibley, no one wants to come face to face with her. This benefits the owner, because at the end of the day, everyone cleans up as quickly as possible to avoid being alone in the building. When they are, they sometimes hear Sybill calling their names. In mid-2001 the owner and others heard the sound of glass breaking in the upstairs lounge. When they ran up to investigate, there was no broken glass to be found.

Many customers who have not heard that the Cabbage Patch is haunted ask the owner soon after entering. One customer was talking with the owner, when she saw a young girl wearing a white dress, floating a few feet behind the owner.

Name: **Oxford Saloon & Eatery**
Address: 913 First Street
Snohomish, WA 98290
Phone Number: **360-568-3845**
Website: www.oxfordsaloon.com
Price: $$
Theme: Turn of the century tavern.
Cuisine: Pub food
Open: Daily, 11:00 a.m. — 1:00 a.m.
Special Facilities: Specializes in live blues music. Pool tables. Wednesday night is 'Murder Mystery Dinners'.

Dating to the late 19th century, the Oxford Saloon led a checkered past. The current owners are careful to preserve the turn of the century Boom Town image of the place. It resembles the kind of restaurant many trendy chains try to look like, but fail to imitate. The main floor is an open bar with old saloon style tables and chairs. The basement has rough walls, benches, and several pool tables.

It has always been an eatery and bar, but the upstairs was a combination rooming house and bordello. Madame Kathleen ran the bordello there in the past. She was forced into prostitution and hated her profession and her customers. The basement was used at times as a men's card room and bar. Local historians record several brawls, knifings and shootings there.

The Ghosts

The owner of the Oxford Saloon has detected at least eight distinct spirits and perhaps many more crowding the Oxford. Kathleen has been seen by a few patrons on the second floor. She is a middle-aged woman, usually wearing a long purple dress and a hat with purple bows and violets. Two other female ghosts, known as Mary and Amelia, may be responsible for things being rearranged or moved on the second floor. A male presence is seen in the upstairs from time to time.

Henry, a very active ghost that inhabits the first and basement floors. Henry was a local policeman and a regular customer at the Oxford Saloon. One night Henry was called to the saloon to break up a fight. During the melee he was knifed, and died. Many women using the downstairs bathroom have complained that an invisible hand has pinched them. He has also been active on the second floor.

Name: **Snohomish Library**
Address: 105 Cedar Avenue
Snohomish, WA 98290
Phone Number: **360-568-2898**
Website: www.sno-isle.org
Open: Monday - Thursday, 10:00 a.m. - 9:00 p.m.

Friday & Saturday, 10:00 a.m. - 5:00 p.m. Sunday (September-June), 1:00 p.m. - 5:00 p.m.

Special Facilities: Ghost Cam with the *Everett Herald.*

At the turn of the 19th Century, Andrew Carnegie was the richest man in the world. One of Carnegie's passions was education. In the early 20th century he and the foundation he created endowed hundreds of cities and towns across the United States with libraries. In 1910, the town of Snohomish received $10,000 to help build their library.

In the years after the library was built, three of the 'McMurchy girls,' worked there. Catharine began working there in June of 1923. She quit in 1939, after ill health made her leave her beloved librarian's profession, or perhaps it was her passion. Catharine never married, but retired to live with another sister, Anna. In 1950, the two women, now elderly, moved to a Seattle retirement home where they later died.

The Ghosts

In 1991, a library employee was sitting in the staff break room, eating her lunch. She heard the sound of someone walking down the stairs, from the library's third floor storage loft, above her head. She looked at the door where the stairs ended on the second floor. The door opened and the employee saw an older woman, wearing a blue dress. The woman walked through the break room and passed through another door into the main library.

The employee got up and followed the strange woman. The old woman was not anywhere within sight. The employee asked around and found that other employees had seen and/or experienced many strange things that they attributed to the library's ghost. Most of them agreed that the ghost could only be Catharine McMurchy, whose life had centered around the library for many years.

Legends of the haunting continued and for the Halloween season in 2000, the *Everett Herald* investigated. Four reporters from the *Herald* spent an eventful Halloween evening at the library. Throughout the night, they heard footsteps in the library loft area. The *Herald* and library sponsored a webcam in the library. The webcam takes pictures of the library at regular intervals and displays them on the newspaper's website (http://lass.heraldnet.com/ghostcam/index.cfm). One reporter was sitting in a chair, which began to shake. A window rattled in the wind and the chair shook even more.

Skykomish

Name: **Skykomish Hotel**
Address: 102 Railroad Avenue
Skykomish, WA 98288
Phone Number: **Unknown**
Rooms: 22 Rooms
Prices: $$
Theme: Turn of the century rustic hotel
Cuisine: Café inside the hotel.
Open: Spring and summer
Special Facilities: The hotel is closed for renovation but may reopen soon.

The Skykomish Hotel was built in 1904 and has 22 rooms. It looks and feels a little like the *Shady Rest Hotel* seen in a 1960s television series. The rooms are not fancy and the bathrooms are down the hall. Depending on where you step, the floors squeak or sag suspiciously under foot. There is a small 1950s style café on the main floor that serves ordinary American food. I love places like this. The Steven's Pass Company purchased the hotel a few years ago and uses it as housing for their winter personnel. They open the hotel up for guests during the summer though, and the haunting still continues.

The Ghosts

In the 1920s, a prostitute named 'Mary' was murdered in Room 32 by one of her customers or a jealous lover. The last owner claims to have seen and felt Mary's ghost several times. Once she followed him down the stairs. On a different occasion he watched the door to room 32 unlock, open, close and he saw the lights come on.

I was told that several people have heard voices talking in and around the third floor bathrooms. The haunting extends from the third floor down into the café attached to the hotel lobby. One morning a new cook heard the sound of a knife and fork scraping and cutting against a plate. He listened and heard a clank, as if silverware was put down on the countertop. He had not started cooking and the café was empty. He told another employee, who confirmed that she had heard ghostly eating herself, more than once.

Name: **The Iron Goat Trail**
Phone Number: **206-283-1440**
Website: www.bccctc.edu/cpsha/irongoat
Price: Free, though donations are accepted
Theme: Railroad and early Washington state settlement.

This trail highlights the development of the settlement of the Pacific Northwest, particularly the railroads in Steven's Pass. The trail begins at Martin Creek, near milepost 55 on Hwy 2, and runs through Stevens Pass to the Wellington ghost town. The Wellington Ghost Town Trail is six miles long. Portions of trail are barrier free. From the trail visitors can see the remains of the old rail lines, supporting structures, and the remains of a train crash at the bottom of a canyon.

The Ghosts

In February of 1910, snow banks stalled two trains overnight as work crews tried to clear the tracks. The next morning an avalanche swept down the mountainside, carrying both trains over a hundred feet to the bottom of the river valley. Ninety-six people were killed. This may account for the rumors of ghost trains, the sounds of crashes, and the screams of people echoing through the pass on winter evenings.

Steilacoom

The Town Ghosts

Steilacoom's founder, Lafayette Balch, brought members of his family with him. A true lunatic, Albert would lose focus whenever there was a new moon. He would disappear, and return after the moon changed its cycle. His condition became worse as time went on. In late December of 1862, he ran out of his house dressed only in his nightshirt. His body was found on the trail to Fort Nisqually the next day. The official coroner's inquest determined that Balch had either fallen or collapsed from exhaustion and died of exposure. He may still wander the trail on the night of the new moon.

In the 1850s Steilacoom was a thriving metropolis with entrepreneurs like Andrew Byrd, who owned a slaughterhouse. J.M. Bates' main asset was a lone cow. One day the cow came up missing. One joker told Bates that he had seen Andrew Byrd taking the cow to the slaughterhouse. Bates found Byrd in the post office. After a brief exchange, Bates shot him. The night Byrd died, a group of vigilantes took Bates into a nearby barn and hung him. Bates has been seen on dark nights, still wearing his hangman's noose, looking for his lost cow.

Name: **Bair Drug Store**
Address: Located at the corner of Lafayette and Wilks Street
Steilacoom, WA 98388
Phone Number: 253-588-9668
Price: $$
Theme: Turn of century drug store
Cuisine: Coffee shop, specializing in desserts
Open: Monday - Sunday, 9:00 a.m. – 4:00 p.m.
Special Facilities: Combination museum and restaurant with gift shop.

W.L. Blair and his wife, Hattie, opened up business in the building in 1895. The drug store was also used as a post office and later converted into a trolley stop. The years brought disrepair until it was renovated and put to its current use as a historic landmark, museum and restaurant. The shelves of the drugstore are stocked with old medicine bottles and the oak mailboxes of the post office, at the end of the store, have mellowed with age. The original soda fountain stands near the entrance.

The Ghosts

Many of the manifestations seem to be centered in the restaurant and kitchen. Appliances have broken down with great regularity. This includes an incident where the oven temperature rose to 500 degrees when the thermostat control was set to a much lower temperature. Coffee is made on a large, multi-pot coffee drip machine. In 1998, employees watched as all of the pots placed on the top burners slowly rotated around in circles. After several seconds the coffeepots stopped moving.

Name: **E.R. Rogers Restaurant**
Address: 1702 Commercial Street
Steilacoom, WA 98388
Phone Number: 253-582-0280
Website: www.errogers.com

Price: $$$
Theme: Turn of the century mansion
Cuisine: Northwest gourmet
Open: Monday - Friday opens 5:30 p.m.
Saturday open at 5:00 p.m.; Sunday open at 4:30 p.m.
Sunday Brunch is from 10:00 a.m. to 2:00 p.m.
Special Facilities: Wedding and banquet facilities, Non-Smoking, lounge.

Merchant Captain E.R. Rogers built this Victorian style mansion around 1891. A few years later he suffered business losses and had to sell his home to Charles Herman. He converted it into a hotel and renamed it the Waverly Inn. W.L. and Hattie Bair purchased the property in 1920 and operated it as a boarding house for many years.

Although Mrs. Bair kept the place immaculate, the finer architectural aspects suffered over time. Stairways were torn out, new ones were added, and many small and great changes were made. After the many years and owners, it was converted into a fine northwest restaurant, named after its original builder.

The Ghosts

Some people claim to have seen Rogers sitting in a rocking chair, looking out of a north-facing window. In 1997, the restaurant bookkeeper was working near the bar when a bell at the end of the bar rang on its own for several minutes. One bar patron was having a drink and nearly choked when he saw a woman’s leg wearing a stocking appear in the air above him. It disappeared into the ceiling. There had been a flight of stairs leading to the second floor, where he had seen the woman's foot disappear.

There are other stories and folklore surrounding a Native American who may have been hung on or near the house site. His apparition is sometimes seen in the yard or looking in through the windows. Many people have heard sounds of footsteps in empty rooms and felt chills and strange sounds.

Downtown Tacoma

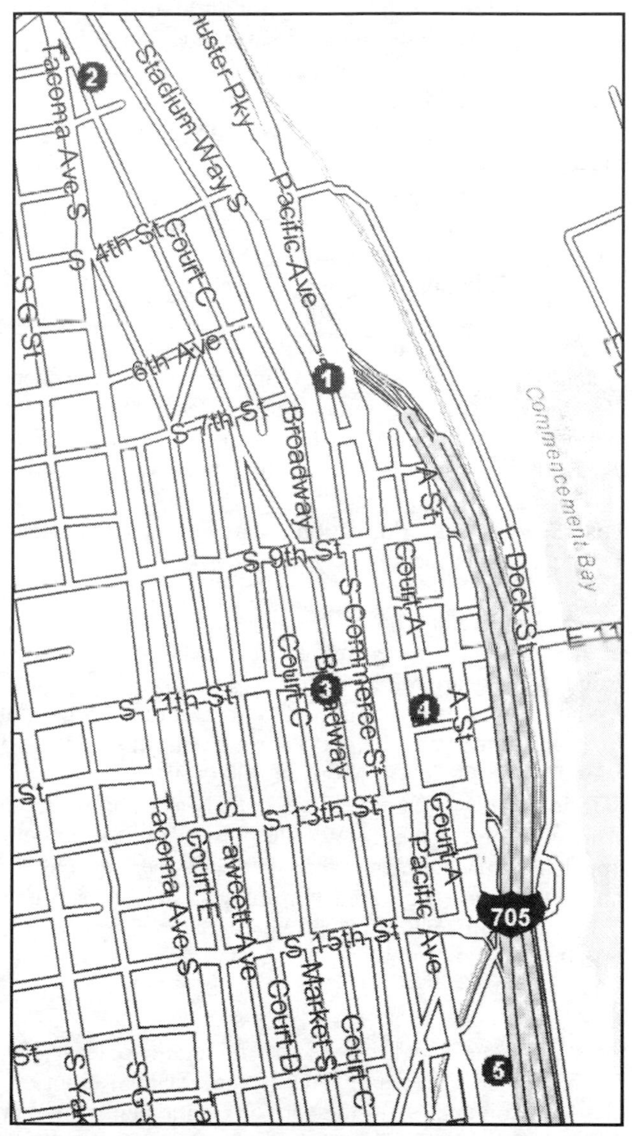

1) Tacoma Bar & Grill, 2) Landmark Convention Center, 3) Pantages Theater, 4) Tacoma Art Museum, 5) Union Station
© GDT 2001

Tacoma

Places to Stay

Name: **Thornewood Castle Inn and Garden**
Address: Technically south of Lakewood, but is usually identified with Tacoma.
Phone Number: **253-584-4393 (between 9:00 a.m. and 9:00 p.m.)**
Fax Number: 253-584-4497
Website: www.thornewoodcastle.com
Rooms: 8 suites. See website for full details
Prices: $$$
Theme: Traditional English Manor
Cuisine: Traditional English Prices: $$$
Open: See website for details

Special Facilities: Many amenities, complimentary chocolates, TV/VCR, radio/CD, coffee, common rooms, Reception rooms, extensive grounds, lakefront, and English garden. Tours of the castle are offered as packages such as, Lunch with Castle Tour, Castle Mystery Series.

Directions: See website for directions. The Thornewood is located within a gated neighborhood.

In 1908 Chester Thorne began to build this 54-room mansion. Many of the materials were imported from England. Some of the windows in the house are original stained glass from 15th century manors. The oak staircase is original, down to the wooden pegs that hold it together. It was three years before Thorne could move in, in 1911. The total cost of Thorne Castle was about $1,000,000.

Thorne and his family were not always happy in this dream estate. One of Thorne's son-in-laws shot himself in the gun closet. The young grandchild of a former owner died in American Lake. In more recent times, the house was used to film several scenes from a Steven King mini-series entitled *Rose Red*. Many of the scenes were filmed in the Rose Red Suite.

The Ghosts

Both Thorne and his wife are reluctant to leave their castle. They have both been seen there. The owner, Deanna Robinson has tried to turn the lights on and off in the former Gentlemen's Smoking Room. When she does that, she has found the light bulb unscrewed. The estate gardener has also seen Mr. Thorne's ghost.

Mrs. Thorne has been seen in her bedroom, which is now the

Bridal Suite. Some guests have seen her reflection in one of the original mirrors in the Bridal Suite. The Thorne's son-in-law who committed suicide has been in the room where he shot himself. Concerned guests report a child standing by the lake, with no adults in sight to supervise. When this has happened there have been no children staying at Thornewood Castle.

Restaurants Clubs and Theaters

Name: **Landmark Convention Center and Temple Theater**
Address: 47 St. Helens Avenue
Tacoma, WA 98402
Phone Number: 253-272-2042
253-593-4095 (ticket office)
Fax Number: 253-272-3793
Prices: Variable, depending on services
Theme: Classical Masonic Theater
Open: Convention Center opens for special events, check box office for show times in theater.

Special Facilities: The Convention Center has many small and large meeting and ballrooms. Catering facilities and large movie-theater with stage for live productions.

The Landmark Convention Center was built in 1927 as the home of the Grand Lodge of the Free and Accepted Masons of Washington State. Its façade includes huge Greek columns rising over a double door entrance. One employee told me the building has eight floors including basements and attic. A broad stairway and two elevators on either side of the stairwell reach these.

The Ghosts

In March of 1972, one of the buildings janitors was killed in an elevator accident. His ghost is supposed to ride the repaired service elevator. The service elevator frequently goes up and down, stopping at random on floors without an occupant. Sometimes the doors will stay open for several seconds, as if an unseen person is keeping them open.

A manager was in one of the large ballrooms. The lights turned off on their own. He opened up some curtains and the ballroom doors slammed shut, temporarily trapping him inside. Keys disappear, only to reappear months later in strange places. Maintenance workers have heard footsteps in the Fellowship Hall Room. When they went into the room they found it empty. Other people reported the ghost of a man in a long robe or coat looking out of the building from an upstairs window. He has been seen standing near the front doors of the building.

The adjoining Temple Theater is another impressive part of the old lodge. The theater seats 1620 people on the main floor and balcony. Most people believe that the theater haunting dates from its opening. In 1930, during a dance performance, the audience saw a ghost appear on or near the stage and watch a girl dance. After the performance he disappeared. In November of 1982, the theater manager went up to the balcony. Although she did not hear anything, she felt a presence there. She turned up the house lights and looked around. She saw a glowing light in the balcony. An employee thought it was the glow of a spirit aura. She did not investigate.

Name: **Pantages (Roxy) Theater**
Address: 901 Broadway
Tacoma, WA 98402
Phone Number: **253-591-5894 (ticket office)**
Website: www.tacomaopera.com
Prices: Variable $$ - $$$
Theme: Classic Greco-Broadway style Vaudeville/Opera house
Open: Variable, check with ticket office
Special Facilities: 1,181 seats, handicap accessible. Live theater and opera performances.

Alexander Pantages began his theatrical career as a boy, when he changed his name from Pericles to Alexander because he liked Alexander the Great. Pantages ran away from Greece as a boy and made his way to the Alaska gold fields in the late 1890s, when he was in his early 20s. The hard life of a gold miner convinced Pantages that it was easier taking money away from miners, than working in the gold fields.

Pantages reasoned that people would prefer a bar with entertainment to a bar without one. Pantages persuaded several people to help him invest in a failed dance hall. It was named the Orpheum and made him rich, and left them penniless. This is where he met Kathleen Eloisa Rockwell. Katherine Rockwell the famous entertainer was better known as 'Klondike Kate.' In 1900 or so, she arrived in Dawson where she began working at the Palace Grand.

Kate and Pantages quickly became business partners and lovers. Pantages had an idea to open a chain of vaudeville houses along the Pacific Coast. He sold the Orpheum in 1902, and sailed for Seattle. Kate continued performing in Alaska and all of her profits went to support his entertainment business. In 1904, the first Seattle Pantages Theater opened. The next year, Pantages married one of the orchestra violinists, Lois Mendenhall. Kate sued him for breach of promise. Kate continued performing, until the gold ran out. She eventually settled in Eastern Oregon. Pantages continued building his vaudeville empire.

Pantages became famous for the size and opulence of his theaters. He insisted on a classical style. He worked closely with architects, defining a style now known as "Pantages Greek." This included marble floors, domed ceilings, stained glass, gilt and bronze fixtures, as well as murals and tapestries on the walls. Pantages theaters were not small either. The largest of them held 2,800 people. The Pantages Theater in Tacoma held around twelve hundred people.

The present Tacoma Pantages Theater was built in 1918. It replaced a smaller, earlier one. In keeping with the Pantages Greek theme, the Tacoma Pantages made rich use of marble and bronze. It was converted into a movie theater in 1932 and renamed the Roxy. The Roxy played first run movies for several decades, until the birth of the multiplex theaters. In 1978 it underwent extensive refurbishment and reopened as a live theatre in 1983. It has been renamed 'The Pantages' again, and is the current home of the Tacoma Opera.

The Ghosts

According to stories, there is a ghost haunting the stage at the Pantages. It is a theater tradition to always keep a light shining on the stage between shows. This is done so that the "ghosts" do not stumble in the dark. Kate is supposed to walk the theater and stage at night. Perhaps drawn to the light? Or looking for her lost love, Alexander Pantages? After reading biographies of both Pantages and Klondike Kate, I do not think that Kate is a likely candidate as the theater ghost. It seems more likely that the ghost of the Tacoma Pantages is some lonely chorus boy or girl who had aspirations of fame and fortune that never came true. Perhaps they return to the place of their last moment of fleeting fame?

Name: **Tacoma Bar and Grill**
Address: 625 Commerce Street
Tacoma, WA 98402
Phone Number: **360-572-4861**
Prices: $$
Theme: Historic building.
Cuisine: Northwest
Open: Nightly
Special Facilities: Full bar.

One of Tacoma's great landmarks is the Old Tacoma City Hall. Its Italianesque tower rose above the city in 1893, celebrating Tacoma's prestige as a rail and shipping center. Mr. and Mrs. Hugh Wallace, a former U.S. Ambassador, donated the buildings bells in memory of their daughter who had died at the age of 12. The building held the offices of city employees, councilmen and women, as well as a series of hearing rooms.

According to maintenance and security staff, the basement had a series of temporary holding cells for prisoners. Tacoma outgrew its municipal center and moved to other locations. Fortunately, the building has been retained as an architectural landmark. It has been converted into upscale businesses as diverse as architect offices and aromatherapy shops. A large portion of the ground floor has been turned into the Tacoma Bar & Grill. Rough wood and brick make for an interesting rustic appearance to this charming restaurant.

The Ghosts

In 1979, the police were summoned repeatedly to the old building when burglar and fire alarms went off. When they arrived each time the building was secured and there were no trespassers on the premises. Even though the bells were disconnected in the 1950s, they were rung repeatedly in the past.

An employee of the restaurant escorted me to the basement. He showed me a solitary confinement cell. This door opens into a small three foot by three-foot room. He told me that several people have seen the figure of a man walking around in the basement. He may be Gus. Gus is harmless and engages in the occasional poltergeist prank. One night, all of the wine glasses resting on a sideboard shattered. The restaurant owner watched all of the bottles tumble off the shelf, one by one. It was as if someone walked along behind the bar, knocking them down with a finger.

Shops, Sights and Sounds

Name:	**Fort Nisqually**
Address:	Information Address; 5400 North Pearl Street, # 11 Tacoma, WA 98407
Location:	Point Defiance State Park, Tacoma, WA
Phone Number:	**253-591-5339**
Fax Number:	253-759-6184
Website:	www.fortnisqually.org
Prices:	$
Theme:	Historic recreation
Open:	September 4th – March 30th, Wednesday – Sunday, 11:00 a.m. – 4:00 p.m. March 31st – May 25th, Wednesday – Sunday, 11:00 a.m.- 5:00 p.m. May 26th – September 3rd, Wednesday – Sunday, 11:00 a.m.- 6:00 p.m.

Special Facilities: Gift shop, well-versed interpreters in period costume, traditional craft demonstrations. Guided tours are conducted.

Recurring events:

May 19th:	Queen Victoria's Birthday Celebration.
August:	Brigade Encampment Recreation.
October:	Candlelight Tour.
December:	19th Century Christmas Celebration.

In 1833 the Hudson's Bay Company established Fort Nisqually near present day Dupont, Washington. In the 1840s and early 1850s, the Fort was moved. The stockade surrounding Fort Nisqually was more for security of their goods rather than as protection against Native American raids. There were some incidents where people were injured or killed around the original fort though. The fort was abandoned in the 1850s.

In the 1930s, the fort was surrounded by a high fence, to protect it against vandalism. Only two buildings remained in decent condition, the Chief Factor's residence, built by Dr. William Tolme in 1854, and the granary, constructed in 1851. Using labor provided by workers employed by the New Deal public works plans, the buildings were moved to Point Defiance Park as part of a recreation of the original fort. It has been open to the public since the 1940s.

The Ghosts

Before the Chief Factor's house was moved to Point Defiance Park, it and the old fort buildings were located on a hill, just off of DuPont Center Drive. Motorists driving along the road were sometimes surprised to see an old man sitting in a rocking chair on the front porch of the old house. Several times people investigated, only to find the fence secured and the compound empty. When the house was moved, the spirit may have moved with it.

Visitors and staff at the fort have seen an older man dressed in a black coat, wool trousers, and an old-fashioned, beaver felt hat walk through the main gate. He always heads down the path and through the white picket fence surrounding the Chief Factor's house. Somewhere down the path he disappears. Other people think that they have seen him sitting on the chairs of the front porch. Although Dr. Tolmie was the person who built the house, its last resident was Edward Huggins. Some people think Huggins decided to stay in his house, even after his death. He may also be the ghost encountered in the fort's bastion by a staff member.

A few years ago the fort held an event that continued until late evening. One of the staff entered the first floor of the bastion tower and stopped. He half-saw, half-sensed, a man standing at the washbasin. He apologized for disturbing the man and backed out. Then he remembered that he was the only one who was supposed to be sleeping there. He went back in, only to find the tower empty. He told me that in the 1800s at the real fort, Huggins had stayed in the original bastion when dignitaries stayed at the fort. At that time, it was common for the lower employees to be kicked out of their quarters to make room for the higher status guests.

Name: **Tacoma Art Museum**
Address: 1123 Pacific Avenue
Tacoma, WA 98402
Phone Number: 253-272-4258
Website: www.tacomaartmuseum.org
Prices: $
Theme: Regional, 19th and 20th century art
Open: Tuesday – Saturday, 10:00 a.m.– 5:00 p.m.;
Thursday, 10:00 a.m.-8:00 p.m.;
Sunday, 12:00 p.m. – 5:00 p.m.
Special Facilities: Museum displays are changed frequently. There is a permanent Dale Chihuly display.

The Ghosts

In the past there was a bank or investment firm on the third floor of this building. When the U.S. Stock Market crashed in 1929, ushering in the Great Depression, many people committed suicide in a number of ways. Many people in New York jumped out of windows. According to a story I was told, a banker in Tacoma could not jump, since the bank was on the third floor. He shot himself in his offices. He has been seen there at frequent intervals ever since.

Last year a female employee of the art museum was walking around a corner on the third floor when she nearly bumped into a man. They both stopped and looked at each other. After a few seconds, the man dissolved. Sometime later an artist who specialized in drawing what she interpreted as 'human souls' came to the museum to look at a display. She could not stay on the third floor. This time because of a loud banging noise.

Name: **Union Station**
Address: 1717 Pacific Avenue
Tacoma, WA 98402
Prices: $ (none)
Theme: 19th Century major railway station
Open: Variable, depending on the shop
Special Facilities: Railway station, many shops, Dale Chihuly art exhibit.

A few years ago, the Union Station was refurbished in part and many shops opened inside. Some of the old time employees seem to have remained behind. An old time ticket agent has been seen in a new shop. Other people have reported poltergeist phenomenon. Shop spaces have changed tenants so often that it is hard to track down which shops are haunted.

Olympia

The Washington State Capitol Dome was damaged during the Millennium Earthquake. Visitors used to be allowed to walk in the dome spaces. The dome is not haunted, but the areas used by the State Supreme Court Justices is. Unfortunately, they are also closed to the public.

Restaurants Clubs and Theaters

Name: **Capitol Theater**
Address: 206 East 5th Avenue
Olympia, WA 98501
Phone Number: **360-754-6670 (Olympia Film Society)**
Website: www.olywa.net/ofs/
Prices: $
Open: check the box office for exact times.
Special Facilities: Olympia Film Society shows classic and art films five or six times a week. The 'Backstage' at the Capitol is also open for live music concerts and private parties can rent it for their own functions.

The Capitol Theater in Olympia opened in 1924 during the golden age of silent pictures and Vaudeville. This meant not only did the theater have a movie screen, but it had a full stage and orchestra pit as well. It had no competition for audiences in Olympia until the nearby State Theater was built in 1949. It was not competition that ended the profitability of the Capitol. It was the advent of television and a decline in movie attendance.

The Capitol made a slow decline until the mid 1980s, when the Olympia Film Society began showing classic films there. In 1986, they played a silent movie, with a live orchestra accompaniment. Over the next decade the OFS quickly grew in membership and financial strength. They signed a lease on the Capitol Theater in 1990 and gradually upgraded the movie showing capability of the Capitol with new film projectors and Dolby digital sound system.

The Ghosts

Somc theater employees claim that the building has bcen haunted for at least 20 years. They believe that the ghost of a former janitor who was killed by an exploding boiler haunts it. A descendent of the original owners denies that such an accident ever took place. Regardless of the origin of the spirit, strange things have happened there. Employees and workers in the past reported incidents such as pockets of cold air, lights flickering on and off. In one instance, heavy work lights strung over the stage began swinging on their own. These lights were too heavy to have been moved by a breeze or draft.

Name: **Seven Gables Restaurant**
Address: 1205 West Bay Drive NW
Olympia, WA 98502
Phone Number: **Unknown**
Prices: $$
Cuisine: Northwest gourmet
Open: At the time this book was being written, the Seven Gables was closed. I hope it will be open again soon.
Special Facilities: Special events and conference facilities.

The Seven Gables restaurant was built in an architectural style known as Gothic Revival. It incorporates typical Victorian designs but includes gothic style gables and bay windows as well as a spindled porch. George Byron Lane built the house in 1893 and used it for political entertaining as well as a home. He came to Olympia in 1891 and became one of the founders of the Olympia State Bank. He also served as mayor of Olympia. Other prominent residents of the house were the Helenius family. Karl Helenius lived there from 1912 to 1930. Some people believe that Karl stays on today as a ghost.

The Ghosts

In 1994 Stephen Taylor and his wife Glennda McLucas-Taylor bought the restaurant and began renovating some of the rooms. She removed some shelving which covered up the large mirror behind the bar. She saw a stain on the mirror, like someone had removed all of the reflective silvering in the shape of a perfect heart. She began cleaning it, to wipe away the stain. She cleaned it several times a day. Nothing helped. Then one day the heart was gone. Other people have heard ghost voices in the upper floor.

The basement seems to be another focus of paranormal activity. Both Glennda and Stephen have felt a presence there. When they are alone in the building they sometimes hear the sound of voices or footsteps coming from the stairwell. The previous owner told Glennda that the ghost of a little girl has been seen in the back of the basement several times.

Name: **State Theater**
Address: 204 East 4th Avenue
Olympia, WA 98501
Phone Number: **360-786-0151 (box office)**
Website: www.orcalink.com/~whitney
Prices: $$
Open: Check the box office for exact times.
<u>Special Facilities</u>: Live theater productions by the Harlequin Productions Theater Company.

The State Theater was a latecomer to the Olympia movie scene when it opened in late 1949. Because it was newer, it was designed differently than earlier theaters. The State did not have a balcony. It was made out of cast concrete, resembling the newer style of football stadium. It was earthquake proof, developing only one small crack during an earthquake, which took place while it was under construction. It had 880 seats, arranged with an eye toward acoustical design and comfort rather than maximum seating capacity. The seats were soft and the carpet thick and plush.

In time, the State suffered from the same decline as the Capitol and other single screen theaters across the United States. In one last bid to compete with newer multiplex theaters, the owners remodeled it into a three-screen theater. This did not work. In 1996 it closed for a year. The Harlequin Productions Theater Company purchased it and remodeled it in 1998. To do this, they had to remove some of the lower level seats to construct a traditional Greek style stage and theater, handicap access and upgrade the technical aspects of the theater.

The Ghosts

According to a director of the theater, the ghost that haunts the State appeared after the remodel. Perhaps it was drawn to the new atmosphere? It was certainly active at the time, with a poltergeist type personality. When things like books and equipment were put down, they would be found in a different location a few minutes later. I spoke with an employee recently who did not know anything about the earlier haunting.

Shops, Sights and Sounds

Name: **Bigelow House Museum**
Address: 918 Glass Avenue NE
Olympia, WA 98506
Phone Number: **360-753-1215**
Website: http://bigelow.simplenet.com/BigelowMuseum.html
Prices: $
Theme: Pioneer Home Museum
Open: Summer, Saturday & Sunday, 1:00 p.m. – 3:00 p.m.
Special Facilities: Bigelow descendants sometimes give tours of the house. Special tours on Thursday and Friday by appointment.

Daniel Bigelow came to Olympia in 1851, fresh from studying law under Daniel Webster. His dream had always been to live in the Pacific Northwest. He settled in Smithfield, which later became Olympia, and opened a law office. In 1854 he married Ann Elizabeth White and the two of them lived in his log cabin for a short time. Soon after they were married he built a two-story home now known as the Bigelow House.

Bigelow rose in government service quickly. He became Thurston County Treasurer in 1852. More importantly, in 1853 he was part of a three-man committee that rewrote several laws of the Oregon Territory. Their changes led to the division of the Oregon territory, which created the Washington Territory. Bigelow served in the Territorial and State Legislature for many years as well as campaigning for women's rights and education. His descendents still live on the second floor of the house and allow the first floor to be part of the museum. In 1995, the house was restored as closely to its original state as historians could tell, using old photographs. This includes reproducing the original porch, chimneys, raised ceilings, and reproduced Victorian pattern wallpaper.

The Ghosts

In 2001, The Indie Club, a group of independent filmmakers from the Puget Sound area, visited the Bigelow House. They were filming a documentary on historic haunts in the Pacific Northwest. Mr. and Mrs. Bigelow gave them a tour. A few years ago, Mrs. Bigelow was ironing clothing in her upstairs room, when she saw something out of the corner of her eye. She looked up, and saw a man wearing dark gray pants with black suspenders and a white shirt. As she watched, he adjusted his shirt, and calmly looked at her.

She recognized him immediately. It was her husband's grandfather, Daniel Bigelow. He was not a young man, as in the photographs, but appeared to be around 75 years old. Her first impulse was to help him with his shirt. She started forward, then remembered that her iron was still turned on. She looked down, turned off the iron and looked back to where Daniel Bigelow had been standing. He was gone. Mrs. Bigelow took it all in stride. She was used to the paranormal and not frightened. After all, he was just a member of the family.

Name: **Washington Governors (Executive) Mansion**
Address: Near the intersection of SE Cherry Lane and SE 12th Avenue, east of the State Capitol buildings.
Phone Number: 360-586-TOUR
Prices: Free
Open: *Wednesdays. Times are variable, depending on the season and activities at the mansion. Typically, morning tours start at 10:00 a.m. and rotate 15 minutes until the last tour at 10:45 a.m. Afternoon tours begin from 1:00 p.m. to 2:45 p.m. Reservations are required.

***Due to earthquake damage, the tours are suspended until at least October 2001.**

In 1908, public officials in Washington State needed a place to entertain dignitaries during the Alaskan Exhibition. For the princely sum of $35,000, they built a temporary structure, which later became the Executive Mansion. Since 1909, Washington's Governors and their families have lived in this 26 room Georgian style mansion. Between 1972 and 1975, seven rooms were added and there were upgrades in utilities and restoration of the older features. It is currently undergoing an extensive repair due to the earthquake of 2001.

Although the Governors Mansion Foundation continues to furnish and maintain the public portions of the mansion, several of the original fixtures remain. The Grandfather's clock at the head of the stairs was purchased from Frederick and Nelson in 1909, as was the furniture in the State Dining Room. The silverware service in the dining room comes from the *U.S.F.S. Olympia.* The *Olympia* was the flagship of Commodore Dewey during the Spanish American War. Many years after the *U.S.F.S. Olympia* was decommissioned, 26 pieces of the original silverware were returned to Olympia and placed in the Governors mansion.

The Ghosts

Several years ago, people touring the Governors Mansion saw a boy wearing a sailor suit riding an antique tricycle. Some of the tourists even waved at him. Later they asked their tour guide who the little boy was. The guide refused to answer at first. Later they heard the sound of a bouncing ball. The tour guide finally told them that the ghosts of two little boys haunt the mansion. During the remodel in the 1970s the little boy on the tricycle disappeared.

According to some sources, the sound of the bouncing ball is still heard. Mary Charles, the mansions executive coordinator, disputed this in 1997. She stated that she had never experienced anything extraordinary nor had the chef or the housekeeper, both long-term mansion employees. Ghosts or not, as a Washingtonian I am pleased that our Governor allows tours of the house. Not all Governors allow this public visit into what Andrew Jackson called "The People's House," when speaking of the Chief Executive's home.

Centralia

Name: **The Olympic Club**
Address: 112 North Tower Avenue
Centralia, WA 98531
Phone Number: 360-736-5164
Website: www.mcmenamins.com
Prices: $$
Theme: Depression era men's tavern
Cuisine: Pub food
Open: Monday – Saturday, 11:00 a.m.- 1:00 a.m.
Sunday, Noon – Midnight.
Special Facilities: Billiards or pool, original lunch counter, micro-brews, live music.

Shortly after the turn of the century, Jack Scuitto (pronounced Suto) left his bar in Victoria B. C. and moved to western Washington. In June of 1908, a fire ravaged portions of downtown Centralia, destroying several businesses. Scuitto purchased a burned out downtown lot and built the Olympic Club. A major fixture of the club is the large mahogany bar, and several Tiffany style lampshades and wall mosaics. Strangely enough, the theme for this working man's club was tulips. During Prohibition Scuitto added a café and billiard tables. There are rumors that the hotel next to his bar was also a place of "negotiable" affection. Women and children were welcome in the café, but were kept out of the bar.

In 1996 McMenamin's purchased the Olympic Club. They cleaned and repaired some of the internal fixtures and wiring without removing any of the Olympics charm. They even left the huge, monolithic urinals in the men's restroom.

The Ghosts

When the Olympic was re-opened in 1997, an employee saw the ghost of a man standing by the large cast iron stove. The ghost, nick-

named 'Elmer', has been seen standing there several times. Some patrons have reported that their chairs have moved without human aid. Several employees have said that they sometimes hear a man's laughter echo throughout the building.

In 1999, two customers at the bar called the bartender over and asked if the bar was haunted. They explained that they heard the nearby double doors open and felt the breeze of someone walking into the bar behind them. They were facing the large mirror behind the bar and did not see the reflection of anyone walking behind them.

In July of 1999, an employee was alone in the Olympic, setting up for the day. She was surprised to find a little candle on the table, already burning. The candle at the booth was a small one. It could not have been left burning all night. It would have to have been lit at 9:00 a.m. or 8:00 a.m. at the earliest.

Elmer the ghost may have been Louis Galba. He rented a room at the hotel that used to stand on the site of the Olympic Club. The hotel caught fire in 1908. Galba was trapped in his second floor room and jumped to the ground below. He died of his injuries months later.

Morton

Name: **St Helen's Manor House**
Address: 7476 Highway 12
Morton, WA 98356
Phone Number: 800-551-3290
360- 498-5243
Rooms: Two with bath. Two with shared bath.
Website: www.travelpick.com/wa/sthelens.html
Prices: $$
Theme: Country bed & breakfast
Cuisine: Gourmet breakfast
Open: Most of the year
Special Facilities: Satellite TV, wrap around porch in country setting, relaxed atmosphere. Ghost hunters sometimes book the Manor House for Halloween.

John Uden spent two years constructing this fine country farmhouse from 1908 to 1910. He built it for his mail order bride Anna, and her daughter, young Anna. After Uden died, young Anna became a local schoolteacher. She married local landowner Clarence Fisher and they moved in with her widowed mother. Within a year or two the elder Anna died suddenly after drinking a glass of herbal tea with her daughter. A few years later, Clarence's father died and his mother moved in with them. She too died, after drinking herbal tea with Anna. Clarence, who used to drink Sherry with the dog on the front porch, died of cirrhosis of the liver.

After Anna died, the house was inherited by two of her old students who lived there many years. They sold the house sometime in the 1970s or 1980s to people who opened it as a bed and breakfast. Or perhaps they were treasure hunters. The house had a reputation for hidden money as well as ghosts.

The Ghosts

Visitors are usually shown a copy of the video of a Halloween visit from a local television station. When they visited, the film crew brought a psychic who had no prior knowledge of the house. The psychic said that she detected the presence of two women, a mother and daughter. She also felt there had been a murder in the house.

One aspect of this haunting is the way the fire door on the stairs closes all on its own. When the house was converted into a B&B, a fire door had to be installed. This door is spring loaded so that it will close if the power fails or the fire alarm goes. At the St. Helen's Manor House the door shuts on it's own nearly every night at precisely 4:20 a.m. It happened while I stayed there.

Several times the owner has heard the sounds of crashing and banging from the guest rooms. It sounds like the furniture is being destroyed. When she investigates she has always finds the furniture intact. One night a couple stayed in the Green Room. The husband woke his wife up in the middle of the night. He complained that the heavy scent of lilac perfume was nearly suffocating him. The Blue Room is the most famous haunted room. People who know about the haunting want to sleep there. Many people wake up sensing a presence, though no one has seen it. A couple was staying there, when a hand shook the husband hard enough to wake him up in the middle of the night. Not too far away is:

Name: **Ike Kinswa State Park**
Address: Central Washington
Phone Number: **800-452-5687 (Reservations NW)**
Website: www.parks.wa.gov/alphasw.asp
Prices: $
Open: Open for camping year round.

Special Facilities: There are 62 tent sites, 41 utility sites, a RV dump station, three restrooms and ten showers. The park is located on the north side of Mayfield Lake. There are two boat ramps and a 40-foot dock on the lake. There are 2.5 miles of hiking trails and two miles of bike trails.

Directions: From I-5, take Exit #68, which is U.S. hwy 12, east to Morton and Yakima. Drive east for 14 miles and turn north on SR122, Silver Creek Road. Drive north 1.9 miles to a Y intersection. Take SR 122, also known as Harmony Road east 1.6 miles to the park.

Lake Mayfield was created when the Mayfield Dam was constructed in the 1960s. The reservoir drowned the traditional lands and dwelling areas of the Cowlitz Indians. Before the dam was finished, several Cowlitz graves were moved, some to the park. In 1971, the park was renamed Ike Kinswa State Park in memory to the Cowlitz tribal spokesman and leader.

The Ghosts

A few years ago, several Cowlitz Indians, including descendents of Ike Kinswa, visited the park. They walked along one of the trails, which led to the cemetery where their ancestors were reburied. They brought a camera and took several photographs. They paused nearby to take pictures of a tree standing in an empty field. When their film was developed all but one of the photographs on the negative were black. The only good exposure was of the tree, which had a wispy figure standing in front of it.

Portland Basin and Willamette Valley

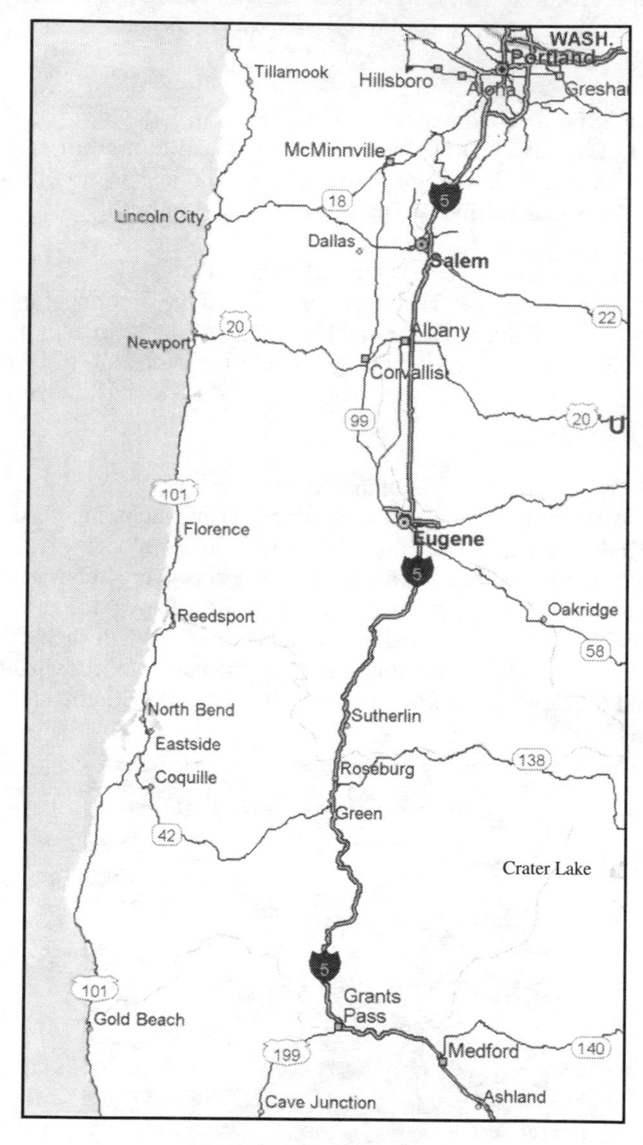

Portland Basin and Willamette Valley

Ashland

Name: **Ashland Shakespearian Festival**
Address: OSF Box Office
P.O. Box 158
Ashland, OR 97520
Phone Number: **541-482-4331**
Fax Number: 541-482-8045
Website: www.orshakes.org
Prices: $$ - $$$
Theme: Shakespearian Festival
Theater Season: February – June, value season.
June – September, full price.
Special Facilities: Multiple theaters, wheel chair access, audio for visually impaired, listening devices, gift shop. The Angus Bowmer Theater has 600 seats, the Elizabethan Theater has 1200 seats, and the Black Swan Theater 138 seats.

In the 1930s the Chautauqua building, which had housed a kind of farmers market was condemned. Angus Bowmer, a professor at the local college, noticed that without its roof, the building resembled an Elizabethan Theater. He persuaded the town of Ashland to stop demolition of the structure and modify it into a theater. He inspired the festival until his death in 1979. Today the festival runs from February to November and attracts audiences from across the country and actors from around the world.

The Elizabethan Theater

The ghost of actor Charles Laughton is said to haunt this theater. In 1962, he planned to travel up to Ashland to act in one of the plays there. Unfortunately, he visited a doctor before the trip, and he found that Laughton had cancer. Laughton never made it to Ashland. He was supposed to play either the lead in *King Lear* or Falstaff in the *Merry Wives of Windsor*. During the 1962 performance of *the Wives of Windsor,* a loud laugh was heard in the back of the theater. Many thought they recognized it as Laughton's. His ghost was also seen backstage wearing the Falstaff costume.

When *Twelfth Night* is performed, props on the stage are moved round during the performances. The third floor of the theater used to be the public relations office. Many nights a mysterious ghostly figure was

sometimes seen and frequently heard singing Elizabethan Madrigals or songs at night. Many employees and actors listened to him.

When I went to Ashland and I stopped by the Theater complex. I was talking with several of the gift shop staff. One of them said; "I don't know about Charles Laughton, but Angus Bowmer is supposed to haunt the theater named after him!" The staff are generally closed mouthed about discussing their ghosts.

Name: **Lithia Park**
Address: Ashland OR (Ice-skating rink)
Phone Number: 541-488-9189
541-488-5340 (recreation department)
Prices: $
Theme: City Park
Open: Daily
<u>Special Facilities:</u> The park is free and open to the public. The fountain runs only part of the year.

Lithia Park began as an unimproved area in Ashland. In 1892, forty five people from the Ashland area formed the Chautauqua Association, and purchased a small parcel of land to hold their Chautauqua, which was a combination country fair and farmer's market, in Ashland. The park grew larger, even after the Chautaqua ceased to be held there.

The park is a few hundred feet wide and nearly a mile long. It was named after the Lithium water found in the two fountains in the park. Architect John McLaren designed Golden Gate Park in San Francisco and helped design Lithia's landscape plan. There are various stands of hardwoods and coniferous trees and a small ice skating rink next to the park. Several ghosts also haunt Lithia Park.

The Ghosts

A famous ghost said to haunt the park is a hunchbacked, dog faced boy. He lived in the 1920s and supported himself by a mix of selling pencils and petty theft. He disappeared in 1926, perhaps the victim of foul play. In the 1960s, people saw a hunchback with heavy facial hair going through cars parked near Lithia Park. When people approached him he disappeared. He was seen again in the early 1980s.

A female ghost has been seen and felt in the park where a pioneer girl was raped and killed in the 1800s. A blue-light, said to be the girl's spirit has been seen wandering around the park at night. In 1975, a car drove through the light. All the passengers reported feeling a damp cold. There may also be the ghost of a logger, killed during a logging accident. He is detected by the smell of lithium water. In life he was addicted to it, and drank so much of the stuff that he smelled like it.

Cave Junction

Name: **Oregon Caves Lodge**
Address: 20000 Caves Highway
Cave Junction, OR 97523
Phone Number: **800-888-2535**
541 592-3400 (reservation)
Website: www.oregoncaves.com
Rooms: 22 rooms
Prices: $$
Theme: Country lodge
Cuisine: 1930's style fountain cafe
Open: Year around
Special Facilities: No phones, no TV, conference facilities, special packages, gift shop, Oregon Caves nearby, stream runs through hotel lobby.

In 1874, Elijah Davidson and his dog, Bruno chased a bear into a cave located on a high shelf on a mountainside. Davidson found an intricate network of limestone caves. The entire network takes up 480 acres of horizontal space, with several vertical levels. There are several open chambers and even a "ghost room," which is two hundred fifty feet long, fifty feet wide, with a forty-foot high ceiling. It is called the ghost room because the stalagmite formations there resemble robed figures. The perfect place to stay when visiting the caves is the Oregon Caves Lodge located across the street from the cave entrance.

The lodge is a ten-sided building, constructed in 1934. The original, 1930s style coffee shop, with its U-shaped birch-wood counter is still in operation below the lobby. In the lobby there is a large rectangular fireplace and huge round beams made from whole pine tree logs. In the dining room, a stream of water from the cave has been diverted and flows through the building. In a picturesque place like this, guests should expect to see ghosts.

The Ghosts

The employees at the historic Oregon Caves Lodge have been sworn to secrecy about the resident ghost, Elisabeth. It is a little difficult for them to keep mum about her sometimes, since Elisabeth is focused on making life hard for them. Years ago, Elisabeth and her husband were honeymooning at the Lodge. One day Elisabeth took a long walk on the trails around the lodge and her husband decided to stay behind. She returned early and surprised her husband in bed with a maid. Later that night she locked herself in her bathroom and slit her wrists.

Elisabeth has a tendency to pester female staff members. When the staff wash towels and sheets the maids always fold the dry linen. If they leave the room for a few minutes, they find the stacked linen turned into heaps of wadded cloths when they return. Elisabeth is supposed to have stayed in Room 308, and remained after her death. Some guests have reported an uneasy feeling when staying in there. Many guests and housekeeping staff have heard the sound of someone pacing up and down the hallway outside Room 308 when it is occupied.

Gold Hill, OR

Name: **The Oregon Vortex**
Address: 4303 Sardine Creek Road
Gold Hill, OR
Phone Number: **541-855-1543**
Website: www.oregonvortex.com
Prices: $$
Theme: Mystical mystery
Open: June – August first tour begins at 9:00 a.m.
Last tour starts at 5:15 p.m.
March - May, Sept – Oct., first tour begins at 9:00 a.m.
Last tour begins at 4:15 p.m.
Special Facilities: Gift shop, large vehicle turnaround. Informative guides

Directions: The Oregon Vortex is a little hard to find, since it is located a few miles outside of Gold Hill. From I-5 North, take exit 43, from I-5 South, take exit 40. There are a few signs, but it is easy to get lost. It is best to visit their website and download their map.

The Oregon Vortex is a location in southern Oregon, near Gold Hill, an early gold mining boomtown. According to local legends, Native Americans made the land forbidden ground because of the strange things that happen there. The Vortex is a circular piece of ground, 165 feet in diameter. Wildlife such as birds and gophers are rarely found inside the circle. Trees grow inclining towards magnetic north. An English engineer named John Litster made this strange phenomenon famous.

Litster arrived in Oregon in 1929. He discovered a dilapidated log cabin at the old mining camp. Litster felt that this energy field of the vortex warps the fabric of space/time. He set up displays outside and inside the boundaries to show observers its effects. A person standing inside the vortex is always shorter than the person standing outside.

There is a large collection of photographs in the Visitor's Center. They show strange light effects on film that were not visible to the photographer when the pictures were taken. Litster set up a series of complex optical illusions inside the log cabin. Some of these effects have been copied at other 'mystery houses' in national amusement parks. Skeptics would enjoy a visit to the Oregon Vortex to try and "discover" the secrets of some of the visual effects.

The Ghosts

Another interesting note about the Oregon Vortex; it is haunted. Several visitors have seen Litster, standing at the high end of the sloping floor of the old log cabin. He is usually seen resting against the wall, laughing and plucking his eyebrow. A tour guide looked inside the cabin, and saw the apparition as well. He recognized Litster from an old photograph. After the quick look, Litster disappeared. Of course, that may have been an illusion too. My tour guide may have been pulling my leg, knowing I was there looking for ghosts. If she did, it's a great story.

Wolf Creek

Name: **Wolf Creek Inn**
Address: 100 Front Street
Wolf Creek, OR 97497

	Exit 76, on Interstate Five in Oregon
Phone Number:	**541-866-2474**
Fax Number:	541 866-2692
Website:	www.wolfcreekinn.com
Rooms:	Eight rooms- two twin beds and five double beds
Prices:	$ - $$
Theme:	Country Inn
Cuisine:	Country gourmet $$
Restaurant:	Lunch, 11:00 a.m.- 4:30 p.m.;
Dinner:	Sunday through Thursday, 4:30 p.m. – 7:00 p.m.
	Friday & Saturday, 4:30 p.m. to 8:00 p.m.

Special Facilities: Gift shop, no phones, no alarm clocks, no smoking. Rooms are decorated with antique furniture.

In 1883 Henry Smith built the Six Bit House as a rest stop for stage coach passengers and local miners. It is the oldest continuously operating hotel in Oregon. It took the horse drawn stages 16 days to travel from San Francisco to Portland. Although automobiles later cut the time down, it was still an overnight trip from Los Angeles to Portland. Many of Hollywood's golden age greats stayed here as a get away.

They included Douglas Fairbanks, Mary Pickford, Clark Gable, Carole Lombard and Orson Wells. Author Jack London wrote the short story, *The End of the Story,* and completed his noel *Valley of the Moon* while staying at the Wolf Creek Inn as it became known. The inn was acquired by the State of Oregon in the late 1970s. The State operates it as a period style historical landmark hotel. It was remodeled in 2001.

The Ghosts

I spoke with someone who stayed there frequently in the past. She told me that some of the employees had told her that the hotel was haunted. Perhaps by Jack London's ghost. I stopped and spoke with some employees who denied knowing anything of the haunts.

Crater Lake

Name: **Crater Lake Park**
Address: Rim Village Drive
Crater Lake National Park, OR 97503
Phone Number: 541-594-2511
Website: www.crater.lake.national-park.com
Prices: $ - $$ (entrance fees)
Theme: Sacred place/natural wonder
Open: Seasonal: See website
Special Facilities: Two campgrounds, gift shop, laundry room, hiking, boating, camping. The Mazama village-store open June through September.

The mountains of the Pacific Northwest are sacred to Native Americans. Crater Lake was once a mountain that stood over 12,000 feet high. It is known posthumously as Mount Mazama. Nearly 7,000 years ago a series of eruptions shook Mount Mazama. Over twenty-five cubic miles of ash and lava were ejected into the air. This left an empty center, which collapsed in on itself, forming a crater several thousand feet deep. The crater gradually filled with rain water and snow melt. The current depth of Crater Lake is 1,932 feet.

The lake was sacred to Native Americans who lived in the area. There is a small island on the edge of the lake, known as Wizard's Island. Wizard Island is a cider cone that gradually poked its head out of the waters of Crater Lake around 900 years ago. It is called that because the shamans used to go out to the island in the summer and perform magic rituals there. They and their fellow tribesmen kept this secret for many years.

Some people also report the presence of a mysterious critter in the lake. This is hard to believe, since there were no fish in the lake until a few decades ago. What would the lake monster have eaten?

Name: **Crater Lake Lodge**
Address: Rim Village Drive
Crater Lake National Park, OR 97503
Phone Number: 541-830-8700 (reservations)
Website: www.crater-lake.com
Rooms: 71 rooms
Prices: $$$
Theme: Rustic log cabin lodge
Cuisine: Northwest

Open: May to October
Special Facilities: Gift shop, no TV, no phones, handicap access, non-smoking rooms, Grand Lobby with high ceiling and large fireplace. Crater Lake National Park recreation facilities. Check for seasonal closures before planning your trip.

Crater Lake lodge was built in 1915, perched on the edge of Crater Lake, the huge log hotel was an immediate sensation. Entertainment at the lodge consisted of mostly recreation, like hiking the trail around the rim of the crater or sailing on the deep blue waters of the lake. At the end of a long day, guests would return to the lodge where they could sit in the Lodge Grand Room, dwarfed by the pine tree trunks that were used as columns to support the high ceiling. Some people would have congregated around the huge basalt stone fireplace.

Unfortunately for the Lodge, the builders made some shortcuts when they built it. Over time the floor rotted and the high beams of the roof began to sag. The Lodge was condemned and closed in 1989. Congress eventually provided money to renovate the decrepit structure, which reopened in 1995. There are increased recreational opportunities, with boating, fishing and hiking around the crater rim.

The Ghosts

A few years ago, at least one couple spent a few haunted nights at the lodge. Their room was on the third floor of the west wing, both husband and wife felt a strange presence. They did not see or hear anything out of the ordinary, but both felt a frightening, overwhelming presence surrounding them. After a sleepless night, they demanded a new room for the next night.

The manager never admitted that there was anything strange or paranormal about the hotel, or that wing specifically. At the same time, he did not seem surprised at the request for a new room, nor did they ask for an explanation. Sometimes a lack of an explanation rather than an admission of facts might give rise to stories. The Crater Lake Lodge is run under government contract by the same company that runs the Oregon Caves Lodge. The management are pretty closed mouth about ghosts at either facility.

Name: **Conser Lake**
Address: Withheld

Conser Lake is located between Corvallis and Millersburg. In the late 1950s people reported a possible UFO landing or crashing in the vicinity of the late. There were also reports of a white, Sasquatch like creature around the lake. It was reported again in 1960. Local newspapers and radio stations carried the story. There was a mass panic. People camped out around the lake, and the ones with guns shot at anything that moved. One person was supposedly able to make telepathic contact with the creature known as 'Flix.' Flix may have been from the crashed UFO or an advanced terrestrial hominid, or a baboon that escaped from a circus early in 1960.

I would advise against anyone trying to visit the lake. Conser Lake is located about a mile from the nearest public road. To get there you have to cross both public and private land. The local landowners are not happy to have people crossing their land. The lake itself is now a muddy wash, located at the bottom of a narrow valley. It is dangerous to climb down to the bottom. Again, I would recommend against anyone trying to visit Conser Lake.

Salem

Name: **Mission Hill Museum**
Address: 1313 Mill Street SE
Salem, OR 97301
Phone Number: 503-585-7012
Website: www.missionmill.org
Prices: $$
Theme: Turn of century mill and historic buildings
Cuisine: Mill Creek Station snack bar $$
Open: Monday through Saturday, 10:00 a.m.– 5:00 p.m.
Special Facilities: Guided and self-guided tours, group tours, gift shop, catering meetings, weddings, parties and special events.

The Mission Mill Museum began in 1964. Thomas Kay began working in woolen mills in England at the age of ten. Trained as a weaver, he came to the United States in 1857, and founded his own mill in Salem in 1889. The mill had several buildings, a warehouse, picker house, dye house and processing house. The mill was operated by the Kay family until 1959 and was gradually shut down in 1962. The Mission Mill Museum acquired the property and set up the various exhibits, including a working water wheel.

In addition to the woolen mill, the museum maintains several historic houses as a display of the early Christian missionary movement. Once United States settlement began in the Oregon Territory, non-Catholic missionaries began arriving. They competed with the early Catholic missionaries, who arrived with the Hudson's Bay Company.

Buildings from both Methodist and Presbyterian missions were moved to the museum grounds when they were threatened with destruction.

The Jason Lee House and The Methodist Parsonage Building represent the Methodist missionaries. The Methodist Parsonage was built in 1841 and was used by missionaries involved in the nearby Indian school. Jason Lee founded Salem in 1842. His house was more of a dormitory, and it had room to house four families. The Pleasant Grove Presbyterian Church was built near Aumsville in 1858. It is the oldest surviving Presbyterian Church in Oregon. It still has its original pews, wainscoting and pulpit as well as original windows.

The Boon House is the oldest surviving single family house built in Salem. It too was moved to the museum grounds when it was threatened. A reproduction herb garden similar to the original one planted by Mrs. Boon has also been recreated.

The Ghosts

There are three haunted locations as well as a kind of roving, caretaker spirit around the mill area. The third floor of the main mill building is now a reception area. I was told by a museum employee that if you stand in the right place, you can feel vibrations from machines, as if the mill is operating. This happens even if the still functional water wheel is not operating.

Museum employees and volunteers have seen lights on in the church across the street at night. A few have investigated. One worker entered the church and heard a mass being given, even though the church was empty. The worker could not see anyone or anything, except a kind of blob of light in the middle of the church.

There is one sinister haunt at the museum. When the mill was operating, a foreman murdered his wife on the bridge near the water wheel. Years later, one night an employee heard the sound of a woman screaming from the bridge. When he arrived, there was no one there and the screaming stopped. Was this the result of strange acoustics or a replay of the murder?

Woolen mills were dangerous places. A worker once fell into the gear mechanism that powers the mill and was ground to pieces. Despite this, there were many devoted employees. One of them, was named Wayne. He worked at the mill for years and donated many of his tools to the museum and helped repair the buildings before he died. Many museum employees saw him or his shadow wandering around the grounds, as if he was making sure things were all right. Many people felt comforted by his presence. The museum staff have not replied to my emails regarding any haunts there.

Name: **Thompson Brewery and Public House**
Address: 3575 Liberty Road S.
Salem, OR 97302
Phone Number: **503-363-7286**
Website: www.mcmenamins.com
Prices: $$
Theme: Historic house converted into brewpub
Cuisine: Pub grub
Open: Monday through Thursday, 11:00 a.m.– Midnight.
Friday & Saturday, 11:00 a.m.–1:00 a.m.
Sunday, Noon – Midnight
Special Facilities: Microbrews

In 1905, Fred Thompson built a house in Salem for his parents. After they died it was sold many times. McMenamins bought it in the 1980s, and turned it into a brewery and public house. They restored some of the original fixtures, but there is no disguising the fact that it began its existence as a house. A great feature is the wide staircase, which leads guests from the entryway to the second floor. There are some large rooms, but patrons are sometimes squeezed into some very cramped spaces. The McMenamins also converted old buildings or built new out-buildings, which are used for their brewing operations.

The Ghosts

Sue was one of the employees at the Thompson house when it first opened for business. She worked there from 1990 to 1992. Shortly after the house opened, she and a co-worker heard the sound of the cash register turning on. After several tries, they managed to turn the cash register off. As they left the building they heard a click as the restaurant coffee machine switched itself on. Employees and customers have felt cold breezes brush past them as they walked up the stairs. A first time customer came into the building, stopped on the stairs, and asked Sue if the house was haunted.

The second floor seems to be a focus for paranormal activity. Many people have heard a tapping noise coming from the cupboard door of an old linen closet on the second floor. A waitress was taking an order when a man almost brushed against her as he walked into the room next to her. She finished taking the order and turned to face the man in the other room. It was empty. The ghost was named Franklin by the staff.

McMinnville

Name: **Hotel Oregon**
Address: 310 NE Evans Street
McMinnville, OR 97128
Phone Number: **888-472-8427**
503-472-8427
Website: www.hoteloregon.com
Rooms: 42 rooms
Prices: $$, includes breakfast
Theme: Turn of century hotel
Cuisine: Fine to pub style $$
Open: Year around
Special Facilities: Several bars with different themes, live music, modems and phone lines in each room, artwork, special packages, local wines, all rooms non-smoking, conference facilities, Annual UFO event.

The Hotel Oregon was originally named the Hotel Elberton in 1905, when it was built. The first floor was taken up by a reception room, lobby, office, large dining room, barber store and candy story. On the second floor, there were 26 rooms, a ladies parlor and bathrooms. In 1912, the third and fourth floors were added but for some reason, they were never finished. Although studs were set up, inner walls were never erected in the top two floors.

After the Great Depression, the first two hotel floors were used as a combination of small business stalls and apartments for long-term tenants. In 1998 the hotel was bought by McMenamins. The top two floors were finished and the bottom floors were renovated. The two favorite theme pubs are the Rooftop Bar, where guests can overlook the city, and the dark Cellar Bar. The hotel has also hosted annual UFO festivals, celebrating a UFO sighting and photographs taken in 1950.

The Ghosts

One of the great features of all McMenamins hotels is the thematic artwork decorating the walls. If you wander around the Hotel Oregon you will see a poster like painting, advertising John's ghost cigars for five cents. John first made himself known, or was seen in the 1980s.

He was a nondescript looking man dressed in heavy clothing. Whenever anyone approached him, he would disappear. John has also been felt in the Cellar Bar. He has not been seen, but he is responsible for the wine glasses that tip over on their own and footsteps that are heard when no one is coming down the stairs.

Name: **Evergreen Air Venture Museum**
Address: 3850 Three Mile Lane
McMinnville, OR 97128
Phone Number: **503-472-9361**
Website: www.sprucegoose.org
Prices: $$ (military personnel are free)
Theme: Historic aviation
Open: Daily, 9:00 a.m. to 5:00 p.m. except for Thanksgiving, Christmas and New Years.
Special Facilities: Gift shop

For historians, the Evergreen airport in McMinnville, is a minor yet significant footnote. It was out of this airport that supplies were (allegedly) ferried to the Contras in Central America. The airport and new museum are not haunted, but historically significant. The museum houses many rare airplanes from World War II. They include a B-17 Flying Fortress, a Mark XVI Spitfire, and the HK-1, the Hughes Flying Boat. Also known as the Spruce Goose. The HK-1 was Howard Hughes' response to a shortage of metal for the war effort.

The Spruce Goose is the largest airplane ever constructed, and made totally out of plywood. It was designed to carry either two, 30-ton Sherman tanks, or 750 troops. The Spruce Goose only flew once, during a trial exercise. After that it spent decades as a tourist attraction before being moved to McMinnville.

The Ghosts

Although no one has reported any ghosts I would be surprised if some of the combat aircraft did not retain some memory of the past.

Forest Grove, OR

Name: **McMenamins Grand Lodge**
Address: 3305 Pacific Avenue
Forest Grove, OR 97116
Phone Number: **503-992-9533**
Website: www.thegrandlodge.com
Rooms: 77 Rooms, most without bathrooms
Prices: $ - $$$ (hostel to suite rooms)
Theme: Historic European style lodging
Cuisine: Pub to fine dining $$ - $$$
Open: Year around
Special Facilities: Gift shop, movie theater, gardens, microbrew, free soaking pool, day spa, special packages, conference facility, artwork. Breakfast is included in stay, except for bunk bed rooms/rates.

In 1922 the Grand Lodge was opened as a combination Masonic retirement home and orphanage. Although made of brick, the Masonic facility tried to be faithful to the Greek revival style of architecture. There are fluted columns and pediments located throughout the building. Ceilings were high, and the orphans were considered a kind of royalty by the local community because of these imposing surroundings.

Between 1927 and 1928 the children were moved to a different facility. It continued to be used as a Masonic retirement home until the late 1990s. At that time, the Masons sold the facility to the McMenamins organization and moved into a new home they had built nearby. In some cases, modifications made by the Masonic residents had to be reversed to return the building to its original state. Sometimes large rooms were divided into smaller ones, such as the room that now houses the gift shop.

The Ghosts

The Grand Lodge opened in early 2000 with a "Grand" celebration. Some of the recently relocated Masonic residents and former orphans stopped in to visit. They commented on how much the building looked like it had in the past. One place they stopped at was the gift shop. I was told that this had been a sick room in the past. I have heard rumors of a mischievous spirit in the gift shop rearranging displays.

Name: **Bugle Blower**
Address: Outside Forest Grove City Limits
Theme: Historic murder
Open: Periodic

Jefferson Davis

This is a story that has grown with the telling over the years. It had faded away, only to reappear again. According to some people, in the 20th century a hermit lived in the woods outside of town. You could tell when he was out and about, because he used to blow his hunting horn. This horn was a bugle which had a distinct, low tone. One day, he was attacked by a cougar, which he killed with his bugle.

Wounded, he eventually made it back to his cabin, where he stayed for several years. He eventually went insane and killed a man with his bugle. He ran into the woods where he died. He is supposed to reappear and attack people at periodic intervals. You can tell when he is about because he always blows his bugle. I have not heard any credible person who has seen this apparition, and there are not as many woods around Forest Grove as there used to be!

Oregon City

Name: **Ermatinger House**
Address: 619 John Adams Street
Oregon City, OR 97045
Phone Number: **503-656-1619**
503-557-9199 (living history tea)
Website: http://proquest.umi.com
Prices: $
Theme: Historic home/museum
Open: Friday through Sunday, 11:00 a.m. to 4:00 p.m.
Special Facilities: Living History Teas, seasonal haunted house tours

Like many Hudson's Bay Company employees, Francis Ermatinger was a world traveler before he came to the Pacific Northwest. Ermatinger was born in Portugal and educated in England. He came to Oregon in 1825 and worked his way up through the ranks of the company. He was placed in charge of the Company Store located in Oregon City in 1844. Ermatinger decided to stay in Oregon, where he became a United States citizen.

Ermatinger built his 15-room house in Oregon City in 1845. It is a two- story building, with a flat slate roof. It was quite a show place at the time. In 1910, it was nearly destroyed by urban planning, until it was bought and moved by the McLoughlin Memorial Association. In 1986 it was moved a second time to its present location. It is now a museum and hosts regular events such as a Halloween haunted house and living history teas. At the teas, guests have a traditional tea with "people" from the past and discuss ideas and issues of the 19th century, like Darwin and Oregon's new statehood.

The Ghosts

No one has seen any ghosts at the Ermatinger house but they know they are there. Caretakers and tour guides will have displays set up for the day. When they leave the room and return, the displays are re-arranged. This happens, even though the museum is closed and the caretaker is there alone. During one of the Halloween haunted houses, a display of cut up ribbons was placed in one of the second floor rooms. Ribbons would disappear from this room, only to turn up in odd places throughout the house.

Name: **McLoughlin House**
Address: 713 Center Street
Oregon City, OR 97045
Phone Number: 503-656-5146
Website: www.mcloughlinhouse.org
http://proquest.umi.com
Prices: $
Theme: Historic house/museum
Open: Tuesday through Saturday, 10:00 a.m.-4:00 p.m.
Saturday and Sunday, 1:00 p.m.-4:00 p.m.
Closed holidays and the month of January
Special Facilities: Gift shop, friendly staff
Annual events:
Dr. McLoughlin's Birthday
October, Halloween ghost stories and haunted tours,
Candlelight tours on the first Sunday in December.

Dr. John McLoughlin is known as the Father of Oregon because he aided and encouraged United States settlers who came to the Pacific Northwest in the 1840s. McLoughlin retired to Oregon City, which was the first Platted City in the Oregon Territory. McLoughlin was a prominent member of Oregon City Society. He began the first lending library in Oregon and practiced medicine for free after he retired.

After McLoughlin's death his house was used as a boarding house, possibly a bordello and a private residence. The house was originally built along the Willamette River. When it was in danger of being demolished, a citizen's group banded together and had it moved to the upper levels of Oregon City. McLoughlin and his wife were buried near the original site of his house, and moved twice before being laid to their final rest in a private plot behind the house.

The Ghosts

Some visitors to the house have sworn that they have seen the ghosts of Dr. and Mrs. McLoughlin walking along the path that leads from their graves to the house. McLoughlin was a very large man and on many occasions visitors and staff have seen the disembodied shadow of a tall man walking in the house.

On the third of September, the anniversary of McLoughlin's death, a ray of sunlight sometimes shines onto a portrait of the doctor. When it touches the gilt frame of the picture, the portrait takes on a golden glow. One morning a caretaker went into the parlor and saw a window shade had been raised, and sunlight was shining on the portrait. She thought that was odd until she remembered it was September third. There are many other ghostly happenings there.

Name: **The Forbes Barclay House**
Address: 719 Center Street
Oregon City, OR 97045
Phone Number: **503-656-5146**
Website: www.mcloughlinhouse.org
http://proquest.umi.com
Prices: $
Theme: Historic house/museum
Open: Tuesday through Saturday, 10:00 a.m.- 4:00 p.m.;
Saturday and Sunday, 1:00 p.m.- 4:00 p.m.
Closed holidays and the month of January
Special Facilities: Gift shop, meeting room

Dr. Forbes Barclay was a friend of Dr. McLoughlin. He donated several of his medical books to the early lending library McLoughlin maintained. This house is not as impressive as Dr. McLoughlin's. It is a small single story home, with a small entry way and an examination room, in addition to the regular family living rooms. There is no admission charge for the Barclay House. It serves as the gift shop for the McLoughlin house. It also has a room, which is rented out for small meetings or parties. This may be the old examination and operating room.

The Ghosts

The Doctor and his wife do not seem to haunt the house. The ghost of a young boy has been seen and felt in the area. Some years ago, a friend of the Forbes family visited the old house and commented that one of the Forbes children, a son, had died in the house. Of course, many people, especially children, died in 19th century doctors offices. He or another child's ghost was seen in 1993.

Oregon City has multiple levels, and the historic McLoughlin, Barclay and Ermatinger Houses are all located on a high terrace above the banks of the Willamette River. The city maintains an elevator that takes passengers from the terrace to the river. One day the elevator operator, Sandy Tunison, saw a little boy waiting at the elevator door.

A little boy has also been seen and heard in the Barclay and McLoughlin Houses. Most of the time he is not seen, but he plays small pranks, where items are moved or played with or hidden, like a small child might do.

Downtown Portland

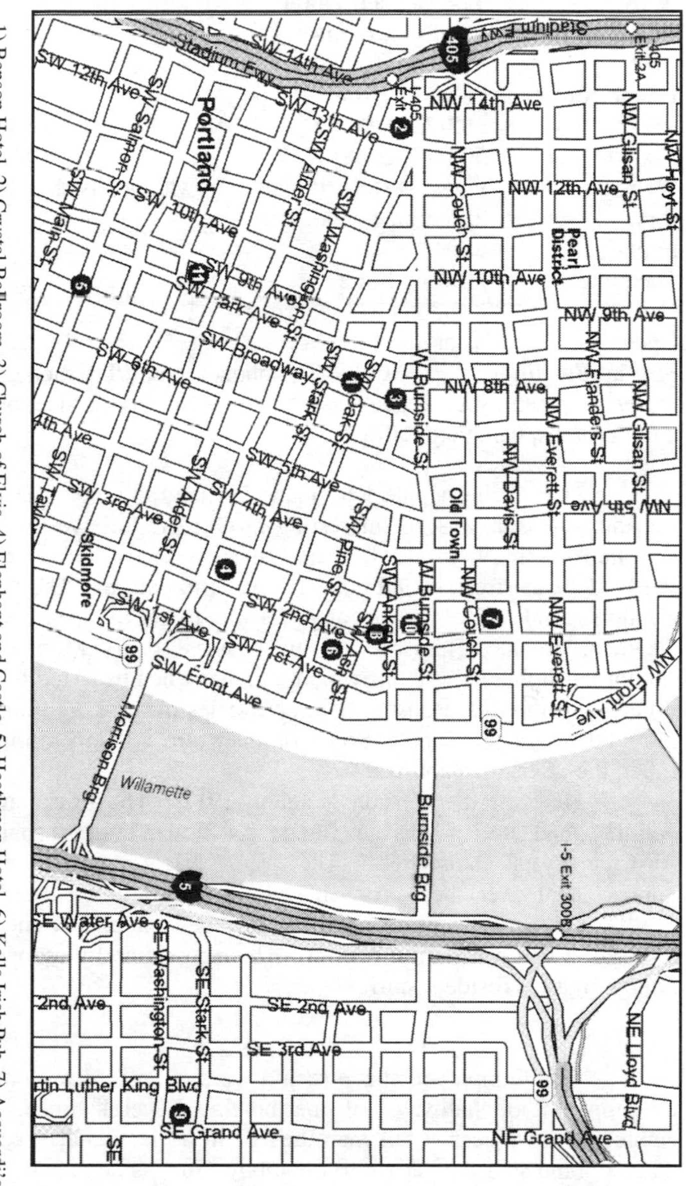

1) Benson Hotel, 2) Crystal Ballroom, 3) Church of Elvis, 4) Elephant and Castle, 5) Heathman Hotel, 6) Kells Irish Pub, 7) Accuardi's Old Town Pizza, 8) Dan & Louis Oyster Bar, 9) Rose & Raindrop, 10) Shanghai Tunnel, 11) Virginia Café © 2001 GDT

Portland

Places to Stay

Name: **The Benson Hotel**
Address: 309 SW Broadway
Portland, OR 97205
Phone Number: 888-523-6766
503-228-2000
Fax Number: 503-471-3920
Website: www.westcoasthotels.com/whc/hotels/showhotels
Rooms: 286 rooms
Prices: $$$
Theme: Historic hotel
Cuisine: London Grill, gourmet $$$
Open: Year around

Special Facilities: Cable TV, phones, email/Internet, exercise room/equipment, special packages, twice-daily maid service, private dining rooms, banquet facilities.

One of the people who made Portland the city it is was Simon Benson. Benson was an interesting mix of progressive business sense and human simplicity. He heard that the bars and saloons lining Portland's waterfront would not serve water to patrons. They only served alcoholic drinks. He saw this as just a way to get the men, most of them his men, drunk. This affected his business every Monday morning. Rumor has it that he was thrown out of a bar when he asked for a drink of water. To stop this, Benson paid for a series of drinking fountains to be installed across Portland. Some of them are still operating, they are called the "Benson Bubblers."

He built the Benson Hotel in 1912. The brick and concrete building had Italian marble floors, Circassian walnut paneling and Austrian crystal chandeliers. The overall effect was to turn it into an improvement over the European style hotels, built on the East Coast, Seattle and San Francisco. In 1991 the Benson underwent a massive restoration and renovation project. This project and a more recent one brought out the resident spirits.

The Ghosts

Hotel employees have seen a woman dressed in white roaming the upper floor hallways of the hotel. Several times guests and employees have seen a tall man dressed in a black coat descending the hotel's grand stairway, down to the lobby. Just as he reaches the bottom of the stairway he disappears. According to one person, he seemed to become transparent and faded as he slowly walked down the stairs. .

One female guest had some trouble getting into bed one night. A ghostly woman in white helped her into her bed. Once in bed, the guest watched the woman exit the room by walking through a closed door. This may have been a past floor attendant.

Name: **Heathman Hotel**
Address: 1001 SW Broadway Avenue
Portland, OR 97205
Phone Number: 800-551-0011
503-241-4100/
Fax Number: 503-790-7110
Website: www.heathmanhotel.com
Rooms: 150
Prices: $$$
Theme: Luxury hotel
Cuisine: Northwest French
Heathman Restaurant $$$
Open: Year round
Special Facilities: Several bars and lounges, High Tea, airport shuttle, concierge, nearby fitness center access or fitness suite in hotel, video library, twice a day maid service, phones with data ports.

The Heathman Hotel, with its Italian Renaissance façade and gorgeous décor, was the last Grand Hotel constructed in Portland. High Tea is still served every day at 2:00 p.m. in the eucalyptus-paneled Tea Court. The builders used exotic woods from all over the world for the many public rooms.

An early tenant of the Heathman was KOIN radio, which moved into studios in a remodeled hotel mezzanine in the 1930s. It left the hotel in 1953, when it moved into the new KOIN television and radio station. At the same time, the hotel began to suffer from an exodus of businesses and people from downtown Portland in the 1950s and 60s.

The hotel was renovated in 1998, and unlike many renovations, the changes did not affect its status on the National Register of Historic Places. The Heathman hired Portland artist Henk Pander to paint a mural on the wall of the Arlene Schnitzer Concert Hall. Forty-eight of the Heathman's rooms face this mural. The paintings that decorate the Heathman are classics, ranging from the works of 18th century European masters, to Andy Warhol silk-screens.

The Heathman has its own film and book library. The film library has 400 films and the book library has several books signed by authors who stopped at the Heathman during speaking engagements. Although upgraded, the hotel is still recognizable as the original Heathman, which may be why the resident ghosts remain.

The Ghosts

Most of the paranormal activity in the hotel seems to be centered around Room 703. Many guests check into the room, unpack, and go about their business. When they return, they sometimes find a half-filled glass of water placed on the desktop. Sometimes the chair at the desk has been shifted, or a towel in the bathroom is removed and put on the counter. They complain, which is why the hotel staff knows that this has been going on for several years.

At first the guests and staff blamed each other. This changed when the hotel installed electronic locks that record how many times a room has been entered, and at what time. In most cases, the electronic record shows that no one has entered the room besides the guest.

In September of 1999, a guest who claimed to be psychic, told management that she had seen a ghost. The spirit energy was concentrated in a row from room 303 to 1003. She felt that someone committed suicide by jumping out of a window, and was haunting the rooms he passed on his way down to the ground.

In the past, guests and staff reported strange incidents. Many people have felt cold spots, or breezes pass around them as they walked down the hall. Others have heard the sound of whispering voices in the same hallways. Then there is the sound of disembodied footsteps walking down the grand staircase.

Name: **John Palmer House Bed & Breakfast Inn**
Address: 4314 N. Mississippi Avenue
Portland, OR 97217
Phone Number: **800-518-5893**
503-284-5893
Fax Number: 503-284-1239
Website: www.innsite.com/inns/a001460.html
Rooms: Three rooms, 2 with shared bath, one with private bath
Prices: $$ - $$$
Theme: Historic home turned into B&B
Cuisine: Gourmet $$
Open: Year round
Special Facilities: Corporate and long stay rates, air conditioning, television, telephones, piano and music room, banquet facility, porch, garden, gift shop, hot tub and massage.

The John Palmer House is another fine Portland Victorian house that has been saved from demolition and turned into a bed and breakfast. Architect John Palmer built the house around the turn of the century. The house is on the National Register of Historic Places and is famous for its stained glass and extra design features. Palmer only lived there for seven years. He left Portland shortly after his wife died in childbirth.

The house was sold to a woman named Lotta. According to stories, Lotta had red hair and had been an opera singer. She lost her voice after several years of singing and purchased the house as a kind of retirement home. The house was once the home of the Multnomah Conservatory of Music. Even though she's now dead, Lotta still likes music

The Ghosts

Mary Sauter and her family purchased the house in 1968. They restored it to its former glory and then turned it into a bed and breakfast. Soon after they took over the house they began hearing noises from the upper floors. They heard footsteps, and their dog growled as its hair stood up on end. A psychic guest confided her impressions to Sauter.

She told Sauter that the ghost was a redheaded woman who stayed on to watch over the house. When people play the piano, Lotta comes downstairs and is heard moving around in the front hallway. In the early 1990s, several guests saw a woman walk through the kitchen and then pass through the kitchen door. True to her history; Lotta is silent, no one has ever heard her voice.

The John Palmer House is up for sale, so visitors had better make their reservations now.

Name:	**McMenamins Kennedy School**
Address:	5736 NE 33rd Avenue Portland, OR 97211
Phone Number:	**503-249-3983** **503-225-5555 ext. 8833 (movie line)**
Website:	www.mecmenamins.com
Rooms:	35 rooms
Prices:	$$ - $$$
Theme:	Historic school, now a European style B & B
Cuisine:	Pub grub to fine food
Open:	Breakfast at 7:00 a.m. to 10:30 a.m.; Pub hours, Monday – Friday, 11:00 a.m.-1:00 a.m. Saturday, Noon – 1:00 a.m.; Sunday, 1:00 p.m. – 12:00 a.m.

Movie Theater Bar opens 5:00 p.m.
Movie times vary, check the movie line.

Special Facilities: Phones, modem, massage, soaking pool, gift shop, movie theater, meeting facilities, own microbrew, live music, special packages.

In 1913 John D. Kennedy donated a large parcel of rural farmland near Portland for a school. The Kennedy School was completed in 1916. It was designed along the lines of a classic Italian villa, with several protected courtyards where the children could play. The school was designed with a single story, so that children would not be trapped on a second story by a fire. Enrollment declined over time and the school was shut down in 1980. It was the haunt of vandals and drug dealers until it was taken over and renovated by the McMenamins. They turned it into a restaurant, movie theater and bed and breakfast in 1987.

The Ghosts

Shortly after the Kennedy School opened as a bed and breakfast the manager and her assistant inspected several of the rooms. They paused outside of Miss Dobie's Room, named after a 1920s schoolteacher. The manager never liked the room and said so. The lock stuck shut when she tried to open it. Her assistant tried next without success. The manager had worked at another haunted hotel and had similar experiences. She apologized to the ghost for offending it. She tried the key again and the door opened.

In 1998 one of the servers took her break. She went into the restroom near the pizza oven. She heard the door of the stall next to her open, close and lock. She looked under the bathroom stall partition. There was no one there. The woman got up, washed her hands, and hurried out of the bathroom. She never uses that restroom any more.

According to one employee, shortly after the school reopened a former student came to visit. He was a boy when a teacher committed suicide. The teacher, a woman, had reached the age of 27 or 28 and was still unmarried. She was so depressed over being an "old-Maid" that she hung herself in the coatroom in the Old McDonald's room. She may still remain.

Name: **White Eagle Café and Saloon and Hotel**
Address: 836 North Russell Street
Portland, OR 97227
Phone Number: 503-282-6810
503-225-5555 ext. 8824 (music line)
Website: www.memenamins.com
Rooms: 9 double rooms. 2 bunk bed rooms
Prices: $$
Theme: Turn of century rooming house and bar
Cuisine: Pub grub $$$
Open: Monday through Thursday, 11:00 a.m. to 1:00 a.m.
Friday & Saturday, 11:00 a.m. to 2:30 a.m.
Sunday, 4:00 p.m. to Midnight.
Special Facilities: No TV or phones in rooms, microbrews, live music in bar, it is possible to rent entire upper floor for a group ghost hunt.

There has been an eating and drinking establishment on this site for nearly 150 years. The present brick bar and café was built around the turn of the century. It is typical of a well-to-do working man's bar from the time. It was owned by the same family until the 1970s. There is a Navaho pattern tile floor in the entrance. It has pre-planned errors, since by Navaho tradition, nothing can ever be perfect. The bar is a huge ornate oak affair which used to be positioned further down the building, by a trough shaped urinal. The urinal was covered over and the bar was moved to its present position in the 1970s.

The second story of the building was empty and uninhabited from the 1950s until 2000. According to folklore, in the past it was used as a combination bordello and boarding house. One of the boarders may still be there. Sam Worek worked for the owners for years in the kitchen. He would go on periodic benders, only to return to work days after disappearing. One night he went to bed and died in his sleep. His body was buried but all of his possessions were left in his room.

When the last owner went to the second floor he found different doors locked and open. Sam's clothes, which might have been in Room One on the last visit, would be moved to Room Four. He used to let visitors go and explore the second floor. That ended when he let a group of people upstairs and soon found them kicking in the locked doors. He later found that they had pried numbers off room doors and stolen Sam's clothing. He sold the bar to the McMenamins and around the turn of the

Millennium, and they restored the upstairs to its former glory. They even improved its décor with several thematic paintings. They did get the room names wrong though. By all accounts, Sam used to live in Room Three, not Two.

The Ghosts

There have been stories for years about Sam haunting the main floor bar and the upstairs. There have also been stories of a ghostly woman leaning against the window in Room Two. She is supposed to have been a prostitute named Rose, who suffered or died there. The basement is supposed to have been haunted by former residents, or prisoners. It was reputed that there was a Shanghai tunnel under the bar and that sailors or workmen would visit the bar and go downstairs to smoke opium with the oriental or black prostitutes that were supposedly kept there.

Shortly after the new staff began working at the White Eagle one of them was carrying supplies into the basement. He walked by the large freezer with his arms full of food. As he passed by the freezer, one of the doors came open and hit him in the back. Another employee, Doug, was serving drinks at the hundred-year-old bar. He felt a presence standing behind him. After ignoring the presence for several minutes he began to feel a light touch on the back of it his head. Doug turned around and as he expected, there was no one there.

In the past, the women's restroom was the scene of several strange events. One patron had a paper throwing fight with the woman in the stall next to her, only to find the stall empty when she got up and checked it. I visited the White Eagle with a female friend in January of 2000. She was using the restroom when she heard a metallic click. When she got up to leave she found that *her* stall door had somehow unlocked itself.

In 2001 I led a group of ghost experiencers in an evening at the White Eagle Tavern. We brought along Ouija boards, Electromagnetic Field (EMF) detectors, cameras and tape recorders. Many strange things happened. The most significant was that when we performed one Ouija session on Room Two, the EMF detectors would spike when questions were asked. There are more stories coming from patrons and employees at the White Eagle. Just wait a while between visits and you hear more.

Restaurants, Clubs and Theaters

Name: **Accuardi's Old Town Pizza**
Address: 226 NW Davis Street
Portland, OR 97209
Phone Number: **503-222-9999**
Website: http://oldtownpizza.citysearch.com
Prices: $$
Theme: Historic building converted into pizza parlor
Cuisine: Pizzeria
Open: Monday – Thursday, 11:30 a.m. to 11:00 p.m.
Friday & Sat, 11:30 a.m. to Midnight.
Special Facilities: Banquet facility, daytime delivery, Shanghai Tunnel Tours start here.

The Davis Block was built in the late 1800s in Portland's growing Business District. Accuardi's Old Town Pizza is located in one of the fine brick buildings that were built in an effort to make Portland look more genteel. Of course, this only hid the seamier part of Portland hidden under the Davis Block. Part of the intricate network of Shanghai tunnels runs under Accuaradi's Old Town Pizza. This is one reason why the Portland Shanghai Tunnel Tours begin here. This building still preserves some of it's better past though. The old elevator is still preserved, though it no longer runs.

The Ghosts

I visited the pizza parlor with a psychic friend in the late 1990s. Although the second floor loft is relatively new, she detected a spirit in the upper spaces. The staff knows there is a ghost, though they do not talk about it unless asked. The spirit here seems confined to moving things around periodically and making odd noises now and then. Any visit to this place would be worth it since they make their own Italian sausage.

Name:	**Dan & Louis Oyster Bar**
Address:	208 SW Ankeny Portland, OR 97204
Phone Number:	503-227-5096
Website:	www.danandlouis.citysearch.com
Prices:	$$
Theme:	Old-Tyme oyster bar and seafood restaurant
Cuisine:	Fresh seafood
Open:	Sunday through Thursday, 11:00 a.m.–10:00 p.m. Friday & Saturday, 11:00 a.m.–11:00 p.m.
Special Features:	Gift shop, historic photos

In 1907 Louis Wachsmuth found his oyster bar near Portland's docks. At first he was confined to selling raw oysters until 1919, when he bought the Merchant's Exchange Saloon. He began with his own special recipe for Oyster Stew and expanded the facility as the years went by. This includes the ship motif extension built in 1937.

The Oyster Bar resembles some of the modern Yuppie bars where the wall hangings and photographs plastering the walls are reproductions of authentic antique maritime artifacts. Don't be fooled! The thing that saves the Dan and Louis from being tacky is the fact that the wall hangings are original. The windows are shaped like round portholes and the wooden walls are hung with ship models, ropes and old pictures of past employees and the Northwest Coast.

The Ghosts

The Wachsmuth family continues to run the restaurant and many of their employees have been there for years. If ever a place deserved to be haunted by a devoted owner or employee, it is Dan and Louis Oyster Bar. I spoke with "Tuck" Wachsmuth in 2000 about any ghosts at the

Oyster Bar. He informed me that they did not have any ghosts; but the Shanghai Tunnel Tour groups frequently stop there after a tour. With or without ghosts, this is a great place to eat.

Name: **Bagdad Theater and Pub**
Address: 3702 SE Hawthorne Avenue ?
Portland, OR 97214
Phone Number: **503-236-9234**
503-225-5555 (ext. 8832)
Website: www.mcmenamins.com
Prices: $$ - $$$
Theme: Historic Theater converted into theater and pub
Cuisine: Pub and varied movies
Open: Pub: Monday through Saturday, 11:00 a.m.-1:00 p.m.
Sunday, Noon – 2:00 p.m.
Call the box office for show times.
Special Facilities: Own microbrew, eating and drinking allowed in theater, private events

The Bagdad Theater is one of many Arabian Knights style of theaters built in the late 1920s. The theater was used for vaudeville as well as movies. One night after the performances were over, the theater's janitor hung himself backstage. His body was not found until the next morning.

The Bagdad Theater will comfortably seat 700 + people in its auditorium and large balcony. Several rows of seats have been removed to make way for the permanent tables, set up in front of many seats for patrons to place their food and drink while watching movies.

The Ghosts

Several paranormal events happened during the renovation of the theater. In 1994 when McMenamins bought it, the electricians turned off the main power. Suddenly the lights came on, and flicked off and on for nearly an hour before they stayed off. Several customers who used the downstairs bathroom told employees that they felt watched. Employees in the kitchen would sometimes feel as if someone was watching them from the windows of the swinging doors that separated the kitchen from the lobby.

One man told me that although he hasn't seen anything strange, he sometimes scares himself when he's in the backstage area alone. When I was back there I saw a mannequin hanging from the ceiling near the stairs, leading to the basement. "Oh," the worker replied as if seeing it for the first time. "There's been a noose hanging from the ceiling ever since this place opened as a McMenamins. The doll is new though."

Name: **Cornelius Pass Roadhouse**
Address: 4045 NW Cornelius Pass Road
Hillsboro, OR 97124
Phone Number: 503-640-0174
Fax number: 503-640-2930
Website: www.mcmenamins.com/pubs/cpr
Prices: $$ - $$$
Theme: Italian style villa farmhouse turned into pub
Cuisine: Pub grub
Open: Monday through Thursday, 11:00 a.m.-10:00 p.m.
Friday & Saturday, 11:00 a.m.-11:00 p.m.;
Sunday, noon to 10:00 p.m.
Special Facilities: An invented haunting, own brewery, fireplaces and gardens, live music, meeting facility.

Over 130 years ago Charles Imbrie built his dream house in Hillsborough, Oregon. It was built at the crossroads of two Indian trails, which are still major travel routes today. The family lived in the house for over a century, until they sold it to the McMenamins.

On the house grounds they carefully preserved the better outbuildings. The Octagonal Barn, built in 1913 has been converted into a meeting facility and music venue. The oldest surviving barn is The Granary, which was put together with wooden pegs and hand hewn beams. It is also used as a quiet venue or for private get togethers. The McMenamins built a brewery near the pub parking lot. Curious customers often stop and watch operations through the large windows.

The Ghosts

When I arrived at the Cornelius Pass Roadhouse I saw several pictures painted on the walls detailing a story of tragedy in the house. At the top of the third floor stairs there is a painting of a little girl who pushed her little brother down the stairs, accidentally killing him. Her parents stand in a portrait above the fireplace on the second floor. And why does a young woman with sad eyes hide in the closet to the right of the fireplace? They were inspired and invented by the artist, because he

thought the place should have ghosts. The Imbrie family informed me that the house was not haunted.

Several of the employees have experienced cold spots around the stair landings. Some of these can be explained by a natural draft of cold air. But why does the draft remain in the summer? Glasses sitting at an empty table have shattered when no one was around and footsteps have been heard walking up the stairs when the building has been closed.

Name: **Crystal Ballroom**
Address: 1332 West Burnside Street
Portland, OR 97209
Phone Number: 503-225-5555, ext. 8811(concert schedule)
ext. 8812 (ticket information);
ext. 8810 (ballroom)
Website: www.mcmenamins.com
Prices: $$ - $$$
Theme: Historic dance hall
Cuisine: Pub grub to Pizza $$
Open: Call for box office information
Special Facilities: "Floating" dance floor, special acts and performances

At the turn of the century dance instructor Montrose Ringler had a large clientele of people from the upper classes. They refused to come to his school, in a less than savory part of town. Ringler wanted to build a large dance hall closer to Portland's center. At the same time, Lola Baldwin, a local woman's suffragette and reformer, opposed dance halls. She believed that modern dances led to immoral conduct. She spurred the city to pass four anti-dance ordinances within Portland.

Despite the opposition, in 1914 Cotillion Hall, as the 'Crystal Ballroom' was then known, opened for business. A major attraction of the dancehall was the floating floor. A layer of fine maple planks was laid on top of a series of wooden rocker panels with ball bearings attached to the ends of the rockers. This added a gentle swaying motion to the whole floor when people danced.

In 1921 Ringler sold his lease to the Cotillion Hall. It gradually fell into disrepair. The building was renamed the Crystal Ballroom in 1950. With the construction of large auditoriums, the old hall could not compete for popular bands. The Crystal Ballroom closed as a music venue in 1968 and was not reopened until 1997 when McMenamins purchased the facility and brought it back to life. At least parts of it.

The Ghosts

On Christmas Eve of 1998 the manager received a call from the Crystal Ballroom's Security Company. The burglar alarms had gone off. He drove there quickly, entered and walked upstairs to the main ballroom entrance. He quietly let himself into the ballroom and walked through the ballroom, (in the dark), and headed down the main stairs to the second floor. He paused at the foot of the stairs. He heard the voices of at least seven people talking very loudly at the top of the stairs, directly above him. He listened to their footsteps and voices grow fainter as they walked away, across the dark ballroom. Whether they were ghosts or thrill seekers, there were too many of them to confront.

The ballroom's elevator seems to have a mind of its own. There have been several occasions when bands have loaded or unloaded the elevator, only to watch it close its doors and travel up to the third floor on its own.

Name: **Elephant & Castle Pub**
Address: 439 SW Second Avenue
Portland, OR 97204
Phone Number: **503-222-5698**
Website: http://elephantcastle.citysearch.com
Prices: $ - $$
Theme: English Pub
Cuisine: English pub grub
Open: Monday through Saturday, 11:00 a.m.-midnight.
Closed Sunday.

Special Facilities: Special English menu items, lunch specials, 14 beers on tap, a large selection of Scotches, darts, Two TVs

The Elephant and Castle is housed on the first floor of the Waldo Building. The Waldo Building was built in 1886 and made use of Italian architecture and cast iron for its fixtures. It is ironic that this building was constructed by Judge John B. Waldo, and a few years later it became a center for Chinese societies, some innocent, some less respectable, like the Tong.

According to some stories, the basement became a combination opium den and Shanghai trap. There were five tunnels leading to and from the Waldo Building. There is a very old stall, with walls, ceiling and a locking door standing in the center of the basement. It was filled with dirt and garbage. Several years ago, the manager, Sharon was cleaning up in there and she found an opium scale at the bottom of the stall.

In the 1960s George Frederici had the idea to open an English style pub close to the police station. He named it after the "Elephant and Castle Pub" in England. Despite the high ceilings and wrought iron interior he did a fair job of including great English pub elements. There are English wall hangings and imitation suits of armor, and a heavy wooden bar as well as a large selection of English foods and drinks. George ran the bar for several years before passing it on to his daughter Sharon.

The Ghosts

Sometimes people have felt a cold spot near the barstool marked "George." This was the place where George held court in between waiting on customers and keeping the bar stocked. Sharon believes that her father forced out any bad spirits during his time as bartender. Perhaps he's still doing it after death.

A suicide victim may be the person people hear walking in the back of the bar, near the keno machines. Sometimes customers have heard the sound of chairs falling or soft footsteps in the back room. Sharon is not afraid of any ghosts in the bar or basement.

Name: **Kells Irish Restaurant and Pub**
Address: 112 SW Second Avenue
Portland, OR 97204
Phone Number: 503-227-4057
Website: www.kellsirish.com
Prices: $$
Theme: Historic building converted into Irish Pub
Cuisine: Irish Pub grub
Open: Lunch, Monday to Friday, 11:30 a.m. to 2:30 p.m.
Saturday & Sunday, 11:30 a.m. – 3:00 p.m.
Dinner, Monday – Thursday, 5:30 p.m.– 9:00 p.m.
Friday & Saturday, 5:30 p.m.–10:00 p.m.;
Sunday, 5:00 p.m.–9:00 p.m.
Special Facilities: Cigar Room, full range of Irish and European drinks, souvenirs for sale

Kells Irish Pubs are a slowly growing chain. The first was opened in Seattle, and the second one is located in Portland. A third Kells will open in California, eventually. Both northwest pubs are haunted. The Portland Kells is located in an 1880s Greek revival style brick building located near Portland's waterfront. It is a strange mix of old brick, arches, pediments and Irish memorabilia. The interior is rough, with a 40-foot bar located in the back of the building, behind the regular tables and seating. The high ceiling is supported by tall, cast iron columns and is covered with dollar bills hung up on the top at night by "the little folk." The money on the ceiling is donated by patrons and donated to charity every year.

Kells sponsors an annual St. Patrick's day festival. They offer a selection of Irish and English alcoholic drinks and several traditional Irish dishes like soda bread. Daily specials are posted on a large blackboard, which is typically Irish. Kells customers recently voted to make the bar smoke free. This does not apply to the basement, which has a long, smoking room. The smoking room really does look like it belongs in an Irish pub. The ceiling is low and the floor is uneven concrete and tile. The walls are hung with Irish theme prints. It is also haunted.

The Ghosts

Kells is located near Chinatown. The "Shanghai" tunnels that connected most of old Portland also ran through the basement at Kells.

Strangely enough, it is not the ghost of an old time sailor that haunts Kells. It is a firefighter who may have died there. According to stories, patrons and workers have seen a fireman dressed in his old-fashioned hat and jacket in the basement. He usually disappears before anyone can talk to him. Psychics told the manager they felt the presence of a fireman there. Recently a bartender was in the basement and felt someone tap his shoulder. When he turned around there was no one there.

Name:	**Pied Cow Coffee House - AKA Buttertoes**
Address:	3244 SE Belmont Street Portland, OR
Phone Number:	503-230-5540
Prices:	$$
Theme:	Hippie/Victorian/Buddhist Coffee house
Open:	Evenings

The Pied Cow Coffee House was formerly named Buttertoes. It is located on Portland's historic Belmont Avenue. The coffee house began as a fine Victorian house and was built in 1894. One of its original tenants was a woman named Lydia. She was supposed to have lived in the house for 25 years. She was seen day after day, sitting in her rocking chair at one of the tower windows. After Lydia died in the 1920s the house was sold to a number of people and one time suffered from a large fire. In 1978, Carolyn Hulbert rented the building and converted it into a combination restaurant and boarding house. The restaurant occupied the first floor. In the 1990s it was sold and Buttertoes moved to a new location

It is hard to adequately describe the Pied Cow Coffeehouse's theme, since it does not seem to have one. The interior design is a mix of Victorian-Hindu-Bohemian. This comes from the original Victorian woodwork and chandeliers, the many Buddhist wall hangings, an odd mix of watercolor paintings, and beads. The menu lists several pages of unique teas, coffees, beers and wines as well as light food and desserts. The customers are an eclectic mix of New Agers, Goths, and people who just like to hang out. All in all it's an interesting place.

The Ghosts

Before the name change, some mornings the staff opened the restaurant to find that the tables and chairs had been rearranged. One day, the cook was alone in the kitchen when several muffin tins flew off a shelf. They moved through the air, about five feet, and landed on the floor behind him. A tenant who lived on the second floor frequently dreamt of an elderly woman. She stood in the apartment, just looking at him, she walked toward him and then disappeared.

The previous stories date from the 1970s. I have tried speaking with the current owners several times. They refused to reply to any messages. One of the waitresses told me that they did not believe in ghosts and did not want to discuss the matter, so if you go there, don't bother asking. But if you do, and you get any answers, contact me at jddavis@rocketmail.com!

Name: **Rose and Raindrop**
Address: 532 SE Grand Avenue
Portland, OR 97214
Phone Number: 503-238-6996
Prices: $$
Theme: English pub
Cuisine: English pub grub
Open: Monday – Friday, 11:00 a.m. to 2:30 a.m.
Saturday & Sunday, 10:00 a.m. to 2:30 a.m.
Special Facilities Live music, 33 beers on tap, non-smoking room in back, kitchen closes at 11:00 p.m.

The Rose and Raindrop was formerly known as Digger O'Dell's Pub. The management has tried to upgrade the former décor into something more than an English pub. The building itself is one of the oldest preserved buildings on the east side of the Willamette River and the owners are careful to preserve its interior. They have typical pub grub as well as English inspired food such as steaks, lamb and other more exotic foods.

The upper dining rooms are closer to a cozy club rather than a tavern atmosphere. I have dined there and have enjoyed the rustic, old brick and wood interior. I was told that when it was first built, the Rose and Raindrop was a funeral home, or embalming room for a funeral home. This may lead to any ghosts.

The Ghosts

I spoke with someone who worked there when the bar was still Digger O'Dells. He told me that he was in the kitchen cooking, when all of the utensils began banging on their own. The stove flared up suddenly as well. It all stopped when he began yelling in panic. The manager came in just as it stopped. The manager was a skeptic and did not believe him. I spoke with the current manager who has experienced many things, and he is a believer.

Name: **St. Johns Theatre**
Address: 8704 North Lombard Avenue
Portland, OR
Phone Number: 503-286-1768
Prices: $$
Theme: Historic movie theater
Open: Check box office for dates and times

The St. Johns Theatre is the oldest movie-theater and live performance venue serving the St. Johns neighborhood. It is also the home of the Cathedral Park Jazz Festival. In late 2000, The Jazz Festival received grants and loans to purchase the theater to renovate it. The support plan included upgrades so the theater could show first run movies, as well as upgrading its live performance venue for the Jazz Festival and other cultural events.

The remodeling is in progress right now. I am curious about whether or not anything will be activated by the changes. The St. Johns Theatre still shows first run movies.

The Ghosts

The ghost stories about the St. Johns Theatre date back to the time when live stage performances were more common than movies being played on its screen. Because the stories are older, they are also vague. From what I can tell, past employees felt a presence on the stage area and sometimes felt cold spots, where there was no draft. The reports faded over time, but renovation and revitalization may bring the ghosts back.

Name: **Shanghai Tunnel Bar**
Address: 211 SW Ankeny Street
Portland, OR 97204
Phone Number: 503-220-4001
Website: http://home.europa.com/~1201cafe/shanghai/htm
Prices: $$
Theme: Underground pub
Cuisine: Pub grub
Open: Tuesday through Sunday, 4:00 p.m.– 2:30 a.m.
Special Facilities: No cover charge, happy hour from 4:00 p.m. - 8:00 p.m.

The Shanghai Tunnels Bar was built in the basement of one of Portland's old-town buildings. You can still see some of the blocked up passages along the wall. The place is frequently smoky, and the low ceilings and dim lighting can give visitors a claustrophobic feeling. Because it has to meet health codes, the place is a little too clean to really give the complete Opium Den feeling to patrons.

The food and drink at the Shanghai Tunnel is not typical of northwest pubs. There are Quesadilla's, tofu, Pan-Asian cooking, and some vegetarian dishes. They do not stock microbrews. They stock a line of non-regional and European brews.

The Ghosts

The area around Ankeny and Burnside is near the center of the network of Shanghai tunnels that honeycomb Portland's old waterfront. When Portland was first settled, the streets were dirt and the sidewalks were made of wooden planks. If there was a sidewalk at all. It was more practical to hollow out a series of holes and tunnels from the waterfront to many nearby businesses. This meant that goods could be offloaded from ships and delivered without getting bogged down in the muddy pits that used to be called Portland's streets.

Although the tunnels were used to transport goods during the daytime, they were deserted by local businesses at night. This was too much of an opportunity for Portland's criminals to ignore. The tunnels became the nighttime realm of opium addicts, smugglers and the Shanghai press gangs. Whenever ships called at a major port there was a strong chance that the ordinary seamen would not return, especially if they were offered a better berth on a different ship, or a land grant, or gold had been discovered nearby.

Most ships captains made it a regular practice to fill these shortages, especially if their next port of call was several months travel away. Many innkeepers and tavern owners made it a practice to size up their clientele every night. They were looking for sailors, farmers, lumbermen and anyone else who might have been useful on a ship. They would drug the prospective sailors and take them through hidden passageways to the waterfront and sell them to the waiting ship captains.

Sometimes an enterprising Shanghaier might make several stops along the way to the waterfront. They built vaults and cells along the tunnels to store their drunken victims. Sometimes these men died of drug overdoses or suffocated in the tunnels. Some may have just been forgotten there. Shanghaiing went on from the 1870s until it ended in the 1940s. Perhaps. Since that time, the tunnels have gradually collapsed or been filled in. But many basements in the old waterfront still have some elements of the tunnels such as bricked up passages or heavy doors as remnants of their past uses.

The Ghosts

I visited the Shanghai Tunnel and chatted with one of the bartenders while she was cutting up some kind of leaves for drinks or food. She told me that the place has a reputation for being haunted, but the ghosts are very discreet. I also spoke with the manager, Zorn. He has had a few experiences too. He was tending bar one night and a shot glass materialized in the air and nearly hit him in the head when it fell. He has seen out of the corner of his eye, and has seen items fall off the shelves when no one was near.

Other employees have felt things, rather than seen or heard them. They manifest themselves as the occasional cold spot, or a cold touch now and then.

Name: **Virginia Cafe**
Address: 725 SW Park Avenue
Portland, OR 97205
Phone Number: **503-227-0033**
Prices: $$
Theme: Bar and grill
Cuisine: American
Open: Daily, 11:00 a.m.– 2:30 a.m.
Special Facilities: Fifteen beers on tap, happy hour, no cover charge.

The Virginia Café is a kind of throwback to the American Bar and Grills that were everywhere in the 1950s and 1960s, but are now fading away. *Perry Mason* has been on television as a daily rerun in the Portland area for the last 30 years. People from Portland will understand me when I say that when I go into the Virginia Café, I expect to see Perry Mason and Della Street eating lunch with Paul Drake.

The Café is divided into two levels, with a second story loft overlooking the high backed booths, separated by glass partitions. The bar and restrooms look like older fixtures that were not changed when the place was remodeled in the 1950s or 60s. It is a good thing that there is a huge red neon sign, hanging over the building entrance, since it can be hard to find.

Over the years the neighborhood has grown up, and the back wall of Nordstrom's dwarfs the other buildings. The Virginia Café moved to its present location in 1922 in what was known as the Tenderloin District. During the Great Depression it managed to flourish because the kitchen sometimes acted as room service, providing food to the prostitutes and their customers. Time and big business may have bypassed the Virginia Café somewhat, but they have a loyal clientele who enjoy the food and atmosphere.

The Ghosts

I spoke with the manager some time ago about rumors of hauntings. She told me that she herself has felt a presence in the back portions of the bar, near her office. The owners are reluctant to talk about any ghostly doings.

Shops, Sights and Sounds

Name:	**24 hour Church of Elvis**
Address:	720 SW Ankeny Street Portland, OR 97205
Phone Number:	**503-226-3671**
Website:	www.churchofelvis.com
Prices:	$ donations
Theme:	'The King' rocks on
Open:	Varies, it is best to call ahead

Special Facilities: Elvis memorabilia, entertainment machines, mock and real weddings

I know this entry may upset some people, because ELVIS IS NOT DEAD!!! So how could I mention his ghost in Portland? O.K., that may be true, but even the most die-hard Elvis fans will agree that THE KING'S SPIRIT IS EVERYWHERE!!!. People who have their bathrooms decorated as a shrine to THE KING, will enjoy this proverbial Mecca of Elvis worship.

The Church used to be confined to a store front closer to the waterfront, but has moved north, near the US Bank Tower. The displays, which were in a window on street level are inside, on the second floor of the church building. The church has some interesting and often arcane displays of Elvis memorabilia. There are several mechanical, coin operated machines on display. Some of them still work. I especially like the machine that says, "insert Quarter here!" I am still waiting for something to happen.

Despite the name, the church is not open 24 hours a day. Call ahead or email via the website to arrange a mock wedding, which costs a modest fee. You can have a legal wedding performed by an Elvis impersonator (or The King himself?), for a larger fee, as well as the price of a marriage license.

Name: **Cathedral Park**
Address: North Edison and Pittsburgh
Portland, OR 97203
Website: www.parks.ci/portland.or/us/parks
Prices: $ (Free)
Theme: City park
Open: Year round
Special Facilities: Boat ramp, stage, soccer field, hiking trail, open air stage

Cathedral Park is located under the St. John's Bridge on the east side of the Willamette River in North Portland. It is named after the cathedral shaped arches that form the supports of the bridge above. Today the park is well maintained and there are periodically live plays or bands performing on the open-air stage. It has not always been such a nice place.

In 1949, a 15-year-old high school student Thelma was waiting for a bus to pick her up to go berry picking. She was kidnapped and taken to the base of the bridge. She was held there for a week, where she was raped and killed. The evidence from the crime scene allowed police to find her killer who was arrested and later executed for his crime.

Sadly, Thelma's spirit may still suffer. Passers-by and residents frequently hear the sounds of screams coming from the park on summer evenings. The police are dispatched and arrive at the park only to find it empty, with no evidence of any crime. Recent ghost hunting groups have recorded some of these sounds, late at night.

Name: **The Money Tree**
Address: Located at the corner of North Mississippi Avenue
& North Killingsworth Court.
Portland, OR
Theme: Buried treasure
Open: Year round
Special Facilities: Fenced in neighborhood site

The money tree is not an official tourist site, and it is located in a residential neighborhood. I would strongly suggest if you want to visit, be discreet, polite and go in daylight hours. People living in that area know it is not the safest at night. Please do not dig for treasure or remove "souvenirs" either.

One of North Portland's less favorite residents was Ed Black. He lived in the neighborhood near Mississippi and Killingsworth. Ed's mother had told him when he was a boy that he would probably never live to see his 50th birthday because he had no common sense about what he said to people. He always aired his opinions, no matter who he offended. When he turned fifty, he celebrated with a few of his friends. Shortly after that, he was found dead at the corner of North Kerby and North Alberta. He had been shot in the head.

Ed may have bragged about his treasure trove at his birthday party. Ed lived in an old van and never seemed to have very much. He told a few people that he had a fortune in cash, jewelry and other valuable items. He told them he hid it under or near the rocks of an old dead tree at the corner of North Killingsworth and Mississippi. Although the neighbors were curious, they never dug for Ed's treasure. Nor have they seen anyone else at the fenced lot. All the same, a few people claim that they have seen Ed's ghost standing by the tree after the morning rainstorms.

Name: **North Portland Library**
Address: 512 North Killingsworth Street
Portland, OR 97217
Phone Number: **503-988-5394**
Prices: $ (free)

Jefferson Davis

Theme: Historic library
Open: Tuesday through Thursday, 10:00 a.m.-9:00 p.m.
Friday & Saturday, 10:00 a.m.-6:00 p.m.
Sunday, 1:00 p.m.–5:00 p.m.
Closed Mondays and legal holidays.
Special Facilities: Special meeting room on the second floor.

The North Portland library was built in 1913. Like many local libraries, it served a small community near the Columbia River waterfront until it was swallowed up by the growing city of Portland. The first floor contains the main book stacks while the second floor is reserved as a meeting room. When not being used, the second floor is always kept locked and monitored with a security camera system.

The Ghosts

In 1990, a librarian sitting at the main desk was monitoring library security. She saw a man sitting on a chair in the second floor. There was no meeting scheduled that day and the doors were locked. She called another librarian and they both saw the man sitting patiently in his chair. When they investigated, they found the second floor locked and empty. Since then the man has been seen on the security cameras several times by library staff.

Pedestrians foolish enough to walk along Commercial Street (near the library) at night have heard the sound of footsteps following them. It is usually not muggers, who are pretty common, but disembodied footsteps, which follow pedestrians for several blocks. I am serious now. I advise against this experiment, since the area is not safe at night. There have been several muggings in the neighborhood over the years!

Name: **Pittock Mansion**
Address: 3229 NW Pittock Drive
Portland, OR 97210
Phone Number: **503-248-4469**
Website: http://www.mediaforte.con/pittock/ptckhis.htm
Prices: $
Theme: Historic mansion museum
Open: Daily from noon – 4:00 p.m.

Henry Pittock, was one of the early pioneer industrialists who made Portland what it is today. Depending on your point of view, this is good or bad. This was his retirement home. Pittock Mansion overlooks Portland. The shell of the house is square, but the rooms are circular or

oval, built off of a central grand staircase like spokes from a wheel. The house incorporated many of the most modern features. There was a dumbwaiter to raise food to the upstairs bedrooms. The house was designed so that morning airflow acted to cool the house without fans in the summer. Instead of bells to call servants, the Pittock's had an internal phone system installed.

The house was the culmination of the life and work of the Pittocks. After the sandstone mansion was completed, the Pittocks and some of their descendents moved in together. Georgiana lived in the house for four years, until her death in 1918. Henry survived her by one year, dying in 1919. The house was purchased by the City of Portland in 1964 and restored with public and donated funds and labor.

The Ghosts

Since the house has opened to the public in 1965, there have been some stories of strange happenings throughout the mansion. A picture of Henry Pittock as a young man seems to move from place to place. Visitors have reported the strong smell of roses, Georgiana's favorite flower. Others have reported the sound of heavy boots walking in and out of the rear entrance. A woman was looking at the picture displays in the basement level when she felt something. She turned around and saw the figure of an elderly woman, standing next to her. The woman vanished, before her eyes.

The windows on the main staircase have a tendency to shut on their own when they have been left open by the staff. When I visited the mansion in 1998 I asked a member of the staff, who told me that had happened that very morning.

Name:	**Portland Underground Tours**
Address:	P.O. Box 398
	Rhododendron, OR 97049
Phone Number:	503-622-4798
Website:	members.tripod.com/cgs-mthood
Prices:	$$

Theme: Historic Portland tours
Open: Check phone information
Special Features: Tour times are posted on the website as well as on their message phone Special group tours are also conducted.

Michael Jones and the Cascade Geographic Society have taken the opportunity to educate the public in a hands-on way. In the late 1990s they combined their efforts to educate and preserve the old system of Shanghai/storage tunnels running under the older parts of Portland. Beginning with volunteers and educational field trips, they gradually had some of the remaining portions of the tunnel network opened up. This allows them to conduct tours that educate as well as horrify members of the general public about Portland's shady past.

The Ghosts

The tours pass under haunted places like the Accuardi's Old Town Pizza, and other haunted locales. I have sent emails and left messages requesting information about ghosts within the tunnels but have not received any response.

Name: **Simon Benson House**
Address: Portland State University Campus
Corner of SW Montgomery ST & Park Avenue
Portland, OR 97207
Phone Number: 503-725-8209
Website: www.pp.pdx.edu/benson
Prices: $$
Theme: Historic house
Open: Wednesday & Friday from 3:00 p.m. – 5:00 p.m.
Special Facilities: Possible group meeting facilities on the first floor

Simon Benson is mentioned in other places in this book. Benson was one of Portland's early entrepreneur benefactors. He made his fortune in lumber and put much of it back into the community. He endowed schools and colleges, built roads, provided free public drinking fountains and donated hundreds of acres of land as parks. One of his more private accomplishments was his house.

In 1900, Benson completed his Queen Anne Victorian home on the corner of Clay Street and SW 11th Avenue. It would take an architectural report to describe all of the details of his home. Because of his lumber background, Benson had each room finished with a different type of wood. He commissioned a dozen leaded, stained class windows for his house.

By the 1920s Simon Benson had moved to Beverly Hills, and the house was divided into separate flats. It was a favorite place for college students to live when Portland State University came to dominate the neighborhood. In 1991 the house was condemned as untenable and boarded up for nearly a decade. The negative effects of time accelerated the decay to the house. Finally in the late 1990s the Friends of the Simon Benson House were able to procure funding and loans to move and restore the house for public uses.

The house was moved to the Portland State University campus at the corner of Montgomery and Park Avenue. It is the home of the Portland State University Alumni Association, which occupies the second floor. The first floor is open as a reception area.

The Ghosts

After sitting vacant for nearly a decade the house became overgrown and downright scary to look at. It generated stories of strange lights and ghostly noises from people who walked by it late at night.

I talked with a spokeswoman for the house about any stories from the restoration workers. She told me that there were some vague stories, but she had no details. She did agree that ghost or no ghosts, the house would benefit from visitors. So if you stop by for a visit, please let me know if anything strange happens.

Name: **The Wall (website)**
Website:http://web-star.com/thewall.html

The wall is a website devoted to remote ghost detecting. There is a web cam pointed at the wall of an old Portland cemetery. The camera takes a picture every five minutes and posts it on the site. People are invited to tune in and watch for any possible paranormal phenomena. They can post their observations on the site's chat room.

Name: **Portland Haunting at the Docks**
Website: http://209.162.216.149/ghost/default.html

The website has several apocryphal stories posted by someone whose brother disappeared under mysterious circumstances. Believe it or not. Just read and see.

Columbia City

Name: **Charles Green Caples House Museum**
Address: 1915 1st St
Columbia City, OR 97018
Phone Number: **503 397-5390**
Website: www.teleport.com/~dareth/DAR/museums.htm
Prices: $
Theme: Historic House Museum
Open: March – October, Friday – Sunday noon – 5 p.m.
Special Facilities: Gift shop, meeting room

Directions: Columbia City is a few miles north of St. Helen's, Oregon, along Hwy 30. Exit Hwy 30 in Columbia City and turn east on I Street, take a right (south) on 1st Street, the Caples House is located near the end of the road. The museum is a whole complex of buildings, which take up an entire city block.

Charles Caples and his family settled in Columbia City in the 1840s when he was a boy. Charles left the family farm and went to medical school in Portland. He returned to Columbia City to practice medicine when he graduated. He constructed his two story family home on the site of the original family log cabin in 1870. He and his family lived in the house, and he practiced medicine there until he died. His family lived in the house until the 1950s. In 1959, his descendents donated the house and land to the Mt. St. Helen's Chapter of the Oregon State Society, Daughters of the American Revolution, who continue to run the museum.

The house includes a display of medical equipment, period furniture, old-fashioned kitchen and bedrooms, there are displays in other buildings. There is a wash house, tool shed and the old family carriage house has been turned into a kind of children's museum.

The Ghosts

In the late 1990s, the caretakers called the International Ghost Hunters Society to investigate the house. One of them had seen the imprint of two bodies on one of the beds. During their investigation they detected anomalous electromagnetic field readings in the doctor's office. They may have captured pictures of the ghost of Mrs. Caples in the mirror in the bedroom. For more information, visit the IGHS website at: www.ghostweb.com/caples.html.

Name: The Interstate Bridge

In the autumn, some people driving across the older of the two Interstate bridges which cross from Portland to Vancouver sometimes see a strange sight. They have seen a tall man wearing an old-fashioned hat and heavy coat walking south, toward Hayden Island. This may be the ghost of one of Vancouver's mayors, who's body was found hanging in a tree on Hayden Island when Jantzen Beach was an amusement town. Was it suicide or foul play?

Downtown Vancouver

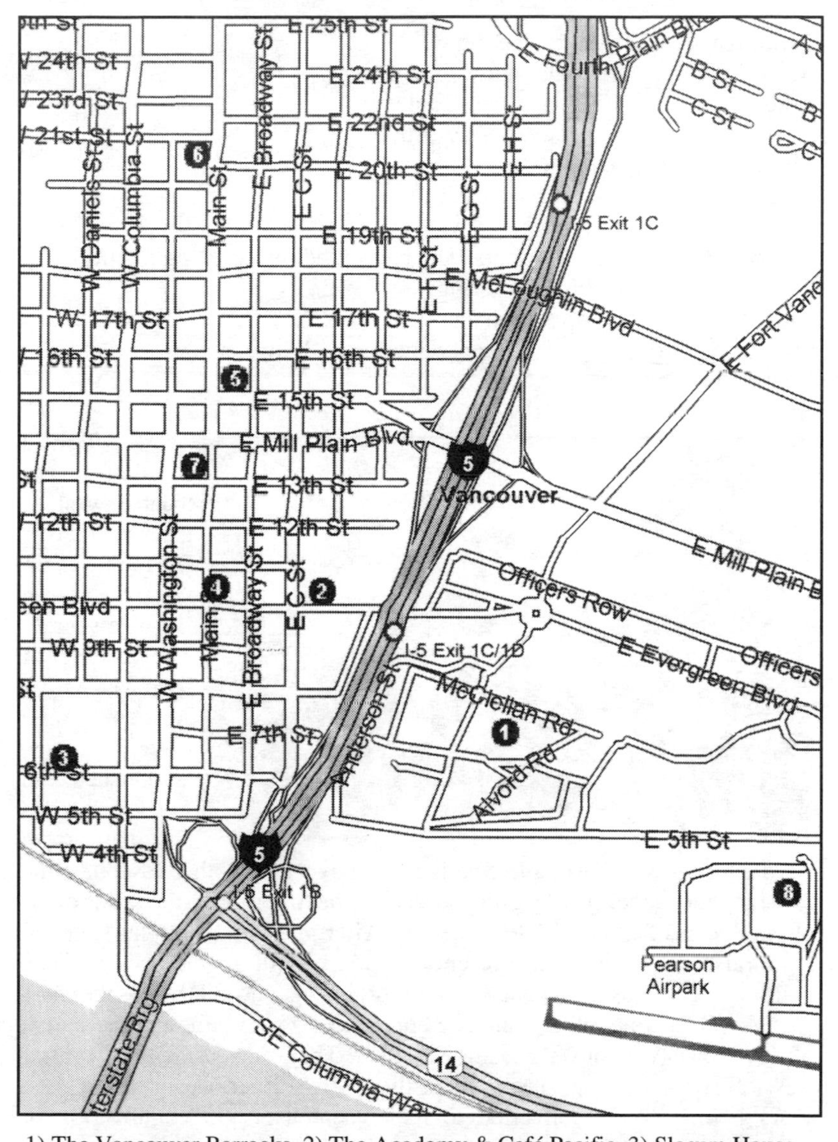

1) The Vancouver Barracks, 2) The Academy & Café Pacific, 3) Slocum House Theater, 4) Kiggins Theater, 5) Clark County Historical Museum, 6) Casa Grande Restaurant, 7) Hidden House Restaurant, 8) Pearson Air Museum © GDT 2001

Vancouver, WA

Restaurants, Clubs and Theaters

Name: **The Academy**
Address: 400 Evergreen Boulevard
Vancouver, WA 98660
Phone Number: **360-696-4884**
Website: www.the-academy.net
Prices: $$$
Theme: Catholic school/chapel turned into meeting facility
Cuisine: Gourmet catering: $$$
Open: By appointment
Special Facilities: Chapel open for weddings, conference and meeting facilities.

The Academy is located west of the Vancouver Barracks on Evergreen Boulevard. The Sister's of Providence Academy and the now demolished St. Joseph's Hospital were the dream of Ester Pariseau. She is also known as 'Mother Joseph.' She came to Vancouver in 1856, and served as the Superior of the small order of the Sisters of Charity of Providence. After many years of planning and fund raising, she had the present Academy built in the 1870s. The buildings served as a convent, mission, orphanage, hospital and school.

Over time, other churches and schools were built and the parish of downtown Vancouver became smaller. They moved facilities further west of The Academy. It closed in the 1970s. It sat vacant for several years before it was converted to its present use as a combination of offices, specialty shops and wedding chapel. Even with its new uses, some of the students may still be there in spirit.

The Ghosts

When it was still a private school, a strange boy walked into the classroom. Everyone assumed that he was a new student. As the school bell rang, the new boy got up and ran out of the room, *through the wall.* Maintenance workers have talked about some of their late night experiences. The have heard children's voices in classrooms. When they open the doors, the sounds cease. The sounds of footsteps have also been heard in the top floor. Now a locked storage area, in the past, this was where the Sisters had their cells. Are they still keeping up their vows and rising to go to midnight mass?

There was a wedding ceremony in the chapel sometime in the early 1990s. Video taping weddings was still rather new to most people. One of the wedding consultant staff members set up a video camera in the chapel. He accidentally left it turned on for an hour or so before the wedding began. After the wedding ceremony, he had to view the extra footage, to see where to begin editing the wedding itself. About a half hour before the wedding ceremony began, he watched a translucent figure of a woman in a nuns habit walk through the chapel. Some people think that this might be good luck.

The Café Pacific, which is attached to The Academy, is also reputedly haunted.

Name: **Café Pacific (formerly RP McMurphy's)**
Address: 400 E Evergreen Boulevard # 114
Vancouver, WA 98660
Phone Number: 360-695-2911
Prices: $$
Theme: Pub
Cuisine: High quality pub grub and bistro style cooking
Open: Evenings
Special Facilities: Smoke free. They have many local bands as well as a house band, the Mother Joseph's Academy Players, on Fridays.

The Café Pacific is located on the north side of the Academy building. It was built as an addition some time after the main orphanage and school buildings were constructed. The builders used brick, which gives it a quaint, old world kind of aura. I have been there several times and have enjoyed the mix of live bands they book. The stage is located in the main pub room, so if you want a quiet drink, this may not be your kind of venue. There is a picture of Mother Joseph hanging in the main entrance. She looks rather stern. I don't know if she would approve of a bar playing rock music in her former domain.

The Ghosts

I spoke with the former owner of the club, Steve, for ghost stories. He told me the place was haunted. Most of the ghostly happenings were in the back, employee only areas. There is a tunnel, leading from the Academy, north, to Mill Plain Road. He took several trips through the tunnel and swears he felt a presence there. I have spoken with the new employees and management. They are unaware of any haunts. Of course, they just moved in. Perhaps the ghosts are taking their measure?

Name: **Casa Grande Restaurant**
Address: 2014 Main Street
Vancouver, WA 98660
Phone Number: 360-694-7031
Website: www.pdxguide.com/columbian/columbianftp/casagrande15/home/html
Prices: $ - $$
Theme: Tudor style home turned into restaurant
Cuisine: Authentic Mexican dishes
Open: Sunday - Thursday, 11:15 a.m. — 8:30 p.m.
Saturday and Sunday, 11:15 a.m. — 9:30 p.m.
Special Facilities: To go orders, lunch menu, vegetarian dishes

The Casa Grande restaurant opened in Vancouver, Washington over 20 years ago. It was a time when most Vancouverites thought that Mexican food only came from Taco Bell. It was a little hard at first to convince some people that corn soup and tamales wrapped in cornhusks really were Mexican dishes.

The Casa Grande opened in an older house, built when 20th Avenue was almost outside of Vancouver's main hub. The owner was so tall he had to order a special bathtub to fit his size. His wife was a small woman who he dominated, for a time. According to stories, she visited his offices in downtown Vancouver and told him that she knew he would be chasing after the wrong kind of "Does" when he left home on an upcoming hunting trip. Later, he was found dead in the house, killed by a gunshot wound. After a brief hearing, it was declared an accident and she lived in the house for many years.

The Ghosts

There have been old stories of ghosts in the house. Some people talked about cold spots on the stairway. There were some electrical problems and lights went off an on without people using the switches. The restaurant owner was reluctant to talk to me about any possible haunting. He and his wife are very religious and feel it may be improper to be flippant about ghost stories. All the same, we talked, and he told me that nothing paranormal has happened since he opened the restaurant. He loves the building and he was happy to share the interesting story of the house and how it fit into the history of Vancouver.

Name: **Hidden House Restaurant**
Address: 110 W 13th Street
Vancouver, WA 98660
Phone Number: 360-696-2847
Prices: $$ - $$$
Theme: Historic home turned into restaurant
Cuisine: Fine dining
Open: Lunch, Tuesday through Friday, 11:00 a.m.-2:00 p.m.
Dinner, Tuesday through Sunday, 5:00 p.m.-9:00 p.m.
Special Facilities: Some vegetarian dishes, special French gourmet. Visitors can tour the building free before or after lunch.

Lowell M. Hidden was an early influence in Clark County. He opened his brick company in 1871. He built the Hidden house thirteen years later as a showpiece. This brick Victorian has some unique decorative touches added by the Danish craftsmen who finished its interior. It was also the first home of Clark Community College.

The Ghosts

The ghost or ghosts seem to be active at all times of the day. One morning, an employee was mopping up in the front entry when she heard a woman singing. Another employee was in the upstairs dining room, vacuuming the floor, when he heard his name called. He paused to investigate but found himself alone. This happened three times before he fled the building. During an employee meeting, the second floor bathroom door was found locked. The door was forced open. It was empty and had been locked from the inside.

Name: **Kiggins Theater**
Address: 1011 Main Street
Vancouver, WA 98660
Phone Number: 360-737-3161 (information line)
Website: www.kiggins.com
Prices: $
Theme: Historic Theater
Open: Check website or information line for times.
Special Facilities: First and second run movies, matinees

The Kiggins Theater is the last remaining old-time movie theater in downtown Vancouver. J.P. Kiggins, one of Vancouver's early mayors, built it in the mid-1930s. This was during the Great Depression, a daring financial move. It was also designed as a return to the old time, ornate movie theaters built during the 1920s. Like many of the historic theaters in this book, it suffered when Congress broke up the film industry monopoly and television stole their audience. In 1996, the Kiggins closed its doors, not in preparation for demolition but to begin remodeling for a grand re-opening. In May of 1997, the Kiggins reopened after a remodel. It now plays first run, second run, and classic movies on a new projection and sound system.

The Ghosts

In 1997 the manager was in his office on the second floor, when he heard footsteps coming from the attic spaces above. He followed the sound of the footsteps above. He walked through the building, following the attic footsteps. He ended up in the projection booth. He left after a few minutes and went back to his office. A few minutes later the lights in the projection booth, which he had locked, began to flicker on and off.

Some movie patrons and employees have seen a couple dressed in old-fashioned clothing sitting in their seats near the front row after the movie is finished. The couple disappear when they are approached. Employees sometimes see a patron get up during the movie and walk from his seat toward the lobby. He disappears between the theater and reaching the lobby.

Name: **Slocum House Theater**
Address: 605 Esther Street
Vancouver, WA 98660
Phone Number: 360-694-2588
Website: www.slocumhouse.com

Prices: $
Theme: Historic home turned into community theater
Open: See website or call for dates and times
Special Facilities: Sixty or so seat theater, open for private receptions

Charles W. Slocum was born in Massachusetts. In 1857, twenty three year old Slocum came to the Pacific Northwest, after completing an apprenticeship as a carpenter. He began working at the Vancouver Barracks. By 1860, his business and trade contacts ranged from Salt Lake City to San Francisco. In 1867, Charles began building his dream house, based on the house he grew up in in New England. He and his brother did some of the fine carpentry work in the house. They built a "widow's walk" tower that used to give a spectacular view of the Columbia River, before it was moved to its present site.

In 1965, the Slocum House was threatened by an urban renewal project that destroyed the fine Victorian houses that used to line Vancouver's old waterfront district. The house was rescued by civic and preservation groups, which included a small group of citizens known as The Old Slocum House Theater Company. Since 1966 they have raised money to maintain the historic building by using it as a theater.

The Ghosts

There are two or three ghosts at the Slocum House. The first is a poltergeist that pesters the caretaker living there. This ghost does not like to have anything placed on top of the refrigerator. When the caretaker places anything there, he quickly finds the object on the floor.

The second ghost may be Mrs. Slocum. She could not have children, so she and Mr. Slocum always welcomed the neighborhood children with cookies and parties. Sometimes when children are present in the house, people have reported feeling a presence there. A few have reported seeing a misty figure, silently looking at the gathered children.

There are more spirits in the theater prop areas. One of the caretakers was taking a bath and saw wall hangings in another room rustling and billowing. He was later told that there were no curtains or windows in that room, just costumes. Was it a ghost in the room, brushing against the clothes hanging on the walls?

Another theater member was in the basement when she saw something move out of the corner of her eye. She turned to look at it directly. There was nothing there. She felt a growing feeling of menace around her. She left and went into a different room. When she turned on the light, she saw a figure, which hid behind some furniture in the corner of the room. It had disappeared by the time the worker moved to look behind the furniture.

Shops, Sights and Sounds

Name: **St. Johns Road**
Prices: $ (free)
Theme: Roadside Ghost
Open: Year round

St Johns Road is one of Vancouver's oldest roads. It is an ancient Native American trail that ran from what is now west Vancouver out to modern Battle Ground. The current road paved over the original trail, and follows the same meandering route of the original ancient trail.

The Ghosts

St. Johns Road has a guardian spirit or two that may date from the prehistoric period to the late 19th Century. St John's Road runs through an area that is still known as Minnehaha. It used to be a lonely, heavily wooded area. There were pioneer stories about 'the guardian,' a dark figure that escorted people through the woods of Minnehaha. When they left the woods, the figure vanished. The Native American guardian spirit may have vanished with the woods, but there is another ghost.

In the 1940s, a family moved into an old farmhouse that stood near the junction of St. Johns and 78th Street. One dark rainy night, shortly after moving in, the father looked out a window and saw a light moving along the road. He saw a small horse and buggy, traveling north along St. Johns Road. A single kerosene lantern hung from a pole attached to the buggy. A shadowy man was sitting in the buggy, guiding the horse through the rain. The man in the house tried to stop the buggy several times. Each time the buggy driver refused to stop and it and the light disappeared before the home owner could catch up.

Some of the old timers in the neighborhood admitted they saw it too. The man had been a country doctor who served the neighborhood several decades before. One night he rushed to an emergency call. The Doctor missed one of the bridges along the road and drove his buggy into a rain-swollen pond. He and his overheated horse both drowned. Ever since then, their ghosts have been seen, hurrying to an appointment they have already missed.

Name: **Clark County Historical Museum**
Address: 1511 Main Street
Vancouver, WA 8660
Phone Number: **360-695-4681**
Website: www.ohwy.com/wa/c/clarckchm.htm

Prices: $ (donations)
Theme: Historic library turned into museum
Open: Tuesday through Sunday, 1:00 p.m.–5:00 p.m.
Special Facilities: Gift shop, genealogy library

The museum was constructed in 1909, as the Vancouver City Library. It was built with donations from the Carnegie Foundation and other local contributors. In the early 1960s, the Carnegie Library was converted into a museum. It has many static displays as well as rotating exhibits. The static displays include a general store, a printing press, a doctor's office and a railroad museum. There are artifacts from historical figures like Andrew Jackson and U. S. Grant to everyday tools used by ordinary people.

The Ghosts

I stayed overnight in the museum basement once. There are three separate rooms down there: the railroad room, an open visitor's room and an artifact storage room. The railroad exhibit is amazing, the room may be haunted by the spirits of members of The Grand Army of the Republic, a Civil War veteran's society. They used to meet there, but were evicted by the head librarian when they needed the space for bookshelves.

We brought a cassette tape recorder with us and recorded part of the evening the night we were there. When I listened to the tape, I heard myself speaking to my wife. While we were talking, there was a low but distinct sound on the tape that neither one of us heard while we were there. Low, but clear, was the sound of quick, and pant-like breathing.

The Vancouver Barracks

The Vancouver Barracks

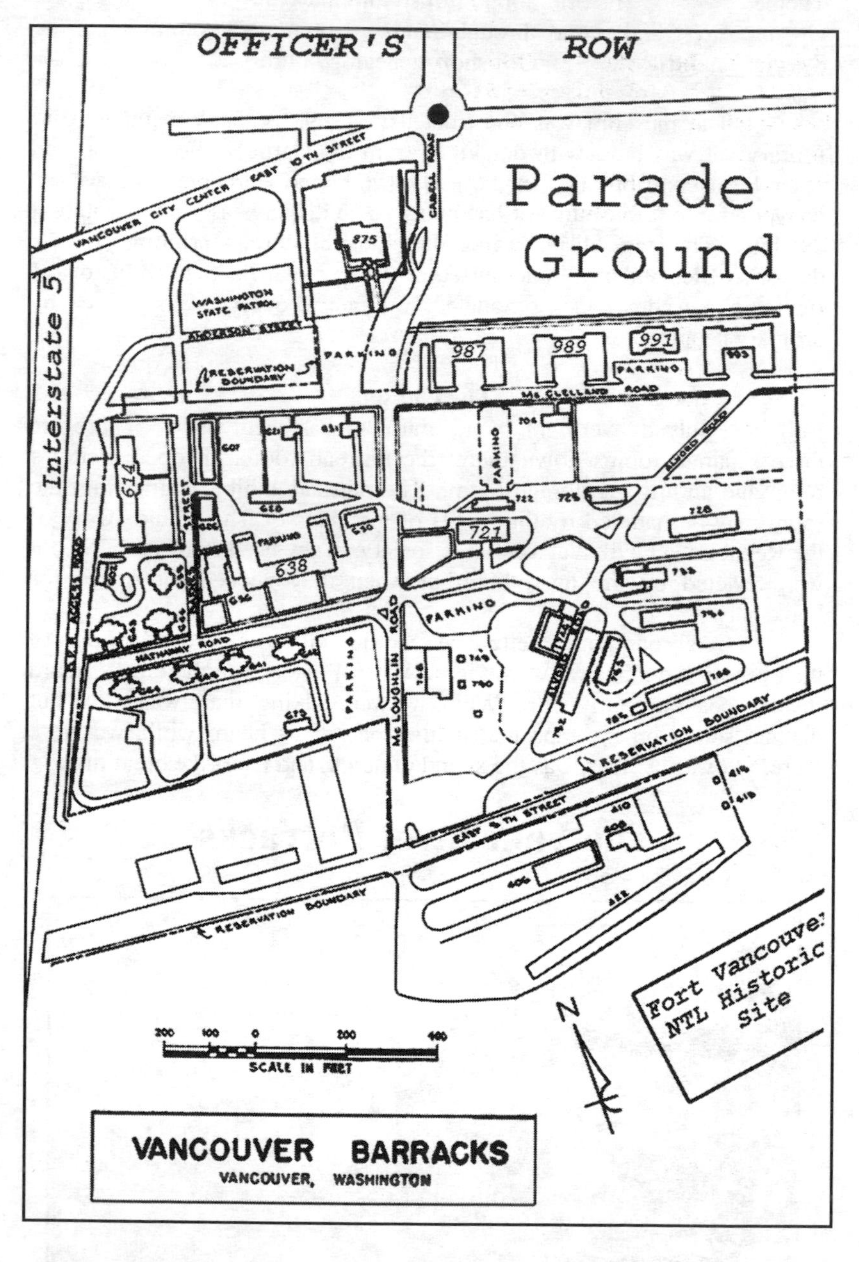

Name: **Ft. Vancouver National Historic Site**
Address: (postal address) 612 E. Reserve Street
Vancouver, WA 98661
Phone Number: **800-832-3599 (info)**
360-696-7655 (info)
Fax Number: 360-696-7657
Website: www.nps.gov/fova
Prices: $$
Theme: Historic Re-creation
Open: March 1st to October 31st, 9:00 a.m.-5:00 p.m.
November 1st, to February 28th, 9:00 a.m.– 4:00 p.m.
Closed, November 23rd, December 24th & 25th.
Special Facilities: Gift shop, interpreters or self-guided tours. Other National Parks Services facilities include nearby O.O. Howard House and Fort Vancouver Visitor's Center
Annual events:
Summer Rendezvous
Winter candle light tours.

Directions: Fort Vancouver is located on Vancouver's east Fifth Street, just east of its intersection with Fort Vancouver Way.

Fort Vancouver was not just a trading post. After 1825, it was the regional headquarters of the Hudson's Bay Company. The Fort was a warehouse, where imported goods like beads were stored for later distribution to smaller trading posts. Wrought iron was imported and turned into knives, axes and traps by the blacksmith and the bakers made hardtack for export. The Chief Factor, a kind of a regional manager for most of this time, was Dr. John McLoughlin. His home in Oregon City is also haunted (see the McLoughlin House).

In 1849, the U.S. Army began constructing the Vancouver Barracks nearby. Homesteading by Americans began around the same time. In the late 1850s the Hudson's Bay Company deserted their post at Ft. Vancouver, and the buildings fell into disuse and burned to the ground. Later, the Fort site was designated a National Historic Site and over the last 30+ years the fort's stockade and other buildings have been reconstructed.

The Ghosts

The cookhouse, next to the Chief Factor's house may be haunted by a poltergeist. The replica of the Cookhouse is complete to fireplace, dishes, dried herbs and maybe the original kitchen staff. A few years ago, a tour guide had finished his tour of the house and escorted the tour group out of the building. He heard a loud banging and clanging. He investigated and found many of the dishes had been gathered and then dropped down the staircase. He was alone and the building was empty.

Most of the guides are very serious about their jobs and don't talk too much about any strange doings at the fort, unfortunately.

Name: **Pearson Air Museum**
Address: 1115 E Fifth Street
Vancouver, WA 98661
Phone Number: **360-694-7026**
Fax Number: 360 694-0824
Website: www.pearsonairmuseum.org
Prices: $
Theme: Historic airstrip and museum
Open: Tuesday through Sunday, 10:00 a.m.– 5:00 p.m.
Special Facilities: Gift shop, interactive displays, guided tours or self-guided

The Pearson Air Museum is located at the eastern end of the Vancouver Historic Reserve. Pearson Airport began as the Army Air Corps airstrip facility for the Vancouver Barracks in the 1920s. Over time it has grown into a combination museum and private airplane storage facility and airport.

The museum has several major components. They include a large display hangar where several historic aircraft such as World War II fighter planes are on display. There is a Computer Resource Center, a Children's Interactive Center, and a theater where national and regional air history films are shown and a restoration center.

The Ghosts

Much of the air museum is new construction, so it does not seem likely that the ghost haunting the large hangar is the result of actions there. It seems more likely that the ghost that haunts the main display hanger is attached to one or more of the airplanes on display. The tour guides are a little closed mouthed about strange doings, but if you get them in private, some may talk about shadows in the corners of the museum.

Officer's Row

Officer's Row is the name given to the former military housing buildings that line Vancouver's Evergreen Boulevard. The oldest buildings date to the 1850s. They are now owned by the City of Vancouver. Some of these buildings are reputably haunted. They are under the management of Key Property Services. They stressed their wish for me to not contact their tenants directly. I am passing this request along to the reader. Please do not go knocking on people's doors looking for ghosts. You can walk down the street and admire people's houses, but please respect their privacy. For the last several years the City of Vancouver has had Halloween "ghost walks" down Officer's Row. I hope they continue in the future.

Name: The Gazebo

South of Evergreen Boulevard, in the Vancouver Barracks there is a Gazebo. This Gazebo was constructed about 15 years ago and has been the sight of many open air concerts and public receptions. In the past, this open area between the Vancouver Barracks buildings and Officer's Row was used as a parade ground. There used to be a sentry post in the parade ground as well. Many couples park near the Gazebo and walk to it at night to be alone in a romantic spot. At least one couple was confronted by the ghost of a past sentry, who threatened to fire, and chased them off.

Name: The Ghostly Housewife

According to legend, in the 19th century, the pregnant wife of a soldier fell down the stairs in one of the Officer's Row buildings and was killed. Her name was Sarah. She has been seen off and on ever since. Sarah appears to women, especially when drinking is involved. She appeared to two women on two separate occasions and warned the women against drinking too much.

Name: The Key Building

The building where Key Property Management has its offices may be haunted. Although this ghost is not unfriendly, he has definite tastes in art. A small shadow box display of a key was kept in the president's office. On two occasions it was knocked from its stand when the building was empty. The "realists" believe that this is also the result of the same building settling that causes the creaks. The employees seem to be evenly divided as to believers and non-believers.

Name: **The Lace Rose Ghost**

One female resident of Officer's Row also shares her house. In her house, lights and clocks were turned on and off of their own accord. The faint odor of perfume seemed to hang in the air. In 1997 she saw a bluish-gray figure wearing a lace rose dress with hair parted in the middle approached her. The figure stared at her. It did not smile, it did not frown, it just stared at her. At that moment the phone rang and the ghost vanished.

Name: **The Nanny of Windemere Realty**

Windemere Realty has offices in two of the Officer's Row buildings. The ghost of a young nanny haunts the attic of one building. In Gothic tradition, she fell in love with the head of the household, and became pregnant by him. In a fit of depression she hung herself in the attic.

One person told me he was outside the empty building one night and watched the lights go on from room to room in sequence. It looked to him as if someone walked in a room, turned on a light, then went into the next and turned on the lights. This happened all the way up to the attic. The staff at Windemere have reported their own experiences. Sometimes all of the telephone lines on the building switchboard will light up as well. Bells have wrung, papers are ruffled and footsteps are still heard in the Windemere Realty building. Like the Key Building, Windemere does not offer ghost tours, so please don't ask to see their ghosts.

Name: **Grant House Folk Art Center and Restaurant**
Address: 1101 W. 13th Street
Vancouver, WA 98661
Phone Number: **360-696-2847**
Prices: $$
Theme: Historic building, multiple use

Cuisine: Gourmet
Sheldon's Café $$
Open: Lunch, Tuesday to Saturday, 11:00 a.m.–2:00 p.m.
Dinner, Tuesday to Saturday, 5:00 p.m.–8:30 p.m.
Special Facilities: Building closed Sundays and Mondays.

The Grant House was built in the early 1850s. It is the oldest building on Officer's Row. The Grant House was originally a log cabin, but changes later added rooms to the cabin and covered the logs with milled boards. A small portion of the original logs can be seen on the main floor in between the main dining room and the outside seating area.

Although it is called the Grant House, Ulysses S. Grant never lived there. He probably spent some of his time there when it was the Post Officer's Club. Many of the Civil War's Union generals probably visited this building when they were junior officers. The building has served as a residence, offices, a museum, and more recently it has been turned into a combination restaurant and folk art center. Some businesses also rent office space on the second floor as well.

The Ghosts

A past restaurant manager frequently heard footsteps outside of her office on the second floor. They would always head down the second story hallway, and down the stairs. She investigated several times and never found an intruder. Not even when the footsteps crossed right in front of where she was standing.

A candidate for this ghost is General Alfred Sully. Sully was a contemporary of O. O. Howard and a Civil War veteran. When he was in residence at the Vancouver Barracks, Sully lived at the Grant House. In the late 1800s, he led several Indian campaigns across the Pacific Northwest. He was plagued by illness, perhaps stomach cancer. Sully died on the eve of a visit by his friend, Ulysses S. Grant. It would be understandable if Scully's spirit walks the hallways of the Grant House.

Name: **Howard House Museum (Building 875)**
Address: 750 Anderson Street
Vancouver, WA 98661
Phone Number: 360-992-1802
Prices: $
Theme: Historic Home turned into museum
Open: March 1st to October 31st, 9:00 a.m.- 5:00 p.m.
November 1st to February 28th, 9:00 a.m.- 4:00 p.m.
Closed: November 24th. December 24th & 25th
Special Facilities: Gift Shop, museum exhibits, and interpretive film, periodic guest speakers

The Howard House is named after Oliver Otis Howard, also known as O. O. Howard. During the Civil War, he rose to the rank of Major General of Volunteers after serving at the first battle of Bull Run and the Battle of Antietam. He lost his right arm at the Battle of Seven Pines, where he got the nickname of 'One Armed Howard.' Howard's command after the Civil War included Washington, Oregon, and parts of Alaska and Idaho.

He ordered many Native American leaders and their families held hostage. He also led the pursuit of Chief Joseph of the Nez Perce. The Howard House was built as his residence in 1879. In the 1960s the building was a non-commissioned officer's club and barbershop. A fire gutted the interior of the building in the 1980s and it was vacant for several years. Eventually, the U.S. Army gave the building to the U.S. Park's Service, which formed a partnership with several preservation groups. After several major architectural changes, the building was opened as a visitor's center.

The Ghosts

In April of 1999, one of the large glass panels for the exhibit, entitled "One Place Across Time," was found shattered. A government representative joked that the ghosts of the Howard House shattered the panel. Through a process of elimination, civil engineers suggested that the new addition had settled, and the stress on the case shattered the glass.

The security system there detects intruders and can track them through the building. There have been several nightly incidents when the alarm sensors have detected someone appearing in one of the second story rooms. This person moves from room to room and then disappears from the alarm monitors. This may tie into earlier reports of ghosts on the second floor.

In the early 1990s the Post Commander and his son saw a ghostly figure silhouetted in one of the second story windows. The Howard House was still vacant and covered with tarps and plywood. The two of them noticed a white figure moving back and forth between the two front rooms on the second floor. Volunteers and staff do not like to discuss any of these happenings.

The Vancouver Barracks

The Vancouver Barracks were established opposite the Hudson's Bay Company's Fort Vancouver in 1849. The original Post extended from the present Vancouver Barracks to the location of Clark College. The alumni of the soldiers who served or passed through here include Ulysses S. Grant, George McClellan, Philip Sheridan, William T. Sherman, Otis Oliver Howard and George Marshall. Under the heading of The Barracks, the military complex included several troop barracks, stables, storage warehouses, a hospital, auditorium and an arsenal made of brick and wood.

In 2001 Congress voted to close down portions of the Vancouver Barracks and turn over ownership to the City of Vancouver. As this books goes to press, the city is still debating what to do with the buildings. Will they become museums, offices, or residences? Some of them are haunted.

Name: **Building 614, The Vancouver Barracks Hospital**

Building 614 was the post hospital from the 1880s until the beginning of World War II. The newest portion was built before World War I. There are spirits here that may date to its early history. When the hospital was built, it was only a decade or two after the practice of the surgeon washing his hands before operating was a novelty.

It would take too much time here to describe all of the strange manifestations that have taken place there over the years. They include, locked doors becoming unlocked, mechanical devises like video cameras and cellular phone batteries going dead. Toilet seat lids in bathrooms

have been raised and lowered between visits, when no one but observers have been in the building.

People working the basement spaces, which had been the morgue, have been bothered by the sound of whispering voices. Other people sleeping in the basement have been awakened when the table they were laying on began shaking. Windows in third floor rooms have been broken from the inside, even when the building was empty. For more information, please visit my website at: www.ghostsandcritters.com

Name: Building 638, Post Headquarters

Building 638 was last used as the headquarters building of the active duty Army garrison. More than one ghost has been seen or heard within its walls. A civilian employee followed the sound of footsteps through the building. When the footsteps reached the end of the hall, the door opened on its own and then swung shut. A soldier heard a curious clicking noise and followed it. He opened the door to the recreation room and saw two men in 19th century military dress uniforms playing billiards. They turned around, looked at him and disappeared.

Several years ago, the Garrison Commander saw a woman walk out of his office, into his secretary's. He investigated and found his secretary alone. In the mid 1990s a visitor was allowed to keep a ghost vigil in the Commander's office. During the night the Ouija board she took along warned her to get out. She later confronted a young man who was dressed in military clothing at least 15 years out of date.

Name: Building 721, The Auditorium

Before the Pacific Northwest was a U.S. Territory, the Hudson's Bay Company built a stockade and a Catholic Church and cemetery. The people buried in the cemetery were employees of the Hudson's Bay Company. Many of the common employees were Scots/Irish, French Canadians, Indian people of mixed heritage and Hawaiians, sometimes called Kanakans. Most could not afford more than a wooden marker, especially for children.

In the 1880s the graves, the marked ones at least, were moved to the current military cemetery. The US Army built the Auditorium over the cemetery sometime after that. In the 1980s, graves were discovered when workers repaired a broken pipe. In 1993, toxic waste clean up forced the military to dig up some of the bones. The U.S. Army Garrison Commander contacted the Cowlitz Indian Tribe's Shaman, who re-sanctified the graves once the clean up was finished.

The Auditorium is now used as a fitness center by the military garrison and its employees. Footsteps have been heard going up and down the stairs when no one was there. The door to the latrine (bathroom), downstairs has been seen and heard opening and slamming shut when no one has been inside.

The Hudson's Bay Company Graveyard as drawn by Richard Covington in the 1850s.. A few gravestones are visible.

Name: **Building 987**

Building 987 was originally constructed as a barracks to house single soldiers. Decades ago, the open bays were converted into smaller rooms. The 104th Division now uses it as offices. A psychic visited the Vancouver Barracks in 1995 and saw the ghost of a young girl looking out of a window at the parade grounds. This is strange since the residents would have all been bachelors. In 2000 workers digging up a leaky natural gas line discovered bones, buttons and other items that may have come from a grave. A record check shows that this building may have been built over the old cemetery as well.

Name: **Building 989**

Like Building 987, this building was built around the turn of the century to scrvc as troop barracks. At least one soldier reported hearing footsteps in the third floor attic spaces above his office. Several times he was the only person in the building and he found the door to the third floor stairway open, when it had been locked earlier.

Building 991

This building is the former post headquarters. Over the last several years workers reported footsteps on the second floor, walking down the stairs to the first floor. The stories of this continued even after one military unit left the building and were replaced by another. The incidents are still happening.

Camas, WA

Name: **Lacamas Lake (Vancouver Parks & Recreation)**
Address: 3016 SE Everett Road
Camas, WA
Phone Number: **360-696-8171**
Fax Number: 360-696-8009
Website: www.ci.vancouver.wa.us/parks-recreation
Prices: $
Theme: Park
Open: Year around
Special Facilities: Trail, swimming and fishing

Lacamas Lake was originally formed by an earthquake several thousand years ago. The lake that we see today is not entirely natural. In 1884, newspaper publisher Henry Pittock had a dam built to supply power for the mill, which made paper for his newspaper. This raised the water level by several feet. The lake is about five miles in diameter, and most of the lake is 24 feet deep or shallower. There are three to seven miles of trails around the lake.

Old timers from Camas tell stories about the Gush-Gush monster of Lacamas Lake. Many old timers remember going down to the lake and hearing a *gush-squelch...gush-squelch* sound. People tried to follow the sound to find its source. The old timer and his friends used to go down to the lake and park with their girlfriends. The strange noise gave them an excuse for snuggling.

Name: **Riverside Bowl**
Address: 3010 NE Third Avenue
Camas, WA 98607
Phone Number: **360-834-4982**
Prices: $$
Theme: Bowling alley/Indian Burial Ground
Open: Monday through Thursday, 10:00 a.m.– 9:00 p.m.
Friday, 10:00 a.m.- 7:00 p.m.;
Saturday, 10:00 a.m.-6:00 p.m.

In 1792, English sailor Lieutenant William Broughton traveled up the Columbia River in a small ships boat. He stopped at a large village in between the cities of Washougal and Camas. Folklore has it that the bowling alley was built on top of this village and its burial ground. At night, chanting has been reportedly heard from the bowling alley parking lot. Lights have been seen flickering in the nearby sloughs.

To protect and preserve this area, the City of Camas has constructed a short trail in the sloughs and put up interpretive signs about the prehistory of the area. The bowling alley patrons and management ignore the stories.

The Columbia River Gorge

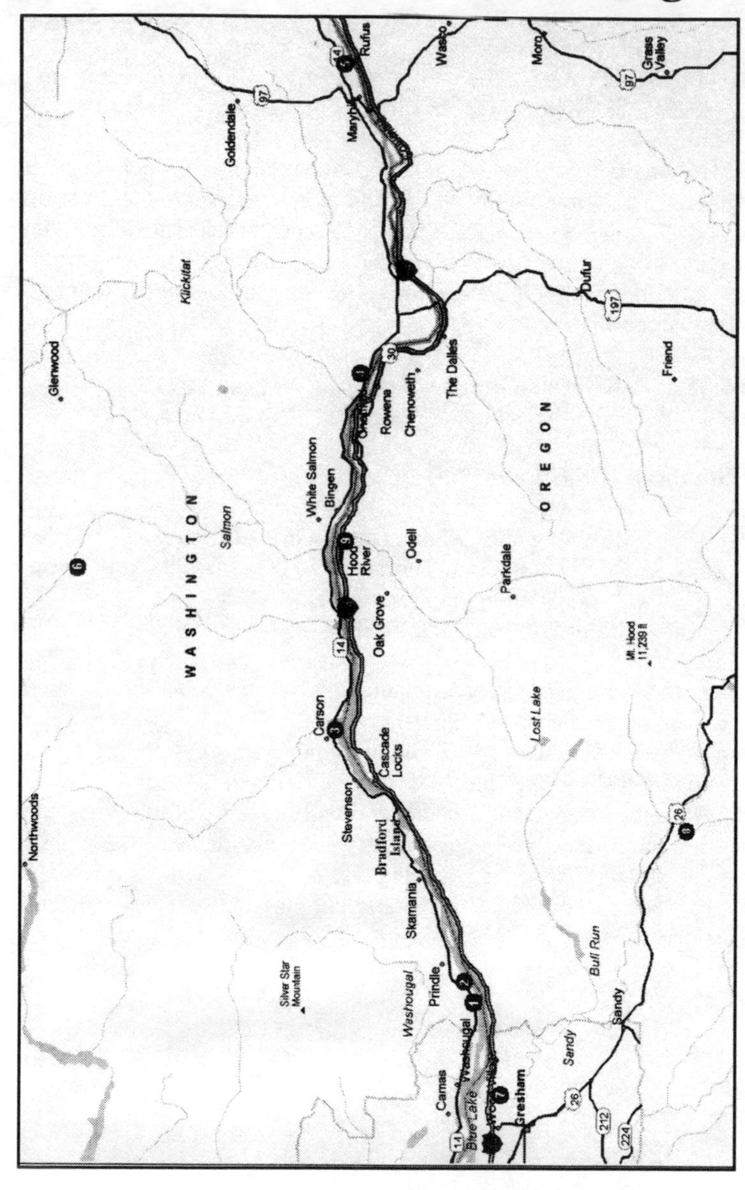

1) Mt. Pleasant Grange, 2) Cape Horn, 3) Carson Hot Springs, 4) Horsethief Lake State Park, 5) Stonehenge Monument, 6) Trout Lake Ranger Station, 7) Edgefield Poorhouse, 8) Welches B&B, 9) Hood River Hotel © GDT 2001

The Columbia River Gorge

This section begins at the west-end of the Gorge, on the Washington side first. Haunts are listed in order, heading east. It begins again at the west-end, of the Oregon side, before visiting eastern Oregon.

The Washington Side

Name: **Mt. Pleasant Grange Hall**
Address: Intersection of Marble Road
And SR 14, at about the 23 mile marker, look for the interpretive sign
Prices: $ (free)
Theme: Historic building

In December of 1867, Oliver Kelly and six men founded a secret society they called the National Grange of the Patrons of Husbandry, or 'The Grange.' Grange members identify each other by a series of passwords and rituals. By 1875, there were over 1,000,000 Grangers in the United States. The Grange did everything from forming cooperative buying clubs, to lobbying for political reform. Individual Grange Halls, like the Mount Pleasant Grange, were often the only public building where farming communities could gather to do everything, from celebrating a great harvest, to planning how to cope with a drought. It was the heart of the community.

The Ghosts

In August of 1999, a couple visited the Grange Hall to look at the interpretive sign about the history of the Grange hall. The husband saw the ghosts of several farmers standing around the Grange Hall. You cannot go into the Grange Hall, but it is an interesting building, which overlooks the Gorge. There used to be live music on summer weekends, but that has ceased.

Name: **Cape Horn**
Address: SR 14, at about the 25 mile marker, look for the traffic turn out/viewpoint
Prices: $ (free)
Theme: Historic highway

For many years, State Route 14 was not paved. There are still frequent landslides and slips on the highway as it hugs the mountainside. One of the most dangerous places is Cape Horn. At Cape Horn, there

was no way to carve a road into the solid rock face. Instead, engineers constructed a concrete bridge, which they attached to the rock face. Since then, many people have driven off of Cape Horn and fallen to the valley below. Most have died, surprisingly, some people have survived!

The Ghosts

In January of 2000, a couple driving east across Cape Horn were having an argument. When they crossed the bridge, a man dressed like a farmer stepped out in front of the car. The wife was driving and tried to stop, but drove through the man, who disappeared.

Carson, WA

Name:	**Carson Hot Springs Hotel**
Address:	1 Saint Martin Road
	Carson, WA 98610
Phone Number:	**509-427-8292**
Web site:	www.ohwy.com/wa/c/carminhs.htm
Rooms:	Nine rooms in hotel, 12 cabins
Prices:	$$
Theme:	Historic health spa
Cuisine:	Northwest
Open:	Restaurant opens for breakfast, lunch and dinner

Special Facilities: European style mineral bath soak, massage, no TV, no phones, some units have kitchens and full baths. Deluxe hot tub suite, 18 hole golf course

The Carson Mineral Hot Springs or 'Hotel St. Martin' was built in 1876, by pioneer Isadore St. Martin. He had lived a hard but interesting life. He was an army scout at the age of 13, during the Indian wars of 1855. He married in 1865 and had ten children. After this active life he settled down to build a hotel and retire. In 1910, St. Martin had a disagreement with 'Old Man' Brown, who taunted him about the medicinal value of the Hot Springs. St. Martin threw Brown off the property and during the struggle, St. Martin was stabbed in the chest with a penknife. He died later in the hotel. Mrs. St. Martin was devastated and did not survive him for very long.

The hotel still keeps its historic character intact. The bathroom is down the hall and the restaurant specializes in seasonal foods. The traditional European bathhouse allows guests to soak in large size tubs and then move to quiet benches where they are wrapped in towels. The baths are segregated by gender.

The Ghosts

The hotel ghost is particular about how the housekeeping staff does their job. If the beds are not made up right, they are pulled apart by unseen hands. Some of the staff have had glimpses of an elderly lady moving about the second story rooms and hallway at the front of the hotel. When they follow to investigate, the woman has vanished. The third floor of the hotel is no longer used. People have also heard the sound of footsteps up there at night.

Name: **Horsethief Lake State Park**
Location: 17 Miles east of White Salmon, WA, (Mile Post 85)
Phone Number: **509-767-1159**
Web site: www.parks.wa.gov/horsthef.htm
Prices: $$
Theme: Sacred Native American site and campground
Open: Tours by appointment summer - fall
Special Facilities: 12 campsites, 35 picnic sites, comfort station, two boat launches, trailer dump, two miles of trail

Horsethief Lake State Park begins at the north bank of the Columbia River and extends north, into a small canyon in the Gorge. It received its name when workers at the park thought that the narrow canyon would have been the perfect place for movie horse thieves to hide. There are several pieces of Native American art on the canyon wall. The most impressive pictograph is called Tsagigla'lal. The name translates into *She Who Watches*. She may have been a territorial marker. Another belief is that she watches over the graves of people killed by the

plagues that struck the Native people after Columbus landed.

Many people believe there is some power in the old drawings. Some leave offerings, such as shells filled with flowers or tobacco. Others have shots bullets at the rocks or drawn over the original pictures. To protect the site, visitors are only permitted to visit *She Who Watches* when escorted by a park ranger. Tours must be arranged in advance and are only conducted on Fridays and Saturdays from April to October.

Please do not desecrate this Native American Spiritual site.

Name:	**Stonehenge Monument**
Address:	East of Goldendale, WA Near mile marker 102 on SR 14
Prices:	$ (free)
Theme:	Monument
Open:	Year round, daylight hours

Directions: Head East of Goldendale on SR 14. Start looking for road signs after the 100 mile marker. Follow the signs south, off of the highway to the monument.

Industrialist Sam Hill was vacationing in England at the height of World War I. He visited the real Stonehenge monument. At that time people believed that the druids performed human sacrifices there. When he returned to the United States, Hill decided to build a replica as a monument to the tragedy of World War I. He wanted to construct the monument as an exact replica of what the real Stonehenge might have looked like when it was first built.

It took over a decade, but the monument was dedicated in 1930. According to one theory, the monument is placed out of alignment so that it does not function as a calendar and druids could not use it. If that is true, it did not work. Every year hundreds of people arrive in spring, summer and fall to celebrate ancient festivals. Sam Hill is buried in a granite cenotaph below the monument.

The Washington Cascades

Serial murder **Ted Bundy** lived in Washington State for some years before he went on a killing spree that ended in Florida. There are stories that one of his first victims was a young coed, whom he killed and buried near a fountain on one of Washington's colleges. I have heard this story attributed to many colleges in Washington and Oregon. Just as suspect is the story that after he was executed, Ted Bundy was cremated and his ashes were spread across the Washington Cascades.

There are several strange and unusual places in the southern Washington Cascades, within the Gifford Pinchot National Forest. For overall information on how to reach some of these places, you might check with the Forest Headquarters, or the nearest ranger station. The recreation and information staff are used to strange questions, but do not maintain a data base of strange sights. You might not get the information you want. Hiking the trails on the Gifford Pinchot used to be free, but federal budget cuts have made it necessary for the Forest Service to begin charging fees. So be careful about where you park, you may need to pay a user's fee.

Name: **Gifford Pinchot National Forest**
Forest Headquarters:
10600 NE 51st Circle
Vancouver, WA 98682
Phone Number: **360-891-5000**
Fax Number: 360-891-5045
Web site: www.fs.fed.us/gpnf
Prices: $
Theme: Natural wonders
Open: 8:30 a.m.– 4:30 p.m.
Special Facilities: Forest information

Name: **Silver Star Pits**

Silver Star Mountain is located north of Camas, east of the Clark/Skamania County line. There are a series of pits and rock features constructed out of the rocky slopes by Native Americans. Were these hunting blinds or were they part of a vision quest ritual? A historic trail passes through the pits.

Please do not desecrate this Native American Spiritual site.

For information on how to reach the trail, I would recommend contacting the Forest Headquarters. The area used to be administered out of Wind River. Their offices are listed below.

Name: **Wind River Information Center**
Address: 1262 Hemlock Road
Carson, WA 98610
Phone Number: **509-427-3200**
Fax Number: 509-427-3215
Prices: $
Theme: Historic USFS compound
Open: Seasonal, call visitor's center
Special Facilities: Gift shop, some permits sold here

Name: **Ape Canyon**

In the early 20th century a mining camp was attacked by a group of bigfoot in an area known today as 'Ape Canyon.' I do not know if there are any Forest Service roads or trails that can access Ape Canyon. The area is within the Mt. St. Helen's National Volcanic Monument.

Name: **Mt. St. Helen's National Volcanic Monument**
Address: 42218 NE Yale Bridge Road
Amboy, WA 98611
Phone Number: **360-274-2131**
Fax Number: 360-274-2129
Prices: $
Open: Seasonal, call visitor's center
Special Facilities: Gift shop, some permits available

Name: **Goose Lake Lava Prints**
Address: Mt. Adams Ranger District
2455 Hwy 141
Trout Lake, WA 98650
Phone Number: **509-395-3422**
Fax Number: 509-395-3434
Theme: Ancient Wonder
Open: Seasonal, call visitor's center
Special Facilities: Gift shop, some permits sold

Directions: The Mt. Adams Ranger District Offices are located in Trout Lake. To get there, head east on either SR 14 or I 84 to Bingen/ White Salmon, Washington. Head north on SR 141 about 25 miles to Trout Lake. Follow the signs to the Ranger Station.

On the wall of the Visitor's Center you will see a large plaster cast hanging on the walls. This plaster cast is a copy of an imprint of hands and footprints made in the soft lava that formed the floor of Goose Lake. Goose Lake was created by a volcano 2,000 to 10,000 years ago.

The Ghost

According to Native American stories, an evil brave pursued a woman to the top of Lemei Peak. The peak overlooked a lava flow. Faced with the threat of the rape or death, she chose death and jumped off the peak. She landed on the lava flow, feet first and then fell forward, burying her hands in the soft liquid rock. Her ghost is supposed to appear on the shore of Goose Lake, combing her long hair.

In the 1930s, Goose Lake was dammed up and the prints disappeared under the water. In the early 1990s, the prints were relocated underwater. The Forest Service built a small dam around the prints, pumped the water out and made a plaster cast of the lake bottom. This is the cast displayed at Trout Lake. They removed the dam and the handprints were again hidden underwater. The Visitor's Center can provide you directions to Goose Lake.

The Oregon Side of the Gorge

Troutdale, Oregon

Name:	**McMenamin's Edgefield**
Address:	2126 SW Halsey Troutdale, OR 97060
Phone Number:	**800-669-8610** **503-669-8160** **503-225-5555 ext 8834 (theater)**
Web site	www.mcmenamins.com
Rooms:	100 rooms
Prices:	$ - $$$
Theme:	Historic building now European style B&B
Cuisine:	Pub grub to fine dining

Black Rabbit $$$
Power Station $$

Open: Year Round
Black Rabbit: Breakfast, lunch and dinner
Pub opens Monday – Sunday, 11:00 a.m.– 1:30 p.m.

Special Facilities: Gift shop, several thematic bars, wine tasting room, original artwork, massage, gardens, 3 par golf course, free historic tours of facility, movie theater

Before modern social welfare programs in the United States, poorhouses were established in many cities or counties. The aged, infirm, disabled or generally indigent were placed there when they could not support themselves. If the land was fertile or had resources that could be exploited, the poorhouse could turn a profit. This was sometimes done using inmates from prisons or jails. Fortunately, the Edgefield was a prosperous and humanely run facility.

The poorhouse was built in 1911 on a 330-acre site as a farm, dining facility, administrative offices, with rooms for residents. The facility stayed open until 1982, changing from poorhouse to nursing home as its inmate's aged. In 1990 the McMenamins purchased the buildings and over a period of several years restored many of them to their present condition. This includes the present Edgefield Winery and brewery facilities and bed and breakfast. Over the years employees and guests have noticed strange things in most of the Edgefield buildings.

The Ghosts

The number of ghosts and hauntings reported by employees and guests is too long to chronicle here. I can only give a short list of the haunted locales and a few sentences on the paranormal goings on there.

The Winery Building entrance: One night, a security guard was blinded by the headlight of a bicycle ridden by an old man. When the guard could see again, the man was gone.

The WineTasting Room: This room had been a final care room for terminal patients when it was an elderly care facility. Wine casks were moved when no one was in the stacking room. A wine server heard footsteps entering the room when no one was there. The same employee trapped a cat in the back room, only to have it disappear.

The Power Station Restaurant: When the power station opened as a restaurant, employees watched food and utensils move without human aid. Invisible presences were felt.

The Althea Room: The ghost of a little girl haunts the top floor room of the Administrator's Residence. She sometimes wakes up guests in the middle of the night, wanting to play. I heard footsteps walking down the stairs from the Althea Room when the only occupant was asleep.

The Study: is located in the main building. In 1999, a worker took a nap there before going home. He slept for a few minutes when he was awakened by a disembodied voice in his ear, saying "PSSSSST!"

Room 20: Guests have reported that the bed will sometimes slide away from the wall in the middle of the night.

Room 34: Has a resident ghost that likes to shake people by the ankles. When they wake up, some of them have seen a tall woman standing at the foot of their beds. She has been known to play tricks on people.

Room 37: A couple woke up to find a woman in 1950s clothing pacing about in their room. She vanished when they approached her.

Room 38: Guests have seen a strange man pacing about in their room. He leaves by picking up a set of invisible keys and walking out.

Room 215: Had a pentagram painted on the floor while the building was vacant. Bagpipers performed an exorcism when the room was opened. The ghost of a friendly dog wakes people up in the middle of the night.

Second floor hallway: Some guests have seen an old man shambling down the hallway. Sometimes he is walking a dog.

The Cat in the attic: When the maintenance workers opened the attic door on the third floor near Room 307, a suitcase fell down. They found a mummified cat inside the case. In April of 2000, a guest staying in **Room 307:** heard a cat meowing outside her room one night. She investigated and opened a door to let the cat out, the room was empty.

Rooms 305 and 306: were originally one room, the Women's Hostel. A security guard watched a rocking chair rock under its own power for several minutes.

The hallway leading to Rooms 311-315: In 1999 a staffer admired one of the new paintings in the hallway. When she brought a friend to look at it, the painting was gone. In April of 2000, the heavy hallway doors closed on an employee. The heavy door at the end of the hallway is sometimes found open, when it should be locked.

Name: **Old Welches Inn**
Address: 26401 East Welches Road
Welches, OR 97067
Phone Number: **503-622-3754**
Fax Number: 503-622-5370
Web site: www.lodging-mthood.com
Rooms: Four rooms & cottage
Prices: $$ - $$$
Theme: Country Inn
Cuisine: Full breakfast
Open: Year round
Special Facilities: Two night minimum stay certain times of the year, fireplace, located inside the Hoodland Recreation Area, smoking areas, some restrictions on children, some pets allowed, no wheelchair access

Directions: From Portland, head east on Highway 26, past Sandy, to Welches. Turn right (south) on Welches Road. The Inn is on the right (west) side of the road.

In 1890, William Welch, the son of Welches founder, Samuel Welch, built the Old Welches Inn, also known as the Welches Roadhouse. It was the first summer resort on Mt. Hood. He operated the resort until 1930, when he retired. He and his wife Jeanne converted the hotel into a home. They tore down a large portion of the original building and remodeled the remainder into the present Old Welches Inn.

The Ghosts

In some ghost circles, the Welches Inn is famous for its haunting. In the past there were stories of a possible love triangle that led to the suicide of a woman and eventual death of the men involved. She was seen several times in the upstairs area and at one point blew out a candle. A male ghost was not seen, but was felt by several people. A rocking chair moved without human aide.

The ghost or ghosts seemed to have settled down in recent years. According to the present owners, there was increased activity when they did some remodeling in the late 1990s. They still lose items, only to have the item appear in a strange place later.

Name: **Hood River Hotel**
Address: 102 Oak Street
Hood River, OR 97031
Phone Number: **800-386-1859**
541-386-1900
Fax Number: 541-386-6090
Web site: www.hoodriverhotel.com
Rooms: 41
Prices: $ - $$$ Seasonal rates apply
Theme: Historic Hotel
Cuisine: Italian
Pasquale's Ristorante, $$$
Open: Restaurant opens for breakfast, lunch & dinner
Special Facilities: Meeting facilities, television, exercise room with Jacuzzi & sauna, email service, airport shuttle

The Hood River Hotel was constructed in 1913 as an addition or annex to the older, Victorian Mt. Hood Hotel, built in the 1880s. In the 1920s, the older wooden structure was demolished and the hotel lobby was transferred to the present Hood River Hotel. Like many older hotels in the Pacific Northwest, the Hood River suffered during the 1960s and 1970s. It was used as a boarding house hotel until Pasquale Barone, the present owner, purchased it in 1988. He spent several months restoring and upgrading the hotels facilities.

Barone used local craftsmen to restore the original look of the hotel, including the marble faced fireplace in the lobby and the brass work on the original elevator. Each room has its own bathroom, though the bathroom in the room I had looks like it was a converted closet.

The Ghosts

I heard an unconfirmed report that the hotel elevator was haunted. This was several years ago. I contacted the hotel for information but they have not responded.

Eastern Washington and Oregon

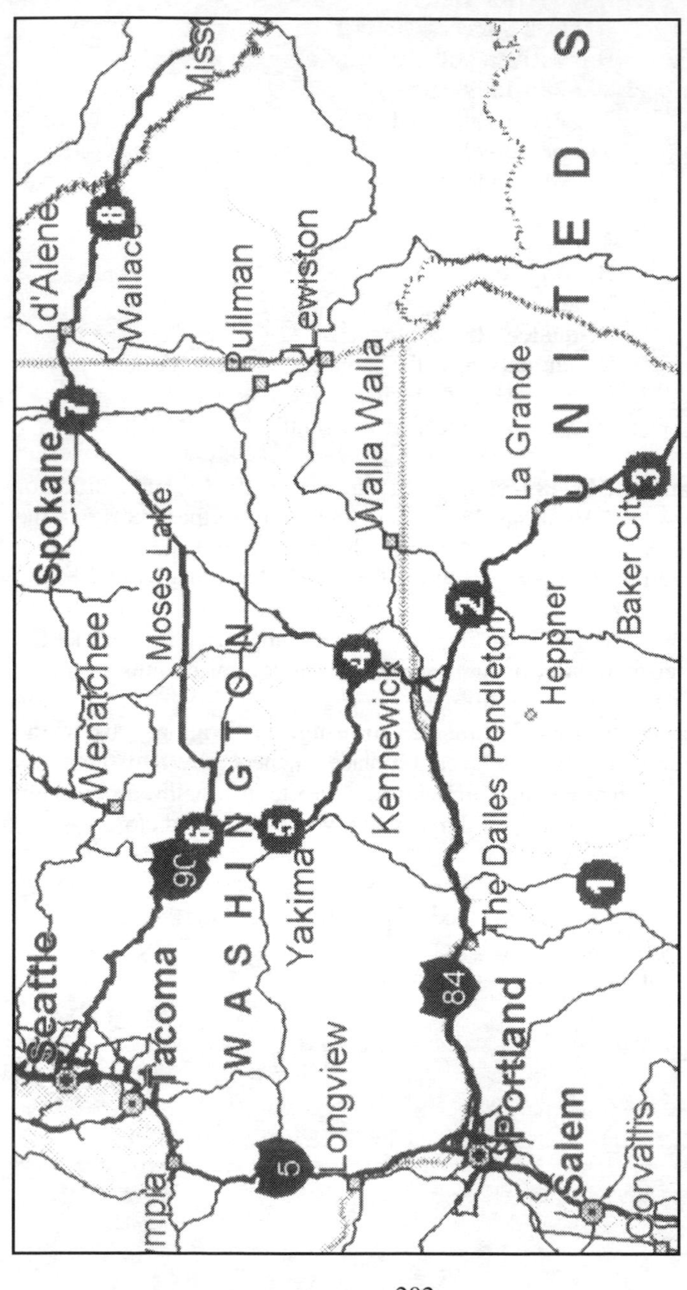

1) Shaniko, 2) Pendleton, 3) Baker City, 4) Pasco, 5) Yakima, 6) Ellensburg, 7) Yakima, 8) Spokane, 9) Wallace, ID © 2001, GDT

Eastern Washington and Oregon

Shaniko

The original name of Shaniko was 'Cross Hollows.' The Cross Hollows Post Office opened in 1879. August Scherneckau was its first postmaster. In 1887 he sold his land to Gustav Schmidt and moved to Astoria. He left his name behind, sort-of. Later residents corrupted the name Scherneckau into Shaniko. Things moved slowly until 1900, when the first train line arrived. Within a few years Shaniko became the central storage and shipping point for eastern Oregon's wool industry. After 1903, wool sales topped over five million dollars before competition and economic pressures ended Shaniko's wool economy. Today Shaniko has around two dozen year round residents.

Name: **Morelli's Bed & Breakfast**
Address: 48812 D St
Shaniko, OR 97057
Phone Number: **541-489-3324**
503-632-3355
Website www.shaniko-oregon.com/bedandbrkfast.htm
Rooms: 3
Prices: $
Theme: Western
Cuisine: Country
Open: Year round

Directions: Take I-84 about 20 miles east of The Dalles. Head south on State Hwy 97 about 94 miles to Shaniko.

The Morelli family have lived in Shaniko for generations. They have turned their turn of the 19th century home into a western themed B&B. Mrs. Morelli is proud of her Elvis room. She is the head of the Chamber of Commerce, and has the keys to the Shaniko Schoolhouse.

The Ghosts

Visitors have reported the sound of ghostly footsteps in the upstairs of the Morelli home. Mrs. Morelli has not heard the footsteps, but she admits she's a little hard of hearing. Others have heard them, and ghost hunters have captured images of orbs in their digital photographs.

I have friends who stayed in Shaniko and were allowed to visit the old school house, which also doubled as a wedding chapel. While they were in the basement they were surrounded by several shadows.

They checked but could not find an outside source for the shadows, which began moving around the basement.

Redmond, Oregon

Name: **Crooked River Dinner Train**
Crooked River Railroad Company
Address: 4075 NE O'Neil Road
Redmond OR 97756
Phone Number: **541-548-8630**
Website: www.crookedriverrailroad.com
Prices: $$$
Theme: Historic train ride
Cuisine: Gourmet
Open: See website for prices, times of events

Directions: See their website for directions

Americans have an open love affair with cars. Many Americans have a secret affection for old fashioned trains. I don't know why they don't ride AMTRACK more often though? The Crooked River Railroad Company has restored numerous old train engines and cars and runs tours through eastern Oregon. Some of the tours are short term excursions, others are dinner theaters, with many themes. There are murder/mystery excursions, dinner theater as well as a live action train robbery. At certain times they also have a buffet excursion.

The Ghosts

One of their dinner cars is haunted. One of their actors was performing in a dinner theater. He may have been admiring himself a bit when he glanced at a mirror hanging on the wall. He saw himself in costume, and a little boy dressed in 1900s period clothing, standing next to him. He looked down at his side, and saw that he was alone. Another employee has heard a woman's voice talking, when everyone in the car was eating quietly. The car itself dates to the 1940s, which is an interesting fact, since the boy is apparently an older spirit. Did they use parts salvaged from an older train car when this one was built?

Pendleton

Name: **Pendleton Arts Center**
Address: 214 N Main Street
Pendleton, OR 97801
Phone Number: **541- 78-9201**
Web site: www.pendletonarts.org
Prices: $ - $$$
Theme: Historic building turned into arts center
Open: Call or check website for times
Special Facilities: Art displays, live performances, community art classes

The Pendleton Arts Center is housed in the city's original 1916 Carnegie Library. The library closed for normal operations in the late 1990s due to structural problems. In 1997 the former library was taken over by the Arts Center. The aim of the Arts Center has been to establish education programs in art performances, fine art exhibits and arts education. Over the last few years they have begun that work and have made significant changes to the old building.

The Ghosts

There are two different versions of how Ruth Cochran's ghost came to haunt the building when it was a library. The first is that she committed suicide there. Ruth was despondent over a failed love affair and she went down into the basement of the library and swallowed a box of lye. She was found later and rushed to the hospital, but it was too late. According to the *Pendleton East Oregonian*, in 1947 Ruth suffered a cerebral hemorrhage. The next morning she was found in the basement and taken to the hospital where she died. Neither explanation is nice.

Librarians heard footsteps between shelves. Ruth liked air in the library, because windows opened by themselves and the building lights flickered on and off of their own accord. Even after the conversion, some people still hear strange noises in the basement but the center's director attributes those sounds to expanding pipes or animals in the attic. It may well be. It may also be that without the stacks of books Ruth had no reason to remain.

Name: **Pendleton Underground Tours**
Working Girls Hotel
Address: 37 SW Emigrant Street
Pendleton, OR 97801
Phone Number: **800-226-6398**
541-276-0730

Website: www.pendletonundergroundtours.org
Rooms: Four rooms, one suite
Prices: $ - $$ seasonal rates apply
Tour Price: $$
Theme: Historic tours & boarding house
Open: March – October, Monday – Saturday, 9:30 a.m.– 3:00 p.m.
November – February, four days a week.
Call for exact days and times

Special Facilities: Gift shop, book tours in advance, hotel has air conditioning, wood stoves, hardwood floors, Victorian décor, no children,

The Ghosts

There are, strictly speaking, no ghosts in the tours, except perhaps for the ghosts of Pendleton's secret past. In 1989 the Pendleton Underground Tours began giving tours of the city's red light district, which included bordellos, casinos, opium dens and other illegal dens that operated underneath the respectable ground level of the city of Pendleton. They met with resistance from conservative elements within Pendleton's community, but the tours continue. A decade ago, one of Pendleton's 18 bordellos was restored and opened as the Working Girl's Hotel.

Baker City

Name: **Geyser Grand Hotel**
Address: 1996 Main Street
Baker City, OR 97814
Phone Number: **888-GEISERG**
541-523-1889
Fax Number: 541-523-1800
Rooms: 30
Prices: $$ - $$$
Theme: Historic luxury hotel
Cuisine: Gourmet
Geiser Grill, $$
Open: Restaurant open daily, 7:00 a.m.– 9:00 p.m.

Special Facilities: Non smoking, indoor pool, meeting facilities, air conditioning, cable TV, Beauty/barber shop, fitness center, handicap accessible rooms.

Directions: Take Exit 304 on I 84, follow the brown historic signs to Main Street. The hotel is located on 19th Street.

The Geiser Grand Hotel was built in 1889 and was the finest hotel between Portland and Salt Lake City. Architects used Austrian crystal chandeliers and mahogany trim was used throughout the lobby to create a European theme. White-gloved waiters handed customers daily menus, written in French. Over the years, the hotel's clientele changed, as it became a casino, brothel, a veteran's hospital and eventually a derelict building when it closed its doors in 1969.

In 1997, the Geiser Grand reopened after a three-year refit. Guests in the dining room are treated to a stained glass ceiling and light bouncing off of 100 crystal chandeliers. The owners have included several interpretive displays of local history in the hotel. They also sponsor dinner theater, living history recreations and live music.

The Ghosts

During remodeling the ghosts became very active. One graveyard shift workman saw one female apparition at least 20 times. She was dressed in a red corset, wearing a peacock feather hat that was popular in the 1920s. He also saw a Blue Lady, wearing a blue, 1930s style dress, hat and veil.

The hotel owner, Barbara Sidway, saw the Blue Lady several times. She took it in stride, though it could become aggravating. In addition to the quiet Blue Lady, there are ghostly parties at night. The hotel owner followed the sound of late partying to a room on the third floor. When he approached the door, the noise stopped abruptly. The room was empty.

Spokane

1) Spokane Civic Theater, 2) Garland & Cedar Street, 3) Patsy Clark's Mansion Restaurant, 4) Cameo Catering © GDT 2001

Eastern Washington

Spokane

<u>Restaurants, Clubs and Theaters</u>

Name: **Cameo Catering & Event Facility**
Address: 1017 West First Avenue
Spokane, WA 99204
Phone Number: **509-363-0505**
Fax Number: 509-363-0098
Web site: www.cameocatering.com
Prices: $$ - $$$
Theme: Historic Lodge
Cuisine: Varied
Open: By event
<u>Special Facilities:</u> Large ballroom, meeting room, original billiard room, Odd Fellows regalia on display throughout building

In 1998 the Spokane Odd Fellows, moved out of their long term building to a new location. They left behind many original items of their organization including some uniforms, records, and a need for a deep clean. After months of hard work Cameo Catering opened for special events. They have done wonderful things to restore the 1909 building to its original glory. A mosaic tile Eye of Horus still winks at you when you walk into the main entrance. The hardwood floors have been restored and the white walls are hung with light draperies. Chandeliers spread light on music recitals, weddings and meetings. If guests tire of the opulence, they can play pool in the original billiard room.

The Ghosts

As might be expected, the Odd Fellows left some spiritual remnants behind as well as paperwork and regalia. A few harmless ghosts tend to follow the staff around the building. One mobile ghost is detected by the sweaty human body odor he creates. He is fondest of the billiard room. A little less offensive are the voices employees have heard late at night and footsteps echoing through the halls and stairs when no one is there. The staff tends to ignore the presences that have probably remained to make sure the building is taken care of.

Name: **Chuck Wagon Restaurant**
Address: Street unknown
Spokane, WA
Prices: $
Theme: Diner
Cuisine: Country Cooking
Open: Whenever
Special Facilities: Friendly Staff

In 1986, a couple visiting Spokane for the first time went out to have breakfast. They found a cheap neighborhood restaurant called *Chuck Wagon*. They ordered the Steak & Eggs special, which was an unbelievable $3.85. Through some mix up with the billing they paid less than a dollar for their breakfast. When they tried to find the restaurant again, it was gone.

This story is based on an account in USA Today's collected work, I Never Believed in Ghosts Until...If anyone finds this restaurant, please let me know.

Name: **Patsy Clark's Restaurant**
Address: W. 2208 Second Avenue
Spokane, WA 99204
Phone Number: **509-838-8300**
Web site: www.nwadv.com/patsyclarks/htm
Prices: $$$
Theme: Mansion turned into restaurant
Cuisine: International gourmet
Open: Lunch, Monday – Friday 11:30 a.m.-1:45 p.m.
Dinner, Sunday – Thursday, 5:00 p.m.-9:00 p.m.
Friday & Saturday, 5:00 p.m.-10:00 p.m.
Brunch, Sunday from 10:00 a.m.-1:30 p.m.
Special Facilities: Banquet facility, fireplaces

Directions: From I-90, take the Maple St. Exit and head north to 2nd Avenue. Turn left (west) and go through Maple Street. Keep heading straight at the "Y." Patsy Clark's is five blocks ahead, on the right.

Irishman Patsy Clark came to the United States in 1870. He made his fortune in gold and silver mining. In the late 1870s he moved to Spokane where he continued his mining operations. He settled in Spokane, and died there in 1915. In that time, he and his wife became civic and social leaders. Words cannot describe the fine detail Patsy Clark lavished upon his mansion when he had it built in 1895.

Stepping through the front door of Patsy Clark's Mansion is like entering a combination Bavarian chateau and cathedral. Most of the dark wood paneling is either carved or has fancy molding added to it. There are leaded, stained glass windows throughout the building, especially on the grand stairway. Visitors find a different, though just as impressive décor in each room, especially the ornate fireplaces.

The Ghosts

Strangely enough, the basement of Pasty Clark's was not concrete, it was dirt. A few days before a concrete basement was poured, two workmen discovered a pair of women's button-up leather shoes and some suspicious bones. The restaurant manager was afraid of publicity and ordered the workmen to get rid of everything. Strange things began to happen when they opened.

Water was seen dripping from a ceiling. When the server got the manager, both were surprised to find that the leak and water stain was gone. In the late 1990s, the bookkeeper was on the second floor and saw a transparent woman dressed in a white nightgown, standing by the stairs. They made eye contact and the woman began walking up the stairs to the third floor and disappeared.

Name: **Spokane Civic Theatre**
Address: 1020 N Howard Street
Spokane, WA 99201
Phone Number: 509-625-2507 (box office)
Web site: www.spokanecivictheatre.com
Prices: $$
Theme: Modern Theatre
Open: Check box office
Special Facilities: Musicals as well as plays produced, theater school, and wheelchair accessible

From the outside, the Spokane Civic Theater was built in phases, from the mid-1960s to the present day. It is also one of the only wholly owned community theaters in the Pacific Northwest. There has been a Spokane Civic Theater since the late 1940s. It has a yearly attendance of 35,000 guests and 1,800 subscribers. A community theater is not a building, it is a group of people who gather together to put on plays. Like all theaters, the true magic is not on the outside, but on the inside.

The Ghosts

No one knows who George the ghost was in life, or how he came to become a ghost. Was he left behind from the building that used to stand on the site of the present theater? Did he move in, when a handful of dust from the stage of the old theater was sprinkled on the stage of the new one to christen it? Wherever George came from, he is a proper theater's ghost. Sometimes a floodlight will sweep across an empty dark stage. Many of the staff and actors have felt a presence in the backstage area during productions. George also flushes the toilets in the men's bathroom when no one is there.

Shops, Sights and Sounds

Name: **Haunted Street Corner**
Address: The corner of Garland & Cedar Street, Spokane, WA
Theme: Disembodied entity

The Ghosts

In 1995 a couple was walking down Cedar street, late one night, when the street light went out. A cloudy mist blew passed them and then returned to surround them. They had a feeling of menace, but that may have been their fear. They ran away from the enveloping misty presence. When they walked by the same street corner again a night later, the lamppost light went out again. They ran!

This is not the nicest part of town. I recommend against anyone walking around there late at night!

Name: **Spokane Scenic Tours & Shuttle**
Address: P.O. Box 4996
Spokane, WA 99220
Phone Number: 509-625-9622
509-623-7995 (Alpha dispatch)
Prices: $$ - $$$
Theme: Historic bus tours
Open: Tours are by appointment only
Special Facilities: Multiple theme tours, various tour pick-up points

In the late 1990s, former law enforcement officer and entrepreneur, Jerome Green, bought three greyhound style buses, a couple of cases of spray paint, and opened the Spokane Scenic Tours & Shuttle Service. Green now lists ten different thematic tours, ranging from Mall/ Antique shopping to Historic City tours. Tours last from one to three hours. He has hosted some notable passengers such as Janet Reno.

One tour that might interest readers is the Forgotten City Tour. In this tour Green discusses some of Spokane's more sensational crimes and criminals, neighborhoods and places. Specialty tours have to be arranged several days in advance. He offers lower rates for tour groups.

Pasco

Name: **Yellepit Railroad Siding**
Address: West of Pasco, WA
This spot is viewable from Amtrak trains.

The Ghosts

Yellepit is a railroad siding near the 215-mile railroad marker, about sixteen miles east of McNary Dam along the Columbia River. Several Amtrak train engineers have reported seeing a woman sitting on top of a pile of rocks where the grade begins rising. She always wears a long dress, and is only seen during rainy weather in the fall and winter. She was last reported in 1999.

According to legend, she was a passenger on a boat that sank in the river, below the railroad tracks. Her husband dragged her to the shore and then stumbled down the railroad tracks to get help. He did not see an approaching train. She sat on the rock, watching as he was run over by the train. She appears on autumn nights, just as the sun is going down, to watch the event replayed again and again.

Yakima

Name: **The Capitol Theatre**
Address: 19 South Third Street
Yakima, WA 98901
Phone Number: **800-876-2446 (box office)**
509-853-2787(box office)
Fax Number: 509-575-6251
Web site: www.capitoltheatre.org
Prices: $$ - $$$
Theme: Historic Theatre
Open: Check box office for times
Special Facilities: 1,500 seats, best of Broadway plays, local symphony, community programs

Directions: On 1-82, take the Yakima Ave exit and go west on Yakima Avenue. This will take you toward the city center. Continue to Third Street and turn left. The theatre is in the middle of the block on the left, or east side of the street.

Frederick Mercy constructed the Capitol Theatre in 1920. It was probably the largest and finest vaudeville theatre in the Northwest. Architect Marcus Pretica, who designed most of the Pantages Theaters, drew up the plans for the Mercy Theatre, as it was named when it opened. A year later the theatre was renamed the Capitol Theatre. Following the pattern of most live Performance Theaters in the Northwest, The Capitol gradually phased out vaudeville in favor of movies and fell on hard times after World War II. In the 1970s, it was sold to the city of Yakima for use as a community arts center.

A fire

gutted The Capitol shortly after it was sold to the city. It took just over two years, but the theater was completely restored with tremendous community support. The artist who painted the ceiling murals came out of retirement to recreate his original artwork. The fine molding in the front of the building was recast from moulds made from surviving Pretica designed buildings. In 1978, the theatre reopened and has been entertaining people ever since.

The Ghosts

There are stories of a theatre ghost known as Shorty dating back decades. Shorty may have been a theater stagehand, with decided musical tastes. When a loud band is booked, there are far too many equipment breakdowns, to be coincidence. There is a door backstage, located 12 feet up the wall, with no stairs leading to it. No one knows if it leads to a room or ends in a blank wall. They call it Shorty's room. The door is sometimes found swinging open. In the 1990s, two ghost hunters detected an unexplained heat source near Shorty's room. They did not exorcise Shorty's spirit from the Theater. Much to the relief of the staff, who like their mysterious co-worker.

Ellensburg

Name: **Haunted Street Corner**
Address: The corner of Pine Street & Seventh Avenue
Ellensburg, WA
Theme: Disembodied entity

In 1895 two farmers visited Ellensburg, where they got into a bar room brawl with a bar tender and saloon owner. The fight ended when the farmers, a father and son, killed their opponents. They were put in jail pending a trial. A gang of drunken toughs broke into the jail and carried the farmers out to hang them. They were going to hang the farmers on the corner of Sixth Street. A house owner there persuaded them that it would disturb his pregnant wife, so the two farmers were carried to a tree down the block and hung there instead.

After the hanging, people avoided the street at night. The corner seemed possessed with a dark aura and strange noises were heard at night. Was it a case of collective guilty conscience or something more?

Name: **Main Attraction Hair Salon**
Address: Lunch Building
421 N Pearl

Ellensburg, WA 98926
Phone Number: 509-925-3159
Prices: $$
Theme: Historic building
Open: Call for appointments
Special Facilities: Massage therapy, full beauty shop facilities

Pat Lynch, one of Ellensburg's more colorful pioneers, built the Lynch Building in 1888. When Lynch was charged with assault with intent to commit murder, he bought the jury some whiskey to help with their deliberations. He was acquitted of all charges.

The Lynch Building has been put to many uses. The space the Mane Attraction occupies was once used as a boarding house. It now houses a mix of gleaming glass and chrome as well as rustic brick and wood. The main floor is where most of the beauty shop stylists perform their duties. There is a loft overlooking the barber chairs, where the massage therapist works.

The Ghosts

There are no good candidates for the identity of the ghost. The brooding ghost at the Mane Attraction is probably not the builder, Pat Lynch. He was too cheerful to remain behind as a quiet presence. Lynch would have been happier as a poltergeist. The presence seemed to center itself in the massage room and upper loft space. It never did any harm, it was just in the way, so the salon owner had a Native American Shaman burn sage to calm the spirit. They periodically burn sage to keep it quiet. There are rumors that the ghost is also felt in other nearby shops.

Idaho

Name: The Jameson Hotel and Saloon
Address: 304 Sixth Street
Wallace, ID 83873
Phone Number: 208-752-1252
(Care of the Best Western in winter)
Web site: http://wallace-id.jameson
Rooms: 6 rooms
Prices: $ - $$ price includes breakfast
Theme: Historic Hotel
Cuisine: American $$
Open: Seasonal, call ahead for reservations
Special Facilities: Banquet/meeting facilities, non smoking, TV, outdoor pool, fitness center, hot tub

Directions: On I-90, take Exit 61 or Exit 62 into downtown Wallace. The hotel is not hard to find. Always call in advance in wintertime.

Theodore Jameson built the Jameson Hotel in 1889. He called it the Wallace Ball and Billiard Hall. The ground and second floors of the hotel are used as an old-fashioned saloon, dining room and meeting area. Despite the upgrades, it maintains its rustic turn of the century appeal. Old-fashioned ceiling fans whir from their ornate ceiling fixtures. The saloon is trimmed in red velvet and the bar is coated with black lacquer.

The six hotel rooms are located on the third floor. There are five rooms with full sized beds and one room has two twin beds. All are decorated in 19th century Victorian style and there is a guest parlor. The Jameson restaurant is not open to the general public for breakfast, so guests are allowed to eat in privacy.

The Ghosts

Over the years there have been many sightings of the resident ghost, named Maggie. Maggie is supposed to have been a hotel guest, who died in the hotel sometime after 1906, when the building opened as a hotel. Maggie spends a lot of time in Room Three. She has been seen as a reflection in the mirror hanging on the wall. When people see her in the mirror and turn around, they confront open air.

A woman was using the upstairs bathroom and heard a female voice asking who was there. When she checked, the first woman was alone. Maggie has been heard walking the halls at night. Fans are shut off or turned on and coffeepots have floated on their own. It may not be Maggie alone. Some people have smelled pipe tobacco, and smoking would have been unladylike way back then.

Index

Recommended Reading

Davis, Jefferson
Ghosts and Strange Critters of Washington and Oregon. **ISBN 1-893186-00-8**

Davis, Jefferson
Ghosts, Critters and Sacred Places of Washington and Oregon. **ISBN 1-893186-02-4**

Davis, Jefferson
Ghosts, Critters and Sacred Places of Washington and Oregon II. **ISBN 1-893186-03-2**

Helm, Mike
Oregon's Ghosts and Monsters.

MacDonald, Margaret Read
Ghost Stories from the Pacific Northwest.

Meyers, Arthur
The Ghostly Register
Meyers, Arthur
A Ghosthunter's Guide

Especially Canada

Belyk, Robert
Ghosts, True Stories from British Columbia.

Belyk, Robert
Ghosts II, More True Ghost Stories from British Columbia.

Internet Resources

Castle of Spirits: *http://www.castleofspirits.com/*
Ghost Stories from Around the World: *http://www.sitemart.com/ghost/18145.htm.*
Ghosts of North Portland Web site: *http://www.hevanet.com/herberb/ghosts/mohawk.htm.*
Obiwan's UFO free paranormal page: *http://www.ghosts.org/*
Paranormal Northwest: *http://www.eskimo.com/~pierres/*
Spectre Search: *http://web2.arimail.net/~spectre1.sprportl.html*
The Shadowlands: *http://theshadowlands.net/ghost/*

About the Author

Jeff Davis was born in Vancouver, Washington in 1962. According to family tradition, he is related to his namesake, Jefferson Davis, President of the Confederacy. Jeff is an Army brat and grew up playing in and around the Vancouver Barracks. This led to an interest in the military and history. Late might horror movies instilled an interest in ghosts, mythology and archaeology.

After a three year enlistment in the U.S. Army, Jeff earned a Bachelor's degree in Anthropology as well as a commission in the U.S. Army Reserves.

For several years he worked for the U.S. Forest Service as an archaeologist. Jeff worked on several of the National Forests, including the Gifford Pinchot, the Boise, the Umatilla and Mt. Hood. In addition to his work as a freelance archaeologist, Jeff is a part-time volunteer consultant to various Pacific Northwest Native American groups.

In 1995, Jeff and his wife Janine moved to England for a year, where he earned his Master's in Arts in Archaeology from the University of Sheffield. His thesis topic was the lifestyle and ending of the Viking settlements in Greenland. That is where he received the inspiration for his publishing company name, Norsemen Ventures. He plans an expedition to Greenland in the future to continue his research. Sometime.

Other Books By Jefferson Davis

Ghosts and Strange Critters of Washington and Oregon. ISBN 1-893186-00-8

Ghosts, Critters and Sacred Places of Washington and Oregon. ISBN 1-893186-02-4

2000 *Ghosts, Critters and Sacred Places of Washington and Oregon II*. ISBN 1-893186-03-2